The Fall of the House of Paisley

Revised edition

David Gordon

Gill & Macmillan

Gill & Macmillan Ltd
Hume Avenue, Park West, Dublin 12
with associated companies throughout the world
www.gillmacmillan.ie

© David Gordon 2009, 2010
First published 2009
Revised edition first published 2010
978 07171 4830 1

Index compiled by Kate Murphy
Typography design by Make Communication
Print origination by O'K Graphic Design, Dublin
Printed by ColourBooks Ltd, Dublin

This book is typeset in 11/14 pt Minion.

The paper used in this book comes from the wood pulp of
managed forests. For every tree felled, at least one tree is
planted, thereby renewing natural resources.

5 4 3 2 1

For Gill, Tony and Kate

Contents

Introduction

So what went wrong?

That seems a strange question to ask about a man who finished his political career as both the leader of unionism and the First Minister of Northern Ireland. Ian Paisley had come to prominence decades earlier as a notorious street preacher, firebrand Protestant hardliner, church-splitter and political pariah. His counter-protests to civil rights rallies in the late 1960s were officially blamed for stoking up tensions, as the province headed towards violent conflict.[1] But by May 2007, Paisley's Democratic Unionist Party (DUP) had completed a remarkable journey from the fringes to the centre of the province's new devolved government. Its 81-year-old leader was being hailed internationally for sealing a monumental power-sharing deal with his long-standing foes in Sinn Féin, the political wing of the IRA. Yet just a year later, Paisley was standing down.

He had previously insisted that he fully intended to serve his entire term as First Minister. When questions started circulating about his future in early 2008, his devoted wife Eileen—Baroness Paisley—defiantly declared that he should stay on. He still went. It was not a neat and tidy end to a political career.

The truth was that Paisley had been damaged in his heartland over his power-sharing deal with Sinn Féin. The Free Presbyterian Church—the church he had built up from nothing—was hit by serious internal friction and he found himself relinquishing his post as its leader. Another blow came when the DUP lost a council by-election in Dromore, County Down, that it had been expected to win quite comfortably.

Then there was the Junior problem. Ian Paisley Jnr had proudly entered government by his father's side, becoming a junior minister in his department. But he was forced to resign his post in February

2008 after a long-running 'cronyism' controversy over links to a property developer. A few years back, Paisley would have swiftly seen off those inside the DUP who wanted to point his son towards the exit door. But he could not save him.

The whispers started getting louder then, about when the father would be going too, and how a growing band of once-loyal supporters wanted it to be sooner rather than later. Paisley was not exactly run out of town. But people below him were ready to put a posse together.

This book charts the developments that led up to Ian Paisley's dramatic resignation—including the Junior-related controversies that helped bring about the Fall of the House of Paisley. Junior and his allies now suggest that he was driven from office by an unjustified media campaign of innuendo. It is a matter of public interest to set the record straight on that front. Junior's tumble from power highlighted damaging faults within the Stormont system, covering such issues as accountability, public standards, use of taxpayers' money and nepotism. There is also some symbolism in the fact that his lobbying for a property tycoon caused his downfall.

In the new Northern Ireland of 2007, the housing market was booming and developers almost looked like a new aristocracy. It all seems a little pathetic now in light of the subsequent property crash and everything that accompanied it. Paisley Jnr's resignation was significant in its own right on a number of grounds. But the way it helped to bring down his First Minister father has echoes of a biblical or Shakespearean drama. Hopefully, it also makes for a good read.

This is not the inside story of the DUP in power, and makes no pretence in this regard. Readers should always be suspicious of journalists who pretend to have been in the room at key moments in history. I was not in the room and I had the hilarious experience of being barred from media interviews held in May 2008 to mark Paisley's departure as DUP leader. Some party sources have co-operated with the research for this book and gratitude for their anonymous contributions should be expressed. DUP headquarters made it clear that no official interviews would be given, and the Paisleys did not respond to requests to speak to them. That was no great surprise. In any event, a DUP inside story would inevitably be a self-serving and partial account of events.

This book seeks to objectively analyse why life did not go according to plan for the Paisleys in government. It can serve as a case-study of the first year of devolution after the DUP–Sinn Féin agreement. The early chapters set out key background factors on why the House of Paisley was not a particularly stable construction. A crucial theme is that Paisley's problems with his traditional base over power-sharing stemmed in no small part from his own mouth. The political messages he preached for decades simply cannot be reconciled with his embrace of partnership government at the end of his career. Crucially, no credible attempt was made to explain his about-turn to his followers, many of whom were left feeling befuddled and betrayed. Instead, a pretence was maintained that there had really been no change at all. This helps to explain why Paisley faced revolts in his church and at the Dromore by-election that were greater than had generally been anticipated.

Another important weakness involved the inherent contradictions between his roles as First Minister and as head of a small, highly conservative religious denomination. Paisley's brief period in power also missed out an expected long-term feelgood factor on the economic front. The credit crunch that swept the world from 2007 dashed hopes of a boom—and exposed some fairly half-baked ideological notions at Stormont. There is also no question that the physical demands of the First Minister's job proved a challenge for Paisley. That was hardly surprising for a man in his eighties. His declining powers left him very reliant on his Junior Minister son. And that proved disastrous.

This book documents—largely in chronological order—the difficulties that hit both Senior and Junior from the autumn of 2007. These included a seemingly obscure policy dispute over commercial development at Northern Ireland's best-known natural attraction, the Giant's Causeway. That's a case-study in its own right, featuring tensions between profit and environmental protection.

The final chapters of the book highlight the chain of events from the start of 2008 that brought the House of Paisley tumbling down, including the Dromore by-election, Paisley Jnr's resignation and internal party machinations about the leadership. The abiding mystery of why the DUP leader said yes after a career built on saying no is also addressed, if not quite solved.

In conclusion, serious questions are raised about the structure Paisley Snr left behind—the power-sharing construction dominated by his party and Sinn Féin. The overall verdict on the devolution experiment to date is not exactly rapturous. The Stormont administration has had its good days. In March 2009, the DUP and Sinn Féin leadership produced an impressive display of unity in response to a renewed murder campaign by dissident republican factions. There have been low points too, particularly a five-month period in 2008 when the Executive—the power-sharing coalition cabinet—failed to meet. It is perfectly legitimate to critically examine current Stormont's structures and politics, while accepting that Northern Ireland has progressed immeasurably from the days of the Troubles. There are also potential lessons for the next generation of politicians from Paisley's brief period in power. For a start, people may not always conveniently forget everything their leaders tell them over the years. That's something the political class here do not seem to grasp sometimes. Delivering good government, with proper standards of accountability, can be pretty important too.

Some nagging thoughts remain about the current Stormont set-up, such as whether a workable settlement could have been achieved many years earlier with much less loss of life. Optimism about the future must also be tempered with the knowledge that Northern Ireland politics remains locked in sectarian patterns. Indeed, as the concluding chapter here argues, the present arrangements are biased against anyone wishing to challenge the status quo and shift political life away from its traditional communal routines. Against this backdrop, it will be a struggle to make politics truly functional or life in the Assembly inspiring.

The era in which Paisley Snr played such a dominant role is now gone. Meanwhile, his son's future remains unclear. Junior's profile has steadily risen since his resignation and his ambition to play a frontline role remains undimmed. It may be that he will rebuild the fallen House of Paisley in some shape or form.

But it will never stand as tall or as grand again.

Chronology

Good Friday 1998: The Ulster Unionist Party (UUP) led by David Trimble backs the Belfast Agreement along with both nationalist parties, the SDLP and Sinn Féin. Paisley's DUP angrily opposes the deal.

A power-sharing government under the Agreement is subsequently formed with Trimble as First Minister and the SDLP's Seamus Mallon as Deputy First Minister. But the devolved structures prove to be extremely unstable. Trimble's hopes of a swift conclusion to IRA decommissioning are dashed, and his party steadily loses support to the DUP.

Devolution is suspended in October 2002, following allegations of an IRA spy ring within government.

October 2004: Inter-party talks at Leeds Castle, Kent, come close to securing a devolution agreement between the DUP and Sinn Féin. A DUP demand for photographic evidence of planned IRA decommissioning is rejected. A speech by Paisley saying that the IRA should be humiliated and wear 'sackcloth and ashes' helps to close down the prospect of a deal.

May 2005: The 2005 British General Election proves a watershed in Northern Ireland, with the DUP heavily defeating the Ulster Unionists. David Trimble stands down as UUP leader after losing his Westminster seat and is subsequently replaced by Sir Reg Empey.

October 2006: Talks involving Northern Ireland parties and the British and Irish governments in Scotland produce the St Andrews Agreement, a framework for a return to devolution. It preserves the main points of the 1998 Belfast Agreement, including a mandatory power-sharing coalition and north–south bodies.

March 2007: A fresh Assembly election sees the DUP cement its position as the main unionist party. Sinn Féin does the same on the nationalist side. The DUP's election manifesto did not categorically commit it to a devolution deal.

Later that month, DUP leader Ian Paisley and Sinn Féin President Gerry Adams hold a historic joint press conference at Stormont, announcing that their parties will enter a new power-sharing devolved government within weeks.

May 2007: A new era begins in Northern Ireland with Ian Paisley as First Minister and Sinn Féin's Martin McGuinness as Deputy First Minister. A feelgood factor is evident in the province and they confound the cynics by establishing a warm working relationship. Their habit of laughing together at joint public appearances sees them branded the 'Chuckle Brothers'.

September 2007: Paisley's Free Presbyterian Church announces that he will be stepping down as its Moderator—most senior minister—in the New Year. At the Assembly, policy controversies start clouding the new government's honeymoon period. The first of these concerns plans for a development by a property tycoon and DUP member called Seymour Sweeney.

Ian Paisley Jnr's lobbying for Sweeney comes under focus and he is criticised for being less than open about his links to the businessman. One answer during a radio interview—in which he says: 'I know of him' about Sweeney—proves particularly damaging.

February 2008: The DUP suffers a shock defeat in a council by-election in Dromore, County Down.

A few days later, Paisley Jnr resigns as a Stormont Junior Minister, immediately casting doubts on his father's future as First Minister.

March 2008: Paisley Snr announces that he will be stepping down as First Minister and DUP leader.

June 2008: Long-serving DUP deputy Peter Robinson takes over as party leader and First Minister.

Chapter 1
Welcome to the House of Fun

'…there is a sort of buoyancy in Ulster at the moment…'
IAN PAISLEY, April 2007[1]

Historic moments abounded in Northern Ireland in 2007. But nothing came close to matching the jaw-dropping moment on Monday 26 March when, at a televised press conference in Stormont, Ian Paisley confirmed the news that a power-sharing deal had been successfully negotiated. The camera panned back to show unbelieving viewers that Sinn Féin President Gerry Adams was sitting beside the DUP leader. That image was thanks in no small part to some clever improvisation behind the scenes.

The DUP had wanted the two leaders to be facing each other, while Sinn Féin insisted on them being side by side. Thanks to a diamond-shaped table formation, the two options were more or less satisfied. Paisley and Adams each sat at the end of their party's table, bringing them beside each other if not quite side by side. The image management could not stretch to a historic handshake, however.

A deal had seemed anything but inevitable just a few days earlier. Monday 26 March had been Secretary of State Peter Hain's absolutely final deadline for the restoration of devolution. But the DUP was determined to bust its way through that date. That meant the only way for it to avoid a total collapse of the process was to negotiate directly with Adams and co. on establishing devolution.

'Today, we have agreed with Sinn Féin that this date will be Tuesday 8 May 2007,' Paisley announced at the press conference.[2] His statement that day was well crafted, giving every sign that he was going to throw himself into the new arrangements 100 per cent. It explained that 'important preparatory work' between the parties would get underway in advance of devolution day. 'This will include regular meetings between the future First and Deputy First Minister,' he added. That meant Paisley and Sinn Féin's Martin McGuinness, a one-time top IRA man in Derry.

The famous Paisley rhetoric was expertly employed at the press conference, bridging the pain of the past and hopes for the future. 'I want to make it clear that I am committed to delivering not only for those who voted for the DUP but for all the people of Northern Ireland,' he said. 'We must not allow our justified loathing of the horrors and tragedies of the past to become a barrier to creating a better and more stable future.' And so the Paisley–McGuinness double act was born.

The First and Deputy First Ministers were soon laughing enthusiastically together at public appearances, even when there did not seem to be anything very funny going on. The nickname 'Chuckle Brothers' was coined in the summer of 2007, and attributed to an unnamed Ulster Unionist. This comment was quoted in a BBC Northern Ireland report marking the first 100 days of devolution.[3] The original Chuckle Brothers were a comedy double act from children's TV. The BBC Northern Ireland report also referred to government officials talking about the 'chemistry' between Paisley and McGuinness.

Although it eventually caused the DUP problems as it continued over the months, the chuckling did not seem like much of a liability at first. Paisley was demonstrating publicly that he was comfortable in his role, and determined to make it work. He gave an insight into the working relationship in one early interview, hinting at private jocularity within their department, the Office of the First Minister and Deputy First Minister (OFMDFM). 'We have had agreement at the end of the day after perhaps a fair bit of argument and stating our views but it has been courteous, it has been honest, it has been straight, and it has also been tinged by a measure of sarcasm by both of us.'[4]

The Stormont honeymoon period went well beyond the two First Ministers. When the devolution project started to struggle in 2008, there was much speculation about a chill between McGuinness and Paisley's successor, Peter Robinson. But they also evidently got on well during a joint trip to the US in June 2007. The pair represented the new Stormont administration at the opening of a major Northern Ireland promotional drive in the States.[5] Robinson declared:

> When you visit us—as I hope you will—you will be in no doubt about the astounding progress that is being made. Our two traditions are serving together in a new government. It is a government that is about change, about building, about progress, about promoting a confident and capable Northern Ireland and I believe there is no limit to what we can achieve together.[6]

In a joint BBC interview with McGuinness in Washington, Robinson said: 'We have been working together for nearly two months and we haven't had a row.'[7]

At times, the joint DUP–Sinn Féin choreography of the early days was almost beyond satire. OFMDFM Junior Ministers Ian Paisley Jnr and Gerry Kelly enthusiastically launched a new 'superheroes' comic for primary schoolchildren. A government press release helpfully explained: 'Herbie Healthy, Sophie Safe, Archie Achiever, Emer the Eco Girl, Donna Does-a-lot and Rory Rights will use their super powers to help in the fight to secure a better society for children and ensure their needs are kept at the heart of government and the community.'[8] Even ardent supporters of the peace process sometimes had to suppress memories of Gerry Kelly's days as an IRA bomber. Likewise, it would have been unhelpful to recall all the abuse that Paisley Jnr and his DUP colleagues had been hurling at Kelly just a few years earlier.

Just in case there is any confusion, incidentally, this was the same Paisley Jnr who in 1999 had condemned the creation of the OFMDFM junior minister posts as a 'waste of taxpayers' money'. That was back when those jobs had gone to SDLP and Ulster Unionist MLAS. Paisley Jnr had at that time also described the two posts as 'superfluous' and claimed that the Assembly was 'quickly becoming a white elephant'. His outburst—in December 1999—was echoed by senior Sinn Féin MLA and future minister Conor Murphy. Murphy claimed the junior minister positions were 'the most blatant case of cronyism and jobbery imaginable'.[9] Time had clearly moved on by the summer of 2007—Murphy and Paisley Jnr were Ministers together for a start. Everyone, it seemed, was on-message by then, and any cynicism or criticism was officially frowned upon.

Feelings of optimism went well beyond the confines of Stormont. Paisley Snr was not far off the mark when he told an interviewer: 'I believe there is a sort of buoyancy in Ulster at the moment among both Roman Catholics and Protestants—that they're seeing a way forward.'[10] The spring weather that year was unusually warm and dry for several weeks.(Like a clumsy metaphor in a bad romantic novel, the summer turned out to be particularly wet and miserable.)

There were other elements to the feeling of optimism that had nothing to do with the Assembly, but nevertheless added to a real sense of optimism. The Northern Ireland football team was enjoying its best run for a generation, thanks to the inspired management of Lawrie Sanchez and the goal-scoring prowess of David Healy. On 28 March, just two days after that Paisley–Adams press conference, Northern Ireland claimed another famous giant-killing home win, defeating Sweden 2–1. In one of his more cringe-making comments of the year, Paisley Jnr said: 'Northern Ireland is doing fantastically well—just like the DUP. They win all their big games and they have a superhero called Healy, we win all our big games and we have a superhero called Paisley!'[11]

Football soon provided another metaphor for devolution disappointment. Sanchez quit his Northern Ireland job a few weeks after the Sweden game to seek English premiership glory with London club Fulham. Healy was one of his first signings in his new job. They both flopped, and Sanchez was out of work within months.

Aside from football, there had been plenty more to cheer about on the sporting front in the first half of 2007. Ireland's cricketers had achieved amazing success at the World Cup in the West Indies, defeating Pakistan and qualifying for the final stages of the tournament. Earlier in the year, sport and Irish history had combined magnificently. Ireland's rugby team had found a temporary new home in Dublin's Croke Park and had received a warm welcome in the GAA citadel. England's rugby players were given a respectful welcome to the stadium and then happily thrashed.

On the music front, meanwhile, Northern Ireland band Snow Patrol had become one of the UK's biggest rock acts. An article in the *Belfast Telegraph* noted: 'They are headlining big summer festivals this year and it seems their songs are being played on the radio around the clock.'[12] A Northern Ireland band had not enjoyed such a level of success since The Undertones in the late 1970s.

The optimism extended to the economic sphere as well. Tourists from various parts of the world were no longer a rarity on the streets. Belfast's locals looked on with bemusement as open-topped tour buses became increasingly common. University of Ulster economist Michael Smyth commented: 'A buoyancy in civil society about its own worth and own identity—helped by the political settlement and underscored by sporting and other achievements— is certainly a necessary condition for us to start to rebuild. But it's not sufficient. We need to have a hard slog of selling ourselves to investors.'[13] The commonly expressed economic hope was that the province could emulate the 'Celtic Tiger' success of the Irish Republic. The phrase 'global credit crunch' had not been coined at that stage.

The property market was enjoying the good times too. As the fine wines flowed, there were many after-dinner chats among the middle classes about the incredible sums their homes were now worth. Tales abounded of apartment blocks in various districts being snapped up in no time by buy-to-let investors. Home-owners were being approached by developers, keen to pay well over the asking price—and then knock down the properties to make way for new townhouses and flats.

One newspaper item published three days after the ground-breaking Paisley–Adams press conference epitomised the period perfectly. It reported that bidding on a red-brick detached home on Alliance Avenue in north Belfast had reached £800,000.[14] The property had been put on the market three weeks earlier for just £285,000. The rich symbolism lay in the fact that Alliance Avenue sat in the heart of one of the city's worst sectarian killing zones of the Troubles.

There was much excitement on the retail front as well. Middle-class spending power in particular was being buoyed by the property bonanza. The imminent opening of the province's first IKEA furniture store was awaited with something close to euphoria in some quarters. And Belfast was looking forward to its new £400 million Victoria Square, bulging with designer clothes stores. Paisley and McGuinness were among the dignitaries present when the trendy centre's long-awaited opening was finally held in March 2008. Belfast was being marketed as cool. Only the bitterest begrudger would surely have recalled the unique Victorian-era Kitchen Bar that had been controversially demolished to make way for Victoria Square.

The economic illusions that underpinned the apparent good times of 2007 painfully emerged over the course of the first 12 months of devolution.   These hard lessons in financial reality will be examined later in this book. But it's worth noting at this point that few if any sceptical voices were raised at Stormont at the time. Nobody seemed to think that the party might be followed by a hangover.

The positive atmosphere that followed the power-sharing deal also had a manufactured aspect to it. That was primarily because one of the first significant acts of the new power-sharing executive was to put looming household water charges on hold.

The hated 'tap tax' formed part of the 'reform agenda'

enthusiastically pursued by Secretary of State Peter Hain and his Northern Ireland Office (NIO) ministerial team. It proved an effective lever for pushing Assembly members towards devolution. Hain, who arrived in the province following the Labour general election victory in May 2005, never tired of pushing his policy programme.

This was a break with the previous Direct Rule approach, where ministers largely held the fort in the expectation that the Assembly would be returning. 'Care and maintenance' was one way of describing the pre-Hain attitude. One senior figure from the Northern Ireland Civil Service coined the phrase 'warm storage' to sum up the thinking. Hain was much more proactive, and in the process managed to annoy quite a few people.

A source close to his NIO team insists that this was not an evil plot to hasten devolution's return. 'It was always a misunderstanding that this was about doing unpopular things deliberately,' he says. 'Decisions were taken on the basis of what was genuinely believed to be the right thing to do.' This source confirms that Hain's hands-on approach was a 'deliberate policy change'. 'It was agreed in Downing Street, but wasn't born in Downing Street. They had to be persuaded. What we wanted to look like—and this was the big difference—was that we were enjoying it.' It was correctly anticipated that this would impact on the mood among Northern Ireland's political parties. 'It built a sense, which helped the situation, that this was unfair, that this was their job. It created an itch to get round the table and make those decisions themselves.'

The NIO source points out that aspects of the Direct Rule policy drive were well received, including reductions in hospital waiting times. It is true to say that some Hain initiatives had admirers, not least in the voluntary and environmental sectors. But water charges were far from being the only contentious aspect of his 'reform agenda'. The list also included the scrapping of the 11-plus transfer test, reform of household rates, and plans to slash the number of councils.

The councils issue was never likely to have people marching in the streets. But it was felt deeply at grass-roots level in politics.

Councillors were not excited at the idea of losing their seats and the prestige that went with them. The drawing of proposed new local government boundaries is also an inevitably fraught topic, with much focus on how many of the new councils would be unionist or nationalist controlled. The 11-plus was also a massive issue, particularly among Protestant middle class voters. In water charges, however, Peter Hain had his best method of applying pressure to the local parties. He and his ministers could point out that direct household charges were in place in Britain, and ask why Northern Ireland should be any different. They could also explain that an estimated £3 billion was needed over the next 20 years to bring the province's ageing water and sewerage infrastructure up to the required standards. Without the introduction of charges, this money would have to be taken from other public services like health, education, etc.

A new tax is never going to be popular. And so, reflecting the mood among voters, Northern Ireland parties railed against the plans. That's where Hain and co. had the perfect response: if you don't like it, agree to restore devolution and sort it out for yourselves. By happy coincidence, the first household 'tap tax' bills had been due to land on doormats a month after the 2007 Assembly elections. One senior NIO source freely admits that this was a deliberate 'twisting of the knife', with a timescale that helped to 'focus minds'.

As the March deadline for a devolution deal approached, it was made clear that the bills were being prepared and would be posted out in the absence of an agreement. Water charges therefore played their part in the sealing of the deal. In his momentous 26 March devolution deal press conference with Adams, Paisley declared:

> The two parties have already asked the prime minister to ensure that no water charge bills should be issued and the matter should be left for a local executive to determine. We hope, trust and believe that the secretary of state will at last listen to the voice of the people of Northern Ireland on this issue.

Adams for his part stated: 'As an immediate step both Sinn Féin and the DUP have asked the British government not to issue the water bills.'

The government was more than happy to 'listen to the voice of the people of Northern Ireland'. What they didn't do was provide £3 billion to sort out the infrastructure crisis. Hain had himself boasted about how much water charges had featured in the March 2007 Assembly election. In an article for the *Observer*, he claimed that 'the main issue in the election campaign was not sectarian mistrust, but the introduction of water charges and a comprehensive reform policy I have introduced'.[15]

This was somewhat disingenuous. Water charges were not the 'main issue in the election campaign' in the normally understood meaning of the phrase. Rival parties did not come up with alternative blueprints for solving the problem and then try to convince the electorate of their merits. All the Northern Ireland parties fought the election with manifestos opposing Hain's water charges. Given such unanimity, this 'main issue' could hardly have had much bearing on how people cast their votes. The election was once again about who the Protestant and Catholic communities wanted to represent them in the Stormont tug-of-war. But the parties did get their ears bent on the doorsteps about getting back into the Assembly, taking control and stopping Hain having his wicked way. And that is what the Secretary of State wanted them to hear all along.

The new power-sharing government did indeed halt the tap tax bills being issued in 2007. But it was a deferral rather than a cancellation. Water charges are generally viewed as an inevitability within the next few years. The only questions are apparently when and how much. The electorate might be disappointed when the demands finally start arriving in the post. They might even recall voting against water charges back in 2007. But what's a little disenchantment among the great unwashed compared to the business of striking historic peace accords?

Chapter 2
The Ghost of Paisley Past

'I have told the Lord if I would ever think of compromising he will put me in a box and get me across the river. It is not the way you start your ministry, it is the way you finish it that matters. May God keep us true!'
IAN PAISLEY, January 1980[1]

The theme of this chapter can be summed up in a biblical phrase that will be familiar to Ian Paisley. When it came to a backlash from hardline unionist elements, he reaped what he sowed. In short, the political and theological messages he thundered out over the years came back to haunt him in his new First Minister era. This was one of the factors that helped to make the new House of Paisley unstable.

It is generally accepted that the 2007 devolution deal could not have been secured without Paisley. His DUP deputy Peter Robinson carefully plotted the route to Stormont power, but it is very hard to envisage him getting there on his own. Only the Doc, as the party faithful call him, had the charisma and the standing to bring it about.

Ironically, a few years earlier, it would not have been uncommon to hear whispered suggestions that there would never be an agreement while Paisley was alive. It was claimed a lasting deal would have to depend on Robinson rising to the top and unionism realigning. Paisley confounded those predictions and brought the vast bulk of his party with him into power-sharing. There were some resignations, but Jim Allister, the DUP's European

Parliament Member (MEP), was the only senior figure to walk away. A Robinson-led party would surely have fractured to a greater extent in the circumstances.

But the deal brought with it a personal cost for Paisley. It won him praise from around the world, while causing unease and hurt within his traditional support base. This dissatisfaction was muted in the early days of the new era. While it was relatively small, it could also be vociferous. By July 2007, Paisley had already been on the receiving end of a form of loyalist protest he had long directed at others. He was heckled with cries of 'Traitor' and 'Lundy' at an annual pre-Twelfth of July rally in Loughgall, County Armagh. A local newspaper reported on police minders 'unceremoniously shunting him into a car which ferried him away from a baying crowd'.[2]

Some of Paisley's longest-serving followers were among those most disappointed and angry at the pact with Sinn Féin. For the Free Presbyterians among them, this was more than a case of personal disenchantment. They had thrown themselves into the Paisleyite cause over the years because they were convinced he was God's anointed leader in Ulster. They believed him when he ranted against Rome-inspired nationalist plots against the last bastion of true Protestantism in Europe. In their eyes, their cause was not just about political opinions or tactics, but religious faith. And many of them did not see the power-sharing deal coming.

Amongst media commentators and other elements of the chattering classes, there was a general view that the DUP would go into government with Sinn Féin at some point after the March 2007 Assembly poll. However, that assumption was not shared by all the party's supporters. The DUP's election manifesto had left its options open on whether a deal would be agreed at all. It paid inadequate attention to the task of preparing its grass-roots for the new era. If sections of them were left befuddled, it was probably because they had believed everything Paisley had told them over the years.

WHAT WAS IT ALL FOR?

Veteran Larne councillor Jack McKee was a Paisleyite well before the DUP had even been formed. He was with Paisley in the 1960s and was a member of the DUP's forerunner, the Protestant Unionist Party. He can look back on decades of working for the cause, at election times, at rallies and in unpaid advice centre work. 'I had to take days off work, for instance when Dr Paisley was going to be in town. Over the years, it's cost me a bag,' he recalls.[3]

McKee says he was 'sick to the very stomach' when Paisley agreed to go into government with Sinn Féin, adding: 'It was as if somebody had reached in and pulled the very heart out of you.' It left him thinking all his work down through the years was 'for nothing'. He now questions the past Paisleyite onslaughts on unionist Prime Ministers Terence O'Neill and Brian Faulkner for their efforts at accommodation in the 1960s and 1970s. And he asks why his erstwhile DUP colleagues 'hounded' Ulster Unionist First Minister David Trimble out of office over the Good Friday Agreement. 'They've actually gone further than Trimble,' he says.

It is clear that McKee would have spent a large chunk of his life very differently if he had known how the DUP's future was going to pan out.

I thought there was a bond there, that there was a personal relationship that had been built up over the years. I saw the DUP as a family and in the early days, it certainly was that. The bit that galls me is that through all those years of barnstorming and table thumping, what was it all for? Why had all those people to die? Why did that have to happen? Logic has gone out the window.

McKee is now a supporter of MEP Jim Allister's anti-Agreement TUV (Traditional Unionist Voice) movement. His brother Bobby, also a Larne councillor, stayed with the DUP and backed its Stormont position.

Veteran Ballymena councillor Roy Gillespie was another defector to the TUV following the devolution pact. The retired lorry driver had been a Paisley follower for some 40 years. He was a long-standing member of the Free Presbyterian Church as well as the

DUP, believing Paisley had been 'raised up' by God for the situation in Northern Ireland. Asked to sum up his feelings after the power-sharing deal of 2007, he uses one word: 'betrayal'. 'I was in mourning. I found it very difficult. I had my tears and I lost sleep. It was hard going,' he admits.[4]

Gillespie suspected that there would be political upheaval after the 2007 Assembly election, but held out hopes that Paisley would block a deal. 'We did probably see big changes but we thought he would probably be the boulder at the end of the tunnel. We thought he would hold his ground,' he says. 'Being a man of God, you think he's going to be standing firm and standing true to what he said. His word should be his bond.'

Gillespie's hurt received media attention in early 2008 when Taoiseach Bertie Ahern paid a visit to his home town. Ahern was warmly welcomed to Ballymena by First Minister Paisley, providing yet more memorable images from the new Northern Ireland. Gillespie carried a union flag to the hotel event and staged a lonely protest with his wife Ruby. An emotional Mrs Gillespie told journalists: 'We used to have a great man who stood for us, who spoke out for us, who led us. We protested, we marched and we believed in what we are doing and we believed in him. Now we're let down, we're let down so badly. Where do we go?'[5]

It may well be that Paisley had no option but to move away from the likes of the Gillespies and Jack McKee. Jettisoning old comrades who fail to move with the times can be one of the burdens of leadership. But having roused them to action, and fired them up year after year, were the ageing loyal followers not at least owed a full explanation from their leader?

David Trimble raised this point himself—on behalf of all the Northern Ireland electorate—in June 2007. He said:

Dr Paisley hasn't made it clear why Sinn Féin's Martin McGuinness is his number two—a man with a terrorist past—yet he criticised me for working alongside people like constitutional nationalist Seamus Mallon, my extremely able Deputy First Minister. It has been suggested that Ian Paisley and his colleagues found themselves in power after 40 years on the sidelines, and embraced it with both arms. Perhaps he always wanted to be Prime Minister of Northern Ireland at whatever cost—I pose the question which only he can answer.[6]

It was quite a reserved comment from Trimble in the circumstances. He could have added that he was entitled to an explanation himself after all the vicious abuse he had personally received from the DUP and its supporters.

Paisley did make some stabs at explaining his position. In his first post-deal interview, he spoke at some length about how the return of devolution had saved Northern Ireland from 'Plan B'. This, he claimed, would have meant 'curtains for our country' and involved joint rule from London and Dublin. 'How would I have faced my people if I had allowed this country to have the union destroyed and a setting up of a joint government by the south of Ireland?' he asked.[7]

However, there is no evidence that 'Plan B' would have been anything close to joint sovereignty between Dublin and London, or the end of the union. It is true that a final collapse of the talks process in 2007 would probably have led to ongoing Direct Rule with a greener tinge—a British–Irish partnership with London and Dublin working closely together. That is some distance short of London and Dublin actually sharing joint authority. A source with an inside track to NIO thinking under Peter Hain says joint sovereignty was 'never discussed'. 'We had the next stage of energetic Direct Rule mapped out,' this source adds. There would have been 'lots of meetings' with a north–south theme, but this would have been 'more window-dressing than legal or structural'.

Greater London–Dublin co-operation, incidentally, would also have been the likely outcome had all of unionism walked away from the 1998 Good Friday Agreement. In contrast to Paisley's post-deal claims, the Plan B issue had actually been played down by his deputy Peter Robinson some months earlier. In a newspaper interview in October 2006—following the St Andrews Agreement that paved the way for the DUP–Sinn Féin pact—Robinson denied having any detailed knowledge of an alternative British government plan. He added:

> All I do know and my experience of the last number of years is that I would not trust my future to Tony Blair and Bertie Ahern. If I have a viable alternative to that I will take it—but it has to be a viable alternative and not just anything that they cobble together and throw at me. The alternative, I have to say, has never been the key issue for me. I will not take the decision that I finally will have to take on the St Andrews Agreement because there is looming behind it the ogre of the British–Irish partnership. Of course I recognise that's there and the threat is about but I'm not going to sign a bad package because there's something worse down the road.[8]

Only a few months later, Paisley was effectively telling voters that 'something worse' was actually 'the key issue' after all.

The DUP's defence of power-sharing does not always centre on how they delivered salvation from Plan B. The party also points regularly to the achievement of getting Sinn Féin to sign up to support for policing. Paisley's own support for the police had not always been on display during his career. In 1974, after police had removed him and other anti-power-sharing politicians from a Stormont sitting, Paisley told the officers: 'You have done something which will ruin your careers. From this moment on, loyalists will have no time whatsoever for the RUC.'[9] In 1986, history repeated itself after another attempt at restoring devolution was abandoned by the British government. Paisley and other DUP members were carried out of the Assembly by police, prompting him to tell the officers: 'Don't come crying to me if your homes are attacked. You will reap what you sow.'[10] This ominous warning was greeted with cheers from DUP colleagues.

Sinn Féin's position on policing was undoubtedly a vital issue by 2007, and it was at the centre of the choreography that led up to the devolution deal of that year. It needs to be recognised, though, that signing up republicans to support for the police was not always at the top of the DUP priority list. The multi-party talks at Leeds Castle, Kent, in 2004 failed over the demand for photographic evidence of decommissioning—with policing barely registering by comparison. The sharp focus on Sinn Féin's stance on policing—and the involvement of IRA members in criminality—came later.

It has been argued that the US Special Envoy to Northern Ireland Mitchell Reiss had a central role in placing attention on policing.[11] The Northern Bank robbery of December 2004 and the subsequent murder of Belfast man Robert McCartney by republicans were obviously also critical factors in the process.

The DUP's joint manifesto for the 2005 Westminster and local council elections contained no specific reference to the need for republicans to sign up to policing. It said Sinn Féin could only be considered for entry to an Executive after 'complete visible, verifiable decommissioning', a 'total end to all paramilitary and criminal activity' and when 'the community is convinced the IRA has been stood down'. The manifesto also underlined the DUP's demand for 'timetabled, verifiable, transparent and complete decommissioning, photographed and witnessed'.

Any hopes of a deal on the verification issue had been scuppered, not long after the Leeds Castle talks, when Paisley demanded photographs as a method of humiliation for republicans. He told a party gathering in his north Antrim base that 'seeing is believing', adding: 'This is the vital matter. Unionists will not settle for another disingenuous and valueless decommissioning event.' Responding to claims that he was attempting to humiliate republicans, Paisley said: 'The IRA needs to be humiliated. And they need to wear their sackcloth and ashes, not in a backroom but openly.'[12]

But his demand was not met, as the IRA went ahead with final decommissioning on its own terms in September 2005. No photographs were produced and the DUP's choice of an independent witness was not present. This left Paisley and co. without the longed-for humiliation. The 'vital matter' he had pinpointed was not addressed after all. This has not stopped the DUP subsequently claiming credit for the IRA's final act of decommissioning. Its Assembly 2007 manifesto, for example, said the party had successfully 'required republicans to give up their weapons'. Likewise, Paisley Jnr has stated: 'Decommissioning for a period of time seemed to become the raison d'etre of the Ulster Unionist Party. Yet significant decommissioning was only achieved when the DUP was in the driving seat.'[13]

And Paisley Snr himself told an interviewer during the 2007 election campaign: 'You are recognising our success in achieving decommissioning...'[14] Paisley may have forgotten that he had previously described the IRA's final decommissioning act as a 'charade'.[15] This claim came during a brief controversy in early 2006 over whether the IRA had put all of its weapons beyond use the previous September. The government-appointed Independent Monitoring Commission cited unconfirmed reports that some handguns may have been retained for personal protection purposes. Seizing on this issue, Paisley told the DUP's conference in February 2006:

> When I look back over the last month, I see the mighty host of forces intent on pushing down the throats of the Ulster people the blatant lie that the IRA has decommissioned all its weapons. That falsehood was so blatant even Lord Haw-Haw would have blushed to utter it.[16]

The handguns question soon faded away. But it must have helped to confuse the DUP rank-and-file. One year, you are being told that decommissioning was a vile fraud. Twelve months later, it was a great victory for your party.

Further points should be made on the question of republicans signing up to policing. Firstly, a central element in this policy shift involved Sinn Féin MLAs taking places on the Northern Ireland Policing Board. This was the most public manifestation of the new era. It provided tangible evidence that Sinn Féin was part of the policing system, and had made the crucial change demanded of it by the DUP and others. But the same DUP had previously denounced the very notion of republicans joining the Policing

Board. In her maiden speech in the House of Commons in 2001, DUP MP Iris Robinson spoke of police officers being betrayed, while 'terrorists' were being 'elevated into government and even offered places on the very body that has authority over the police'.[17]

In February 2006, Ian Paisley Jnr used his DUP conference speech to warn Secretary of State Peter Hain of the consequences of Sinn Féin joining the Policing Board. He challenged Hain to 'state clearly that it would not be credible or possible to include the Godfathers of terror and the Mafia of Ulster onto the Police Board' and pledged: 'If he brings Sinn Féin/IRA anywhere near the Police Board then it too will be over!'[18]

That was uttered little more than a year before the devolution deal was sealed between the DUP and Sinn Féin. Again, some loyal Paisleyites must have been left wondering if they had missed something. At one time, the idea of Sinn Féin joining the Policing Board was a betrayal which would bring about the body's collapse. And then it was suddenly part of a vital and remarkable move that had finally cleared the way for power-sharing.

It should also be noted that republicans would hardly have changed their position without the Patten Commission reforms on policing—especially the remodelling of the RUC into the PSNI.[19] The DUP lambasted the Patten reform process from beginning to end, and blamed it on David Trimble at every opportunity.

BROKEN PLEDGES

Various factors can be cited for the DUP's success in ousting David Trimble and becoming the undisputed leader of unionism. Some will accuse Trimble of failing to effectively lead his party and community, or to positively sell the Belfast Agreement. On a more general point, the divisions in the UUP over the accord were also a turn-off for voters. Others will point the finger at the British government, in relation to concessions to Sinn Féin and the impact these had on the unionist community. Continued IRA activities did not make things easier for Trimble.

Republicans, meanwhile, would counter that a significant number of Protestants just could not stomach the idea of power-sharing at all and would always find an excuse to say no. But one simple phrase must be given a star billing in any history of this period. It is 'no guns no government'—the mantra that encapsulated the UUP's pledge not to go into government with Sinn Féin ahead of decommissioning of IRA weaponry.

The DUP relentlessly hammered Trimble for not living up to this commitment. It was a very effective criticism. One of the first sections in the DUP manifesto for the 2001 Westminster elections was entitled 'Broken Pledges of UUP'. Quoting the 'no guns no government' phrase, the manifesto stated: 'The UUP leadership simply can't be trusted anymore.'

The DUP knew the unionist electorate well, and knew the power of this simple message. It is therefore remarkable that it sometimes failed to learn from Trimble's experience when on the road to a deal itself. In its eagerness to see off the UUP, it gave pledges to the public that it did not keep, and made comments that would inevitably be thrown back at it by hardline opponents.

The most famous of these came from Ian Paisley at a Twelfth of July demonstration in 2006. It was made in a speech to members of the Independent Orange Order gathered in Portrush, County Antrim. Just three months before the St Andrews talks in Scotland that produced the framework for power-sharing, Paisley declared: 'There can be no compromise.' And on Sinn Féin taking its place in government, he vowed: 'It will be over our dead bodies. Ulster has surely learned that weak, pushover unionism is a halfway house to republicanism.'[20]

The DUP's 2005 Westminster manifesto had contained the following uncompromising words:

Inclusive, mandatory coalition government which includes Sinn Féin under d'Hondt or any other system is out of the question. If executive devolution cannot be set up on a satisfactory democratic basis, then the only option is to make Direct Rule more accountable and acceptable. It is clear from recent events that republicans have proven themselves to be incapable of making the move to exclusively democratic means. It is time to move on. Send a clear message to the Government that it must proceed without Sinn Féin. We believe a voluntary coalition supported by democratic parties across the community offers the best way forward.

Underneath these words, the manifesto stated in bold lettering: 'Unlike the UUP, when we set demands, we mean them and adhere to them.'

But by the following year and the St Andrews talks, 'mandatory coalition government' involving Sinn Féin was very far from 'out of the question'. It was the basis of the new power-sharing era.

And when the new Stormont government was finally formed, the much-maligned d'Hondt system was used to allocate ministerial posts.[21]

STEPPING BACK IN TIME

It's also worth revisiting some of the earlier comments from the House of Paisley on republicans and power-sharing. The DUP was among the most vociferous opponents of the first attempt at power-sharing, the 1974 Executive headed by UUP leader Brian Faulkner and his SDLP counterpart Gerry Fitt. Paisley was a leading supporter of the loyalist strike that brought down this short-lived partnership administration. Outright antagonism to the principle of power-sharing was a key part of his political platform. The slogan 'Reject the Republican–Unionist Executive' featured prominently in a full-page newspaper advert placed by Paisley and other anti-Faulkner unionists in January 1974.[22] By 'republican', they meant the SDLP rather than the Provisional IRA.

The Provos—whose leadership included a youthful Martin McGuinness—had no interest whatsoever in power-sharing government at this time. Their somewhat over-confident New Year message had stated: 'We look forward with confidence to 1974 as a year in which the British rule in Ireland shall be destroyed and the curse of alien power banished from our land for all time.'[23]

Bellicose opposition to power-sharing would meanwhile remain a constant theme of Paisley's politics for many years. At a

DUP conference in 1977, Paisley said his party was 'seen as the effective resistance to republicans in any future government'. He rounded on those who advocated a voluntary power-sharing coalition, claiming there was a reason why such politicians had started to 'howl'. He added: 'We kept them from their goal—the surrender of Ulster for a few thousand a year, a government car and a government job.'[24] A power-sharing deal at this time would again have been with the SDLP, rather than Sinn Féin.

In the 1980s, the DUP fought elections under the slogan 'Smash Sinn Féin'. Its manifesto for the 1985 local government poll, for example, vowed to 'challenge, confront and confound' Sinn Féin councillors wherever they raised their heads.

> The DUP will seek to exclude them from all council committees, delegations and places of authority, nor will any of our councillors be fraternising with them before, during or after council meetings. The Sinn Féiners must be ostracised and isolated whether it be at council meetings or associated bodies such as education and library boards, health and social services boards, the Housing Council, the Association of Local Authorities or council group committees.

This uncompromising attitude continued right through the 1990s as well, regardless of IRA ceasefire moves. In 1997, Paisley said: 'I will never sit down with Gerry Adams ... He'd sit with anyone. He'd sit down with the devil. In fact, Adams does sit down with the devil.'[25] The same kind of absolutist rhetoric was to the fore in DUP opposition to the 1998 Belfast Agreement. His critics like to point out that the 2006 St Andrews Agreement that Paisley endorsed made no major changes to the Belfast Agreement.

Constitutional lawyers could doubtless argue long into the night over the importance of specific differences between the two documents. The key changes negotiated by the DUP at St Andrews included accountability provisions for both Stormont ministers and cross-border institutions. But the party's opposition to the Belfast Agreement was not based on such matters. The need for Sinn Féin to support policing was not uppermost in its thoughts at this time either.

Nor was its campaign for a No vote in the 1998 referendum exclusively about a lack of clarity on decommissioning. Alongside all the outrage about 'murderers in government' back then, Paisley took the opportunity to reiterate his continuing rejection of any power-sharing arrangement. In one interview during the referendum campaign, he proclaimed that he was 'opposed to power-sharing with nationalists because nationalists are only power-sharing to destroy Northern Ireland'.[26] That clearly meant the SDLP as well as Sinn Féin. In the same interview, he also called for majority-rule-style devolution on the same lines as other parts of the UK, adding: 'It's good enough for Wales and Scotland. It should be good enough for us.'

With his clerical dog collar on, Paisley and his Free Presbyterian colleagues also confidently claimed in 1998 that voting No was nothing less than a moral imperative. His church's General Presbytery placed a sizeable newspaper advert on the week of the Belfast Agreement referendum vote, which stated: 'It is the duty of Christians everywhere to actively and fervently oppose this Agreement.'

The Free Presbyterian ad was accompanied by a long list of Protestant ministers' names, including those of Paisley and his clergyman son Kyle. It also stated that the Belfast Agreement bore 'all the hallmarks of devilish craft' and was a 'blueprint for the strangulation of Biblical Protestantism'. For good measure, a 'Roman Catholic manipulated media' was accused of promoting a Yes vote.

Arguing that it was the God-given duty of governments to punish evil and reward good, the advert also stated: 'The fundamental principle which lies at the heart of any stable and peaceable society has been dispensed with in this Agreement. Set against a backdrop of lies and deceitfulness it ensures that those who have supported and advocated violence will sit in government over our people.'[27] Not all of Paisley's followers had forgotten those particular words nine years later, when he and Martin McGuinness became First Ministers together.

Convinced that God was on his side on the Belfast Agreement, Paisley set about attacking David Trimble for backing the pact in the most extreme terms. He told the DUP's annual conference in 1998: 'He is a liar, a cheat, a hypocrite, a knave, a thief, a loathsome reptile which needs to be scotched.'[28] Paisley was not using language like that because he believed the Agreement was lacking some technical accountability measures for ministers. As Trimble himself has pointed out, his crime involved heading a coalition government alongside the SDLP's Seamus Mallon.

Paisley was not the only DUP figure to indulge in such hardline posturing. Also at the 1998 conference, DUP deputy leader Peter Robinson said: 'The only cabinet the Provos should be in has brass handles on it.'[29] In the same year, Paisley Jnr told a loyalist rally in Portadown that the UUP was consorting with Sinn Féin to 'sell Ulster down the river to Dublin'. He continued: 'This is no way to deal with the IRA. The only good IRA man is a dead one and they should be exterminated.'[30] Junior also told a newspaper interviewer that he had no intention of ever speaking to Gerry Adams. 'I find him repulsive,' he continued. 'If he was in physical danger and I had an opportunity to save him I would not step across the road to do it. In fact, I think I would smile as he suffered.'[31]

Rank-and-file DUP and Free Presbyterian members who took this kind of talk seriously could be forgiven for feeling a tad perturbed by March 2007. They had been taught in the past that the enemies of Ulster included not just republicanism, but all shades of nationalism, the Dublin government, the London government and liberal unionists. Even the middle-of-the-road Alliance was also on the list once upon a time, as 'the pro-Popery Party of Northern Ireland'. That description came courtesy of Paisley's church magazine back in 1981, which added for good measure: 'Basically the Alliance Party has the same spirit as the Roman Inquisition, and would silence and put to death all who would raise their voices in protest against the errors, pernicious doctrines and idolatrous practices of the Roman Catholic system.'[32]

Having received such a warning about the seemingly harmless Alliance, what exactly were the loyal followers to make of a new partnership government between the DUP and Sinn Féin? They had, it should be acknowledged, been warned that a deal would come about some day. Paisley's church once told them during the Troubles:

> In the face of this onslaught and challenge, the Protestant people must not trust in princes nor in the sons of men in whom there is no help. Let them remember that whatever the Church of Rome and its hierarchy may seem to do now, it will in the end make its peace with the I.R.A.—just the same way as it has made its peace with the Communist dictatorship in Poland. Let them also remember that for all its protestations the British Government will also make peace with the gunmen as it did in Rhodesia and elsewhere.[33]

The bit about Paisley making his own peace with republicanism clearly didn't quite make it into the final version of this message.

A TIME FOR CHANGE

It is entirely reasonable and in many cases essential for politicians to adapt and change. Strong arguments are not difficult to compile in support of unionism reaching an accommodation with republicanism. Maybe, in light of the IRA ceasefire, it was always going to be about when and on what terms a deal would eventually be done. But changing while pretending you have not changed is not a viable or sustainable position.

That's essentially what Paisley did. He even declared in one of his last interviews as DUP leader, in May 2008, that there had been 'no real change as far as our policy was concerned'.[34] Yet his previous firm stances on the Belfast Agreement, power-sharing and republicanism are impossible to reconcile with his entry into government. He dealt with these contradictions by simply acting as if they were not there. He seemed to want people to believe that the central issue down through the decades had really been securing Sinn Féin support for policing.

Paisley may in the end have had little option politically but to part company with the old hardliners and leave them to their political cul-de-sac. But given that he had personally marched them into that cul-de-sac, they were at least owed an honest exposition of his new position. It never came. Nor was there any acknowledgment, let alone an apology, for the likes of Faulkner or Trimble—previous unionist converts to power-sharing who were driven from office for their 'sins'.

However, none of this seemed to matter too much in the first few months of Paisley's power-sharing era. All was well, Stormont was getting stuck into the business of government, and anyone feeling in any way uncomfortable about the whole thing was surely just locked in the past.

At this stage, the anti-deal brigade in unionism looked pretty much like a spent force. The angry protest against Paisley at the pre-Twelfth rally at Loughgall, County Armagh, seemed a throwback, and unrepresentative of the prevailing mood.

There was little evidence of opposition to the new First Minister at the 2007 Twelfth of July demonstration of the Independent Orange Order, held in Ballymoney. This was just 12 months after he had pledged that Sinn Féin would be in government 'over our dead bodies'. A *Belfast Telegraph* report from the Ballymoney parade stated:

> There had been fears of hecklers and jeering, particularly from disheartened members of Mr Paisley's Free Presbyterian Church, but these proved to be unfounded. There was at least one poster in the town talking of an unholy DUP alliance and graffiti on the main road between Ballymena and Ballymoney which read 'No DUP sell out', but Mr Paisley received much support. There were rumours that some of the lodges and bandsmen would boycott the field but, again, they proved untrue and Mr Paisley was applauded on to the platform to make his speech.[35]

The rump of hardline unionism would nevertheless make a dramatic comeback over the next nine months. It made a decisive impact, firstly in Paisley's own church and then in a council by-election in the quiet County Down town of Dromore. These revolts had dramatic repercussions for the First Minister. But in the summer days of 2007, few pundits were predicting any great turbulence for Paisley. At that stage, the principal controversy on the political front had not been about power-sharing at all. The main discord at Stormont instead involved attitudes to homosexuality.

Welcome to the strange world of post-devolution Northern Ireland.

Chapter 3
With God on our Side

'With its domineering mothers, muscle Mary gangsters and toy-town soldier flute bands, Northern Ireland is plainly as gay as Christmas.'
Columnist NEWTON EMERSON[1]

It was not particularly surprising that the first big row of the new Stormont was caused by Junior Minister Ian Paisley Jnr. The fact that it was about gay rights was a little less predictable.

Well known for his brashness, Paisley Jnr was never going to let the mere trifle of being in government stop him from spouting his views. The living embodiment of the phrase 'My dad's bigger than your dad', he is unlikely to have been challenged too much during his rise up the ranks of the DUP. A one-man brat pack, he was never that popular with party members, and some grumbled quietly about him lacking his father's charm and warmth. Tackling him openly was a different matter, given his daddy's great affection for him.

Paisley Jnr was always something of a stirrer in political terms, with a liking for mischief that is said to go back to his childhood. His father once stated: 'Ian Jnr was particularly mischievous. Ian was a mouse man. He was always putting mice on the teachers' desks and waiting for the screams!'[2] How they must have laughed.

Paisley Jnr has himself been quite open about enjoying a good disagreement. 'I love controversy,' he said on one occasion. 'I think it's very healthy, it's the spice of life.'[3] That attitude is not a problem for an Opposition politician, but it can cause problems when you are a minister.

When Paisley Jnr was interviewed by a journalist from the Dublin magazine *Hot Press* in the spring of 2007, he gave full vent to his views on homosexuality. 'I am pretty repulsed by gay and lesbianism,' he said. 'I think it is wrong. I think that those people harm themselves and—without care about it—harm society. That doesn't mean to say that I hate them ... I mean I hate what they do.'

Asked by the *Hot Press* interviewer if gay people should abstain from sex, he replied that they should 'free' themselves from 'being gay'. He also said:

> These are people in a country which previously had a very strong family value and moral fibre—and that is slowly but surely being eradicated. I'm not saying that is all the fault of people who've a gay and lesbian outlook, but all of that adds to the problems society goes through.[4]

Paisley Jnr was not in this case simply striking a controversial pose, to kick off a row for the fun of it. He has been a long-time follower of his dad's brand of Protestantism, undergoing a religious conversion at the age of five.

His outspoken comments to *Hot Press* did not come as a particular shock. In 2004, he had vowed to oppose civil part-nerships for same-sex couples, saying it was 'an abhorrent demand that turns the stomach of any decent thinking person'. He added for good measure on that occasion: 'The DUP will continue to oppose attempts to enshrine immorality in the law of this land.'[5]

This crusade failed. Gay civil partnerships became legal in Northern Ireland in December 2005, a couple of days ahead of England.

Earlier in 2005, Paisley Jnr had denounced an adviser to David Trimble, Steven King, for marrying his male partner in a civil ceremony in Canada. Paisley Jnr described such gay relationships as 'offensive and obnoxious'.[6] That earned him a rebuke from fellow members of the Northern Ireland Policing Board. He hit back at that vote of censure with a press release entitled 'Police Board moves from farce to fairygate'.[7]

His remarks to *Hot Press* in 2007 were made public a few weeks into the new devolutionary era, creating a much more serious dispute. That was because Paisley Jnr was by this stage a minister in the Office of the First Minister and Deputy First Minister (OFMDFM), the Stormont department responsible for equality issues in Northern Ireland. This equality remit included equality for gay people. There was widespread criticism of him—possibly more than he might have anticipated and unquestionably more than would have been the case 10 years earlier. Northern Irish society had become more liberal despite the best efforts of the Paisley family. The Church of Ireland *Gazette* published a sternly worded editorial on him entitled 'Apologise or resign'. It stated: 'His comments are a complete disgrace to the Stormont administration and reflect sheer crassness.'[8]

Among those from the Assembly to speak out was Deputy First Minister Martin McGuinness. He made it clear that Paisley Jnr had not been expressing the views of the OFMDFM, and added:

> I don't know what he's going to do, but I certainly think that we have a problem insofar as a junior minister in that department has expressed views which are a total contradiction of everything that the OFMDFM is charged to do in terms of protecting the rights of all sorts of people within our society, including minorities.[9]

It provided an early discordant note at Stormont, jarring with the general positive atmosphere surrounding devolution. A formal complaint was made to the watchdog for MLA behaviour, Standards Commissioner Tom Frawley. An investigation was duly launched to see if the Assembly Code of Conduct had been breached. Frawley took the view that no rules had been broken and that MLAs had freedom of speech. His report stated:

> I consider that Members of the Assembly, as publicly elected representatives, must be free, within the law, to express their personal views on all social and moral matters not least because freedom of expression lies at the heart of any democratic

society. It will inevitably be the case that in some instances such expressions of opinions may be found to be unacceptable by some sections of society.[10]

The Code of Conduct, in truth, contained little of relevance in the circumstances. It was an outdated document, dating back to the previous Assembly that had collapsed in 2002. The text appears to have been simply copied and pasted from the House of Commons Code of that time.

Frawley's report on Paisley Jnr did contain a word of warning for MLAs. It stated: 'I consider, however, that Members of the Assembly, as public representatives, do have a particular responsibility for the manner in which they express their personal beliefs and views.'

When children misbehave, it is not uncommon to blame their upbringing and their parents. A case can be made for Paisley Jnr on these grounds. His father's views on homosexuality were long-standing, regularly aired and even more extreme. In 1977, Paisley Snr famously launched a 'Save Ulster from Sodomy' campaign in an unsuccessful bid to stop the Labour government decriminalising gay sex in the province. Junior would have been just 11 at this time. He might very well have read an edition of his dad's church magazine from 1977 which declared:

> The crime of sodomy is a crime against God and man, and its practise [sic] is a terrible step to the total demoralisation of any country and must inevitably lead to the breakdown of all decency in the province. It is a crime against God, man and woman. It is unnatural, a perversion of sex and a generator of all forms of uncleanness and bestiality. It is as unnatural as sex between man and the beasts of the field.[11]

By comparison, Junior's comments to *Hot Press* were really quite mild. The furore over what he had said to the magazine formed part of a series of political rows concerning homosexuality.

Just as devolution was being established, it was revealed that one of the DUP's new ministries—Culture, Arts and Leisure—was helping to fund the forthcoming 2007 Belfast Gay Pride parade. The grant had already been pledged by a promotions quango financed directly by the Department. The DUP's new Culture, Arts and Leisure Minister was Edwin Poots, a member of Paisley's Free Presbyterian Church. He had been to the fore in an unsuccessful attempt to prevent same-sex civil partnership ceremonies being conducted in the marriage room of his district council's civic centre. Poots, despite his personal views, recognised that he was not going to be able to stop the Gay Pride funding from his department's budget. He commented: 'There is little point making decisions that will end up being overturned in a court of law.'[12]

Poots was nevertheless roundly condemned by Tyrone-based Free Presbyterian Minister Rev. Ivan Foster. Foster, a one-time close ally of Paisley, was fiercely opposed to the power-sharing arrangement and made no attempt to hide his feelings on his church leader's new role in government. Commenting on the Gay Pride funding, he said: 'Far from the DUP elevating the morals of society, it seems that the DUP is going to come down to the level of morality that society demands.'[13]

If the Paisleyite base was a little perturbed by the small Gay Pride grant, worse was soon to follow. It turned out that the new First Minister's own department was signed up to pay some £180,000 over to gay groups.[14] The money had been agreed by Secretary of State Peter Hain prior to the return of devolution. It was being provided, as part of the OFMDFM's equality role, to assist lesbian, gay, bisexual and transgender groups. Now First Minister Paisley found himself inheriting the financial commitment. The political reality was that there was nothing he could do to stop the payments—they had already secured ministerial approval from Hain. Rescinding that decision could have led to a court challenge, and would also have required the backing of the Deputy First Minister.

But this kind of logic held little sway in the absolutist world of Free Presbyterianism. These people had been reared on the biblical story of Daniel, who not only risked his job in government but was prepared to brave a lion's den rather than forsake his principles. Ivan Foster constantly attacked Paisley on the gay funding, using it as a disturbing example of the consequences of the devolution deal.

In the media world, the OFMDFM's grant-aid was no big deal. It made a few headlines, doubtless prompted a few laughs at the irony of it all, and faded away as a story. But it festered within the Free Presbyterian Church for months and was still being addressed by Paisley in front of his congregation the following year.

Homosexuality offends the very core of fundamentalist Protestantism in Northern Ireland. But they do leave themselves open to the accusation of being obsessed with this particular 'sin'. Many in the DUP have needed no second invitation to voice their fury. One of the party's councillors in Ballymena, Maurice Mills, declared in 2005 that the Hurricane Katrina disaster that had devastated New Orleans was God's judgment. Mills said:

> The media failed to report that the hurricane occurred just two days prior to the annual homosexual event called the Southern Decadence Festival which the previous year had attracted an estimated 125,000 people. Surely this is a warning to nations where such wickedness is increasingly promoted and practised. This abominable and filthy practice of sodomy has resulted in the great continent of Africa being riddled with Aids.[15]

The outcry against these remarks did not stop Mills later becoming DUP Mayor of Ballymena.

There were some suggestions that hardline religious outbursts from the DUP would become a thing of the past after Paisley stood down as leader in June 2008. New leader Peter Robinson, although a member of a massive Elim church, was viewed as being from the more secular wing of the party. Yet within hours of him taking over, his politician wife Iris was on the radio denouncing homosexuality as an 'abomination'.[16] She also subsequently declared that the government had a 'responsibility to uphold God's laws'.[17]

This comment highlights the wider significance behind the repeated DUP gay rows, and helps explain why this subject mattered so much in the overall picture. The DUP was not just a political-religious pressure group or a sect any more, but the largest governing party in Northern Ireland's devolved administration. It was not just there to look after its own people, but to govern for the whole of society. That meant gays and bisexuals as well as heterosexuals; agnostics and atheists as well as Protestants and Catholics and those of other faiths. This clearly covered a great many other people who did not share the creed of Iris Robinson, or agree with her particular interpretation of the Bible and 'God's laws'. There was then a potential conflict for DUP figures to grapple with at Stormont. Could they hold true to their core beliefs and provide quality inclusive government at the same time?

Iris Robinson herself provided one example of this conflict. She had been appointed by her party to chair the Assembly's health committee, scrutinising the work of the Department of Health. One of the pressing issues facing Northern Ireland's NHS is suicide among young people, particularly young men.[18] Iris Robinson has repeatedly pressed for action on the problem. In an article in September 2007, she wrote: 'Too many young lives continue to be lost to suicide in Northern Ireland.'[19]

But surely she must have realised that sexuality-related issues could be a contributory factor in youth suicide rates, particularly in religiously conservative communities? Can it ever assist young people grappling with their sexual identity to have it publicly condemned as an 'abomination'? Is that a positive contribution from the chair of the Assembly health committee? Peter Robinson, meanwhile, publicly endorsed his wife's views, saying: 'It wasn't Iris Robinson who determined that homosexuality was an abomination, it was the Almighty.'[20]

Inevitably, the conflict for the religious fundamentalists on finding themselves in government was most acute for Ian Paisley. Paisley became First Minister in May 2007 while at the same time remaining Moderator of the Free Presbyterian Church. He always maintained that politics was secondary to his religious calling, stating as far back as 1972: 'Let me tell you friends that I am first and foremost a Protestant preacher of the old time religion, and I am only in politics incidentally because of the tragedy of our country.'[21]

While Paisley could regularly top the poll at election time, his Free Presbyterian Church never made it beyond the margins. Its membership across the province is estimated to be in the region of just 12,000. As First Minister, Paisley found himself heading a society that was dramatically out of step with his core beliefs. This inevitably led to some interesting contradictions.

When devolution arrived, Paisley's new department, the OFMDFM, was locked in a court battle with a coalition of Christian groups over gay equality legislation introduced under Direct Rule. Paisley's church backed the legal challenge through support for one of the groups involved, the Christian Institute. Others in the coalition included an organisation called Christian Camping International, which seemed a somewhat unfortunate name in the circumstances. The Catholic Church also intervened in the case to oppose the legislation.

The judicial review case against the OFMDFM continued for the first four months of Paisley's period as First Minister. That meant his government department and his church were on opposite sides of High Court proceedings. OFMDFM officials attended court, and retained high-powered lawyers during this period. The Department's legal costs in defending the case came to some £102,524.[22] There was nothing Paisley could realistically have done to halt an OFMDFM legal battle that predated his time in office. But the bizarre position still highlighted the pitfalls of heading a government in a less-than-holy land, while leading an old-time church at the same time.

The inherent contradictions were also evident with other traditional preoccupations of Free Presbyterianism. The church has been fighting a losing battle in its major social priorities over the years. These have included protesting against 'indecency' on the stage, keeping Sunday special and promoting abstinence from alcohol. Paisley has long been exasperated with the levels of drinking among the people of Belfast. In a sermon entitled 'The Curse of Booze' in 1982, he said:

Here we are in this great city with all its evangelical background, with all its gospel preaching, with all its Bibles and evangelism, and the tide of alcoholic liquor is taking this generation down to Hell, and polluting and poisoning and corrupting the coming generation, and the temperance battle of a past generation has got to be re-fought today in this city.[23]

Things have not got any better for him since then. Even the Twelfth of July, the biggest day in the calendar of Orangeism, is now a major booze festival for the Protestant working class. To listen to the Orange Order, the Twelfth is about reaffirming Biblical Protestantism and the principles of the Reformation. But on Belfast's Lisburn Road, one of the main parade routes, spectators are knocking back the lager and alcopops all day. Such a party atmosphere is probably not far removed from community festivals in many other parts of the world. But it does say something about the limited impact of the Paisleyite religious message.

There was a time too when the arrival of anything vaguely racy at Northern Ireland theatres would be the subject of a major rumpus. Not any more. Adult-themed plays and other shows are regularly on stage now, with their subject matter barely remarked upon. An article in the *Belfast Telegraph* in February 2008 pointed out that two plays featuring nudity and sexual content—*Equus* and *Closer*—were being performed in the city's Grand Opera House in the space of a week. It noted that 'seemingly not a word has been uttered, nor a sacrament quoted, in opposition from any of the province's more conservative quarters'.[24]

Sundays too have become very different days. The era when swings in children's parks were tied up on the Lord's Day is long gone. Now Sunday in Northern Ireland can involve an online bet on an English premiership match, watching the game in the pub over a boozy lunch, sobering up enough to go shopping in the afternoon, and then taking in an 18-certificate horror movie at the local multiplex.

Such realities of life created mini-conflicts for Paisley. It was only fitting, for example, that the First and Deputy First Ministers should be guests of honour at the opening of Belfast's upmarket Victoria Square shopping centre in March 2008. Paisley captured the feel of the event by describing the launch of the mall as heralding 'a brand new chapter in the history of Belfast and Northern Ireland'.[25] But were there any reservations in the back of his mind about the fact that Victoria Square not only traded on Sundays, but also included booze-serving restaurants?

Likewise, it was entirely natural for a First Minister to issue a statement welcoming a planned concert by rock band The Police in the grounds of Stormont. 'This is a fantastic coup for Northern Ireland, an event of this magnitude has a sizeable benefit for the economy, not least our tourism industry,' Paisley enthused. 'The beautiful grounds of the Stormont Estate are a fantastic venue for this event and it is fitting that they should be used by the public in this way.'[26]

But surely the Moderator of Free Presbyterianism should have been reiterating his view that rock music is of the devil? 'Rock music is satanic' is how he put it in a sermon in 1986. 'Let me repeat that, rock music is satanic, and those who have studied it have proved that conclusively.'[27] Paisley had previously objected to an Elton John concert at the same venue in 1998, telling an interviewer: 'It degrades Stormont.' Paisley Jnr helpfully explained on that occasion: 'We don't like poofs.'[28]

Alongside his many triumphs on the political scene, Paisley has faced defeat after dispiriting defeat when it came to spiritual battles with the modern world. It is in this context that the deep concerns within Free Presbyterianism about grants to gay groups should be viewed. Its campaign to 'Save Ulster from Sodomy' had failed miserably, just like so many other struggles. And it was presumably too much to bear that its leader now headed a department that was handing out money to these very same people. The fact that Paisley had no role in authorising the money, that it had all been Peter Hain's doing, would not have been much comfort.

Members were actually assured in their very place of worship that Paisley had personally blocked the gay grants. In January 2008, he told a Martyrs Memorial Church meeting that he had refused to sign papers, resulting in the matter having to be taken to Westminster. He claimed he had been told by officials that he had to hand over the remainder of the money agreed by Mr Hain. 'Says I they are not getting one ha'penny from me,' Paisley continued. 'The civil servants said we need to sign there. Says I—no signature, take it away, don't come back to me.' His statement to the church added: 'They took the paper to Westminster and signed it at Westminster and they gave them the money they had promised, but I never gave them a penny, not a penny.' He also told his congregation: 'They told me that if I didn't do it I would be put in prison. Says I roll on the prison, I've been there before.'[29]

Some two months later, in a 30 March address to the church entitled 'False accusers, proven liars', Paisley claimed his account of the gay funding dispute had been vindicated. He strongly attacked claims about the grant-aid made 'by people who call themselves Christians and I used to call them my friends' and added: 'This week, the whole thing has come out into the open.' Paisley continued:

The liars are answered and I have a House of Commons document in my hand in which it states plainly that I was the man who made the objection, refused to sign anything and that the whole system had been jammed up by me. In fact, one of the Tory MPs at the committee meeting this week—for I went to hear what was being said—he said: 'They just told us do your own dirty work, we're not doing the dirty work for you.' And I said amen, that's exactly right, that's exactly what happened.

Paisley concluded: 'So continue to pray for me and thank God it's all on the record now.'[30]

What was really on the record was something quite different. The Commons committee meeting he referred to was dealing with the implementation of an EU directive on gender equality—not grant-aid for gay groups. The legislation required by Europe had to be enacted on a UK-wide basis, after Paisley and Martin McGuinness could not agree on a way forward in Northern Ireland.

This was because Paisley objected to the inclusion within new regulations of references to transgender and gender reassignment.

The Commons committee on 'delegated legislation' met on 27 March, just three days before Paisley made his claims to his church. The Hansard record of the Westminster discussions quotes Tory MP John Bercow saying:

> Is it the case that senior Northern Irish politicians, who have a genuine objection to the measure, said, 'We don't want to soil our own hands with it and therefore we're not going to touch it, but if you, the UK Government, wish to touch it, we are not pleased about it, but you must do your own dirty work because we are not going to do it for you.'?[31]

That presumably was the source of the 'do your own dirty work' reference by Paisley to his congregation. Bercow, it should be noted, was fully in favour of the gender equality moves. And it is clear that neither he nor the committee had anything to say on funding for gay groups in Northern Ireland. The grant-aid was an entirely separate matter. It was never blocked by Paisley, because it had never been brought before him. But £100,000 of it was allocated by his department during his time as First Minister.[32]

The Martyrs Memorial worshippers were clearly fed duff information. Perhaps it was just as well in the circumstances. Given the way the world has turned out for them, denial might be the best way to cope.

Chapter 4
Dodgy Foundations

'The foolish man built his house upon the sand'[1]

It was incoming First Minister Ian Paisley who set the bar for measuring the effectiveness of the new devolved government in Northern Ireland. In his momentous March 2007 announcement of a power-sharing deal, made alongside Gerry Adams, the DUP leader said: 'Devolution has never been an end in itself but is about making a positive difference to people's lives.'[2]

That was a worthy sentiment. Good government is a crucial part of making a political settlement sustainable and popular. It had been a long wait for a stable-looking devolved administration at Stormont. And it was up to the four main Executive parties, and principally the DUP and Sinn Féin, to prove the delay had been in any way worthwhile.

So how did they do? In the early days—in keeping with the general 'feelgood' factor around Northern Ireland—the new regime made a solid enough start. The deferral of the hated household water charges was predictably popular. Ministers struck the right statesmanlike pose when dealing with a fairly short-lived threat of foot-and-mouth disease coming across from Britain. And compensation was swiftly made available to householders affected by flash flooding in the summer of 2007. But it was not long into the autumn before a vague air of disappointment began to be felt. Some of that was inevitable, given the way devolution's potential had been hyped up in the run-up to May 2007. The reality was that the Stormont administration's powers were fairly tightly constrained. Indeed, some critics have even compared it to a glorified—and expensive—county council.

The Assembly is subservient to Westminster on major affairs of state like taxation, borrowing, Europe, immigration, defence, international relations and the major levers of economic policy. Policing and justice powers were not devolved, so law and order was also off the menu. And while there is discretion on how to allocate Stormont's block grant from Whitehall, the actual room for manoeuvre is limited.

The block grant is estimated as between £7 billion and £8 billion higher than the tax raised in the province. This means the Executive is not normally in much of a position to pick a spending fight with the London Treasury—let alone win one. In these circumstances, parity with Britain is normally as good as it gets. That means key decisions on benefit and public sector pay levels can be effectively out of Stormont hands. The situation was frankly acknowledged by Sinn Féin Regional Minister Conor Murphy, some 16 months into the devolved experiment, when he said: 'unfortunately, so much of what we do here depends on the Treasury'.[3] That's the British Treasury, just in case you were wondering. And it was quite an admission by Murphy, a prominent South Armagh republican and former IRA prisoner.

All the rhetoric during the Assembly election period about replacing the hated Hain regime helped to raise expectations to unachievable levels. So too did talk of a massive peace dividend from the Treasury. On 1 November 2006, the four parties that would eventually form Stormont's coalition executive had trooped over to London to meet the then Chancellor of the Exchequer, Gordon Brown. Their aim was to secure a generous financial deal to underpin a new devolved administration, following the St Andrews Agreement of the previous month.

What they actually got from Brown was an exercise in spin of breathtaking proportions. As the talks with Brown dragged on well into that afternoon, the assembled journalists from Northern Ireland started getting restless. Deadlines were approaching—teatime TV news programmes were expecting details of what was on offer and newspaper editorial teams were planning the next day's editions. Just in time, word started coming out of the Treasury.

It was exciting. A £50 billion package was available if the St Andrews Agreement was implemented. This included an initial four-year spending commitment totalling £35 billion for the period up to 2011. According to a Treasury press release, this was equivalent 'to over £50,000 per household' in the province.[4] With figures like that being bandied about, the announcement was inevitably going to make huge headlines. People watching or reading the coverage could have been forgiven for expecting £50,000 cheques to come through their letterboxes.

The attention-grabbing totals were on the airwaves long before anyone had really checked the details. Brown and Peter Hain strolled out to talk to the waiting cameras and hammer home the significance of it all. The Chancellor's offer was 'significant' and 'extraordinary', gushed Hain. Pointing to the date, he added: 'On All Saints' Day, it's a very good, saintly day, for Northern Ireland.' For his part, Brown explained the other main element of the £50 billion package that accompanied the £35 billion spending pledge: 'I also said today that we would be prepared to have a 10 year agreement about investment in infrastructure for the future, not just four years but 10 years, worth about £18bn in that period.'[5]

Within hours, enthusiasm about the Brown offer was starting to quickly dissipate. The Confederation of British Industry (CBI) in Northern Ireland went so far as to claim that the package added up to little more than a 'nuisance payment'. The business body's chairman, Declan Billington, added: 'The offer, while good for an eye-catching headline, is in substance very little more than what is needed to keep our economy afloat.'[6]

Analysis of the figures showed that there was little, if anything, new in what Brown had said. His comment about being 'prepared to have a 10 year agreement about investment in infrastructure' suggested this was an entirely fresh initiative. In reality, an investment strategy had already been planned by Direct Rule ministers in Northern Ireland for some time.

It was officially launched in draft form in December 2004 and by 2006 was worth an estimated £16 billion for the period 2005–15. A portion of the investment money would not be coming from the government in the first instance. It would be delivered through Private Finance Initiative (PFI) deals, with developers supplying the upfront capital in return for long-term repayments from the public purse. The £35 billion four-year expenditure commitment was not overly dramatic either. Indeed, Hain subsequently accepted that it meant maintaining government spending at existing levels. In a letter to party leaders later in November, the Secretary of State said:

> Along with the benefits which the peace process has brought for the Northern Ireland economy and society more generally, Northern Ireland has enjoyed very substantial increases in public spending since Labour came to power, and the package confirms that the current level of spending will be sustained in real terms over the period to 2011.[7]

An adviser to the local parties, University of Ulster economist Michael Smyth, said they were 'spitting rivets' in fury at Brown's behaviour. 'They were patted on the heads and told they were getting a really good deal,' he added. 'Smoke and mirrors, I'm afraid, doesn't even come close to describing the whole exercise.'[8]

There is a case for the defence for Brown, however. He and his Treasury mandarins could be forgiven for thinking that Northern Ireland was already doing pretty well out of the UK exchequer. The subvention to the province is not exactly an irrelevant consideration. Moreover, by the end of 2006, public finances in the UK were becoming tight. The big spending increases of previous years under the New Labour government looked to be over. This was one of the problems that faced the new Stormont regime: bad timing. If power-sharing had been made to work a few years earlier, on the back of the 1998 Belfast Agreement, there would have been significantly more funding options at the disposal of local ministers. Faster policy delivery on the ground could have been achieved, securing greater confidence and enthusiasm among the electorate.

By the time of the DUP–Sinn Féin power-sharing agreement of 2007, the situation was changing. A lot of time and energy could be expended on debating why it took so long to secure a deal, and who was to blame for the delay. The point here, however, is that it had practical repercussions. There was less spending freedom to enable the Executive to build on the goodwill. That was soon joined by a rapidly deteriorating economic situation, due to global factors. It had also been hoped that significant extra funding for Stormont would be secured by selling off government-owned land and other assets. But then the property market slump came along and spoilt that plan.

The spending limitations facing the Executive were frankly acknowledged by Peter Robinson as Finance Minister. In his foreword to the administration's first budget, Robinson stated: 'Recent years have seen above average rates of growth in public spending which will sharply decelerate in the coming three years. This will undoubtedly cause difficulties and challenges in terms of the need to prioritise resources on where they will result in most benefit.'[9]

The Stormont parties did not give up on their quest for a cash bonanza from Brown after the November 2006 meeting. Indeed, there was even talk at one stage of power-sharing plans being scuppered if the Chancellor did not produce more goodies.

The DUP, which made the economy its top priority, had this to say in its manifesto for the March 2007 Assembly election:

When devolution returns, it is essential that an incoming Executive has the necessary resources to make a difference to people's lives. This will require a financial package for Northern Ireland. We have made it clear that resolution of this issue is a precondition for establishing devolution. Northern Ireland will never have a better opportunity to make up for the decades of underinvestment during the Troubles or to help us compete economically with the Republic of Ireland. Without such a package, Northern Ireland will face the prospect of massive local taxes, being economically uncompetitive and lacking the funding for essential infrastructure. This is not a welcome prospect for any incoming Executive. While other parties have talked about a financial package, we were the first party to put it on the agenda and the only one to make it a precondition for devolution.

In the event, Brown's funding never did live up to the hype.

There were further negotiations with the Treasury following the Assembly poll, in the run-up to the 8 May devolution day. These secured the deferral of water charges for a year. But, apart from this concession, it is hard to point to any further significant improvements on the '£50 billion' package unveiled the previous November. Even the water bills postponement proved difficult to obtain. The Treasury had been pushing for years for water charges, and Brown is said to have regarded another delay as effectively rewarding a 'failure to reform'.

A source close to Hain's NIO at the time concedes that the financial discussions in the run-up to devolution were 'difficult'. 'Often the Northern Ireland Office was coming in on behalf of the parties,' the aide adds. While stressing the significance of the funding commitments that were secured, this NIO insider agrees that a bumper deal was never really on the cards:

> I don't think the Treasury were ever in that territory. Gordon is an incredibly tough negotiator, the toughest in government. That they didn't come away with as good a deal as they wanted isn't a great surprise. As many people have seen when they looked at the small print of budgets over the years, they're not quite all they sounded at the time.

The Northern Ireland parties complained to Prime Minister Tony Blair about the funding, seemingly without much success. A source close to Blair's 10 Downing Street team says of Brown's approach at the time: 'I think he was at least optically trying to be helpful. He was trying to make it look as big as possible. I think all the parties unified trying to demand substance, rather than just optics.'

After devolution was restored, there was much less leverage with the Treasury. The Stormont parties could hardly make the lack of extra funding a dealbreaker, when their deal was done. But they still clung to the hope of a major concession from Brown, who took over from Blair as Prime Minister in June 2007.

A central wish from the new Assembly and Executive was for a radical cut in corporation tax (a tax on company income or profits). With the backing of major business interests, the Northern Ireland parties asked for the province's corporation tax rate to be split from the rest of the UK and moved towards the lower rate in the Republic. This always seemed an unachievable goal. Indeed, the 10 Downing Street source quoted above says of the corporation tax demand: 'You were never going to get that.' The NIO insider is equally blunt, commenting: 'That was never going to happen.'

There were some basic political realities involved that Stormont seemed unable to understand or acknowledge. Brown had no votes to worry about in Northern Ireland. That set it apart from Scotland, Wales and England. Slashing corporation tax in Northern Ireland but not in Scotland would have been an electoral disaster for the New Labour government. The Scottish Nationalist Party would have made major capital out of the special concession across the Irish Sea and it would have caused similar problems in Wales. Meanwhile, English taxpayers who helped to bankroll Northern Ireland's bumper subvention could hardly be expected to welcome such a measure.

Brown fobbed Stormont off by agreeing to a review of its corporation tax request by Sir David Varney, a former head of HM Revenue and Customs. Varney's report, delivered in December 2007, pointed out that lowering Northern Ireland's corporation tax would 'run the risk of encouraging profit shifting from the rest of the UK'.[10] That is not something the Treasury could take lightly.

A dissenting view on the clamour for a corporation tax cut came from prominent Irish economist Dr John Bradley. He has described the demand as 'ill-thought out' in the context of the province's dependency on UK financial support. Bradley also commented: 'It gave me no pleasure to watch this politically and economically misguided initiative being shot out of the skies by the mandarins in Her Majesty's Treasury.'[11]

Varney was subsequently commissioned to produce a follow-up report on Northern Ireland's economic competitiveness. It was issued in April 2008 and pressed the case for more privatisations and public asset sales in the province. That set the scene for more classic Brown spin, this time as Prime Minister, when he made a visit to Belfast in May 2008 for a showcase US Investment Conference. The Treasury had already agreed that the Northern Ireland administration would be able to keep all the proceeds from a projected £1.1 billion worth of public asset sell-offs in a set period. In other words, none of these funds would be clawed back to London.

Brown announced during his Investment Conference visit that this limit was being doubled, meaning that up to £2.2 billion could now be retained from asset disposals. Stormont's Department of Finance put out a swift public statement, spelling out some unfortunate facts about the Prime Minister's apparently generous offer. The Department, headed at that time by DUP deputy Peter Robinson, said the existing £1.1 billion sales target was already 'extremely ambitious' and added:

Delivering this £1.1 billion figure is going to be a considerable challenge for the Executive—more so in today's environment of depreciating land and property values. Moving the limit from £1.1 billion to £2.2 billion is a quantum increase that challenges the boundaries of reasonable expectations—thus this should not be perceived as a £1 billion cash injection into Northern Ireland.[12]

The statement also noted that the Prime Minister had confirmed that the province would not be gaining 'any form of fiscal dispensation' to promote economic growth. 'This bears out Finance Minister Peter Robinson's view that the economic destiny of Northern Ireland resides firmly in the hands of the Executive,' it added. It had all seemed so much sunnier just a year earlier.

Aside from the Investment Conference, May 2008 also saw the publication of a special *Belfast Telegraph* opinion poll to mark the first year of devolution.[13] Published just a day short of the first anniversary of devolution's return, it revealed that the public mood about Stormont was far from ecstatic. A thumping 72 per cent said devolution had made no difference to their lives. Only 21 per cent judged the Executive's performance as either very good (6 per cent) or fairly good (15 per cent). Neither good nor poor was the verdict of 47 per cent, which was hardly a major vote of confidence. The negative views outnumbered the positives, with 20 per cent rating the performance as fairly poor and another 8 per cent choosing very poor. 'Forget Happy Birthday,' was the paper's verdict. 'Today's poll blows out the candles early on the Executive's cake, with a stern "must do better" warning,' it added.

They were quite startling results, given all the early optimism and international goodwill surrounding the peace deal to end all peace deals. It was also somewhat off-message of the good people of Ulster, coming as it did alongside the much-vaunted US Investment Conference. This showcase event in Belfast was Paisley's last major engagement as First Minister. The opinion poll, which made few headlines outside the *Telegraph*, provided important evidence that the devolution train was badly running out of steam before Paisley's departure.

The tensions between the DUP and Sinn Féin that marred the rest of the year prompted nostalgia in some quarters about the Paisley era. Robinson and McGuinness were dubbed the 'Brothers Grimm' to emphasise the change of mood from the Chuckle Brothers period. But the truth is that public disillusionment was already setting in, behind the unrepresentative chuckling frontage.

The findings of the *Belfast Telegraph* poll jarred with Paisley's declared hope of 'making a positive difference'. The factors behind this go beyond the relative powerlessness of Stormont. They include some dodgy ideological foundations and basic poor judgment. Perhaps most significant, however, was the fact that much of the economic buoyancy surrounding the feelgood factor in 2007 was bogus. There was soaring hope and confidence in Northern Ireland's economy in the early days of the new Executive. But it was based on a huge housing and credit bubble. When that bubble so dramatically burst, Stormont's relative powerlessness and inadequacies were cruelly exposed.

The collective mania that surrounded rising house prices up the summer of 2007 was part of an international phenomenon. So too was the devastation created when the credit-fuelled bonanza spectacularly fell apart. Northern Ireland was afflicted by a particularly virulent form of the housing market lunacy. And, by unhappy coincidence, the fever was raging at its wildest just as Paisley and McGuinness were taking up their new government jobs. People were spending and investing with great confidence, not because their pay packets had dramatically increased, but principally because the value of their homes had soared. Anything seemed possible in this financial wonderland. The following prediction from a Dublin perspective, published in March 2007, was not untypical of the mood of the time:

> For ordinary working folk, the most obvious response from the Republic to the new Northern Ireland that is emerging from the historic Sinn Féin/Democratic Unionist Party power-sharing agreement will be a pile of money for property and business development. Business interests south of the border have been poised for at least two years to capitalise on a lasting peace. The picture of Ian Paisley and Gerry Adams sitting side by side on Monday and pledging to form an administration signalled money in the bank to investors across the island of Ireland. Billions of euros from the south are expected to flow into the purchase of sites and the creation of jobs to develop them in the North.[14]

A few months later, another commentator wrote about the ending of the British Army's operation in the north freeing up 'prime development' land in former army camps. 'Dubliners will move in as the army moves out—not United Irelanders but property developers and speculators. When one system ends and a new one emerges there's money to be made.' The article continued:

Businesses are already raking in some of that cash. AIB (Allied Irish Banks) yesterday announced profits of €101m in the North in the first six months of 2007, a 21pc growth compared to last year. To put this in perspective, growth was 9pc for the group as a whole. So climate change Northern-style—politicians from opposing traditions cooperating at last—is paying out dividends.[15]

Property was king and Northern Ireland was being wonderfully blessed in the new kingdom.

The Nationwide Building Society revealed some startling statistics in its UK-wide house price survey for the first quarter of 2007. In a press release issued on 4 April 2007, it said market growth in Northern Ireland had set a new record. And while demand was cooling generally in other regions, the province and London were bucking the trend. 'Northern Ireland made housing market history in the first quarter of 2007 with the fastest annual rate of growth anywhere in the UK since Nationwide records began in 1973,' it said.

> Prices increased by a staggering 57.6% in the last 12 months. This brings the average house price in Northern Ireland to over £200,000, a figure comparable with prices in the Outer South East. Prices in the province are still accelerating too, increasing by 14.6% during the first quarter, faster than anywhere else in the UK.

The new Northern Ireland average house price of £203,815 compared to the UK-wide figure of £175,554. In keeping with the new era unfolding at Stormont, Nationwide's commentary continued:

> The strength of the Northern Irish market has exceeded all expectations in spite of the recent economic success of the province. Northern Ireland has one of the strongest regional economies alongside London. The benefits of peace in Northern Ireland should not be discounted. House prices have increased by 281% since the Good Friday Agreement in 1998

compared to the UK average of 179%. Strong net inward migration, success in attracting jobs, infrastructure investment and spin-offs from the booming Southern Irish economy have all helped to boost the Northern Irish market. Belfast saw the fastest rate of house price growth of all of the UK major towns and cities in the first quarter of 2007—the fifth consecutive quarter that it has topped the league.

There was, however, a note of caution in conclusion: 'While additional confidence in the province may grow out of the latest political agreements, continued growth of this level is unlikely to be sustained for long, and such rapid growth in house prices might suggest that this market is more vulnerable than some other parts of the UK.'[16]

Nobody seemed particularly interested in letting such thoughts spoil the party. There was concern about those unfortunate enough to not have a stake in the housing bonanza—the would-be first-time buyers unable to afford a new home, and those dependent on depleted public sector housing stocks. But if anyone at Stormont lay awake at night worrying about the housing bubble going pop, they did not make a big public issue of their fears. It was well known that buy-to-let investors, for example, were inflating prices. But that was just the free market at work, after all.

It seems almost in poor taste to chart how dramatically it all went wrong. By October 2008, Nationwide's latest quarterly house price survey was showing Northern Ireland as experiencing seriously rapid price declines. Fionnuala Earley, the building society's chief economist, said:

Northern Ireland continues to show by far the steepest correction in house prices across the UK. Prices in the province were down another 10.8% from the previous quarter, leaving them almost 30% lower than a year ago. Even with this large fall, the price of a typical property in Northern Ireland is still only back to where it was in the third quarter of 2006. Between the end of 2005 and the end of 2007, house prices in Northern

Ireland increased by nearly 80%, compared to only 17% for the UK as a whole. This meteoric rise clearly left prices in Northern Ireland even more vulnerable to a correction, and this is the context within which the recent price fall should be viewed. At their peak, house prices in the province were above the average house price in England and 24% above the UK average house price. After the recent fall, the price of a typical property in Northern Ireland is 3% below the UK average. Confirmation that the neighbouring Republic of Ireland's economy is now in recession has certainly also not helped the property market in the province.

It's difficult with hindsight to understand how more people could not see that Northern Ireland's housing market surge was not going to end well. Delusional thinking was pretty much in vogue around the world. Super-rich whizzkids in the American and European banking industry failed to spot that granting mortgages to people with bad credit histories was not necessarily a sure-fire long-term winner.

The fall-out from the US sub-prime farce started impacting from the summer of 2007. But growing talk of a credit crunch did little initially to offset the mood surrounding the rejuvenated Northern Ireland headed by Ian Paisley. In late January 2008, the Stormont Executive's budget document for 2008–2011 declared: 'The economic outlook for Northern Ireland remains favourable.'[17] That assumption echoed the view of the experts. Shortly before Christmas 2007, First Trust Bank's latest Economic Outlook and Business Review had given a positive forecast for the province. Its study by economist and Assembly adviser Michael Smyth said:

> With the investment strategy representing a huge vote of confidence in the future of the economy and business rates on hold for the next three years, we are seeing the introduction of a new pragmatic approach to politics in Northern Ireland. Overall in this context the outlook remains broadly positive for the Northern Ireland economy over the next 12 months despite the signs of slowing growth in the national economy. Optimism

remains high.[18]

There were a number of factors responsible for the crushing of economic hopes around the world over the next 12 months, among them rising energy and commodity prices. Pride of place must go to the bursting of the housing bubble, and the associated fact that individuals and nations were living beyond their means. It was a global morality tale—of poor regulation, inadequate credit control, toxic banking debts and greed.

Northern Ireland merits its own small chapter in the story. The 'correction' in its housing market in 2008 did not just mean a bit more realism on the property prices front. Many householders found themselves in negative equity. As the property market rapidly slowed up, the construction industry starting shedding jobs and confidence. The banks stated to get jittery about all the money that developers owed them. Jobs in related sectors, like estate agency and law, also took a hit.

One of the most dramatic casualties was the County Derry building company Taggart Holdings. It had been one of the big winners of the boom years. The family firm headed by brothers Michael and John Taggart rose from modest beginnings in 1989. It recorded a turnover of £128 million in 2006 and a profit of £28 million. That year also saw it announce two massive expansion deals, reported to be worth in excess of £165 million in total.[19] There was talk of plans to build 1,000 new homes in Belfast, while the company's property portfolio also stretched overseas. Michael Taggart was said to have hired pop stars to perform at his high society wedding. The brothers appeared in the prestigious *Sunday Times* Rich List for Ireland. In October 2007, Michael was presented with the 'Emerging Talent' award at a black tie business event in Dublin. In a glowing profile piece published in 2004, rising hotshot Michael had declared: 'We enjoy doing what we do – and we'll keep doing it until we don't enjoy it any more.'[20] Or until you go belly up. Only four years later, their empire was dust and the administrators were brought in.

Even the most ardent critics of Stormont and its Executive could hardly blame them for the credit crunch or the excesses of property markets. But should Northern Ireland's political leaders not have sent out a message of caution? Or did the Executive simply not see the crash coming?

There is a strong argument that governments had a vested interest in inflating the property market delusions. In his book *The Credit Crunch*, Graham Turner noted how rising house prices became symbolic, a 'modern era indicator' of wealth and success. He wrote:

> House prices were soaring, we must all be better off. Never mind that debt was rising too. Never mind that house price inflation is a zero sum game. Society as a whole does not benefit from a rise in house prices. Those already on the ladder can only gain at the expense of a growing number unable to reach the first rung. In the short run, housing bubbles can provide a stimulus to economic growth if they hoodwink people into believing they are wealthier.[21]

There had been some warnings sounded away from Stormont about growing debt levels in Northern Ireland. The Citizens Advice Bureau had been voicing concerns on this subject for a number of years and in 2006 launched a government-funded advisory service called Dealing with Debt. It reported in 2007:

> One year on that service has dealt with over £15,000,000 worth of new debt and helped almost 2000 people. The service handled an average of £1,257,000 of new debt per month and over 160 new clients came to the service every month for help to find a way out of their debt situation.

It also put its bulging caseload into a wider context:

> The deregulation of the financial markets in the late 1980s created a widespread availability of credit and problems with debt. In 2004 the amount of debt amassed by households in the UK stood at over £1 trillion (including mortgages) for the first time, double its level of £500 billion just seven years earlier.

Since then personal debt has continued to increase.[22] Belfast trade unionist Mark Langhammer, meanwhile, highlighted flaws behind the Stormont Executive's first budget, which had been proudly described as 'business friendly'. Langhammer reminded a public debate in March 2008 that Northern Ireland was part of a bigger economy 'which relies heavily on the performance of the City of London, on housing speculation, government borrowing and spending, on vast consumer borrowing and on the availability of both easy, regulation-lite credit and the availability of low cost consumer goods from around the world'. The trade unionist and former independent Labour councillor also stated: 'In today's economy, the United Kingdom as a whole lives a lifestyle well beyond its visible means.' He further said there was nothing in the Executive's budget 'that could not and would not have been undertaken by New Labour', adding: 'It is written firmly within a free market, neo-liberal orthodoxy.'[23]

The developing economic downturn of 2008 came as a blow to central parts of the new Executive's economic strategy. These included attracting major new US investment, and encouraging an expansion of financial sector jobs. Both the US and the financial industry soon had more on their minds than Northern Ireland. The global economic crisis also served to expose some of the half-built ideological foundations of the new Stormont. It would be misleading to speak of fully fledged socio-economic creeds among the governing Assembly parties. They are basically 'catch-all' organisations who seek to appeal to their respective communities across the classes. Each is capable of making populist leftist noises when it suits them, and of adapting right-wing stances should the need arise. Over the decades of Direct Rule, the main function of the parties on bread and butter issues was to keep demanding more funding from London.

Sinn Féin has, on paper at least, left-wing policies, including opposition to the Private Finance Initiative route for funding public investments. But that policy has not stopped its Stormont ministers approving major PFI schemes in the health, education and regional development sectors.

The DUP has been equally flexible over the years. In its early days, it challenged the 'big house' unionism of the dominant Ulster Unionist Party and portrayed itself as on the side of working class Protestants. DUP founder Desmond Boal, a prominent Belfast lawyer and long-time mentor to Paisley, described the party as being 'right wing in the sense of being strong on the constitution, but to the left on social polices'.[24] But over the years, there was a slow shift to the right within the DUP on economic matters.

This may not have been a conscious decision for all the party's politicians. At times, however, a few of them have sounded as if they were reading 'Thatcherism for Beginners' in their spare time—or overdosing on strident opinion piece columns in the *Daily Mail*. They were reflecting the dominant world view of the times, an approach that had held sway since the era of Thatcher and Ronald Reagan.

This free market ideology seemed particularly deep-seated in deputy leader Peter Robinson. In June 2006, Robinson made a keynote speech to a 'management conference' in Belfast's Europa Hotel. It provided a strong flavour of the approach his party would bring to government the following year. A central theme was the pressing need to cut down on the economy's reliance on the public sector. 'The culture that is created by the public sector dominated economy will not be changed overnight,' he told the conference.

The challenge of changing the nature of the economy is a formidable one when one considers the number of people in Northern Ireland directly and indirectly employed by the public sector. An overlarge public sector also acts as a disincentive to the private enterprise which is needed to boost the local economy. At times Government is not the solution but is the problem. The role of Government is not to create jobs but to create the environment in which the private sector can create them. Too often Government activity can hurt rather than help the private sector through regulation and taxation.[25]

Robinson's party fought the 2007 Assembly election boasting of being a 'low tax', pro-enterprise party. 'The DUP believes that business is the job of the business community and that Government's role is, where possible, to remove the impediments to growth in our economy,' its manifesto declared. It further stated: 'The DUP is the only party that can solve the local tax problem. We have demonstrated at every level of Government that we are a low tax party committed to obtaining for Northern Ireland taxpayers the best value for money.'

The party had successfully lobbied Direct Rule ministers to impose a rates cap, to limit the bills householders with properties worth above £500,000 would pay. When in power, it moved to lower the cap to £400,000. The DUP, the one-time leftists on social issues, had quite a following by now among the Protestant middle class. In truth, the party had never been entirely shunned by such people. Poet John Hewitt, in his savage work 'The Coasters', captured the attitude of many better-off Protestants to early-era Paisleyism:

> When that noisy preacher started,
> he seemed old-fashioned, a survival.
> Later you remarked on his vehemence,
> a bit on the rough side.
> But you said, admit it, you said in the club,
> 'You know, there's something in what he says'.[26]

By 2007, the DUP was openly courting the middle class. It underlined its pro-business credentials by claiming the Finance and Enterprise Ministries in the Executive.

Its free marketeering agitation was not confined to Robinson. Others within the party regularly voiced similar sentiments. East Antrim MP and MLA Sammy Wilson helped to lead the charge with repeated criticism of the planning system—accusing it of holding back development. Wilson had once been known as 'Red Sammy' for his occasionally populist stances as a Belfast councillor. But in more recent years, he has become openly right-wing, happy to refer to the DUP as a 'centre-right' party that 'leans towards the Tories'.[27]

Ian Paisley Jnr was also known to spout simplistic Thatcherite-style slogans from time to time. In 2000, he described a proposed restriction on major new supermarket developments as 'an attempt to interfere in the natural course of market forces'.[28]

There was also antagonism within the DUP towards the province's small but active environmental lobby. Paisley Jnr derided them as tree huggers, as he lobbied for faster planning and for more land to be zoned for housing development. Not to be outdone, Paisley Snr gave a decidedly cool reception to an environment official in a meeting held after taking over as First Minister. The clear impression was given that the environmental agenda was an inconvenience in the new go-ahead Ulster.

However, global economic developments in 2007 and 2008 were not entirely favourable to the goal of rolling back the frontiers of the state. As the giants of the financial world started to bleed to death from the self-inflicted wounds of the credit crunch, people around the world started to question the Thatcherite/Reaganite nostrums. The idea that unregulated free market enterprise was the best way to guarantee economic growth and rising prosperity for all was suddenly not so popular.

Northern Ireland's former energy regulator Douglas McIldoon introduced an official electricity price review report in late 2008 with the words:

> The timing of this report, amidst all the distress and suffering which flows from the turmoil in the world's financial markets, at least means that there cannot still be many people left who believe that unregulated markets know best and that the short term private interests of individuals or companies in some inexplicable way is automatically aligned with the public interest.[29]

The cause of free market capitalism was hardly helped by the fact that huge banking institutions had to be saved by government intervention in the UK and US, costing taxpayers billions upon billions of pounds. In Northern Ireland, there was a low-rent version of this upsurge in corporate welfarism. The struggling construction industry started pressing the Executive to give it work, through social housing developments and the speeding up of other planned public investment projects. But Robinson—by now First Minister—seemed to be trying to keep some vestiges of the free market faith. He even managed to quote Reagan in a speech at the height of the banking crisis, telling a business dinner in his constituency: 'The events of recent days have borne out Ronald Reagan's comments that Government's view of the economy could be summed up in a few short phrases: If it moves, tax it. If it keeps moving, regulate it. And if it stops moving, subsidise it.'[30]

If Robinson actually believed the US and UK governments had been wrong to subsidise the ailing banking sector, he did not say so. In any event, the looming recession had by this stage dented any hopes of a Stormont drive against regulation, subsidy and government intervention. It was a sorry sight. The new Northern Ireland was all dressed up, ready for a whirlwind romance with free-market capitalism. Sadly, the old chap had been less than virtuous around the world, cavorting in the wrong places and becoming infected with toxic sores. The romance was over.

Instead, the much-maligned public sector was being proclaimed as a much-needed protector for the province's economy. In September 2008, the First Trust Bank's latest Economic Outlook report stated: 'Public expenditure, though under pressure from higher inflation, will safeguard living standards and jobs for hundreds of thousands of people in Northern Ireland.'[31]

That same month, Robinson's successor as DUP Finance Minister Nigel Dodds told an Assembly committee: 'The extent to which the local economy can degenerate into a recession is minimised by the size and influence of our public sector.'[32]

As 2008 was drawing to a close, Dodds was sounding positively Keynesian on the potential for public works to assist the construction sector, saying: 'Whilst things are difficult, the fact that 40% of all the construction industry's output is in the public sector—far greater than other parts of the United Kingdom—does provide greater help and support to the construction industry than other regions.'[33]

Bless the good old public sector. Who could say a bad word against it? It should be noted that the DUP's zeal for the private sector had already taken a battering around a year earlier, before the credit crunch had really started to bite. That was due to a huge political row over a rock formation on Northern Ireland's north coast.

Chapter 5
Causeway for Concern

'Using private money is one of the new ways of doing things'
DUP MLA SAMMY WILSON, Stormont debate on a Giant's Causeway visitor centre[1]

In September 2007, the Giant's Causeway, Northern Ireland's top tourist attraction, became the subject of the new Assembly's first big policy bust-up. The issue quickly became complicated by controversy over the lobbying activities of DUP politician Ian Paisley Jnr. However, it is useful to separate both subjects out to some extent. That is what the next two chapters will attempt to do. The unfolding revelations about Junior's lobbying had the wider political significance, as they eventually cost him his ministerial job. But the Causeway row is of separate importance, as an example of DUP policies in action. It provides an early example of the party's over-enthusiasm for the private sector.

There were other major policy disputes at Stormont during the year of Paisley rule. But they were mainly fuelled by the age-old division between unionism and nationalism. For example, the debate over whether an Irish Language Act should be introduced was predictably divided on traditional lines. And even the question of where to locate a new multi-sports stadium could not escape the taint of communal tension. A plan to use the old Maze Prison site was bitterly opposed by many within the DUP, on the grounds that it would become a shrine to past republican inmates. But the Giant's Causeway controversy was different. It basically involved the DUP up against everyone else in the Assembly. Given the government ministries the party held, the battle was not as unequal as it might have at first appeared. But it still had to retreat in the end.

ROCKS AND A HARD PLACE

The Giant's Causeway is located in the Paisleys' north Antrim constituency, on the coastline overlooking the Atlantic Ocean. It is set within a designated area of outstanding natural beauty, and is subject to official planning guidelines aimed at protecting both the site itself and its wider surroundings. The Causeway is also Northern Ireland's only World Heritage Site, a status awarded by UNESCO, a United Nations body. As official tourist literature explains, it is 'renowned for its polygonal columns of layered basalt', having resulted 'from a volcanic eruption 60 million years ago'.[2] Creationists, it should be noted, argue that the famous stones are only 5,000 years old and were formed by Noah's flood. But the bitter row that flared up in the autumn of 2007 had nothing to do with the age or origins of the planet. It was about much less profound matters like money and property development.

Four months into the new devolved administration, a DUP minister announced a preliminary approval for a lucrative private sector visitor centre development close to the Causeway. This left conservation campaigners appalled. The debate about constructing suitable new facilities for visitors had dragged on for several years and involved a number of public bodies. In 2000, the existing visitor centre on the headland above the Causeway was gutted by fire. It had been operated by Moyle District Council, the local government authority for the area, which also owned and ran the Causeway car park. The National Trust, which owns the Causeway itself, ran a gift shop and tea room beside the Moyle Council centre. The council's fire-ravaged visitor building was replaced by temporary premises, as deliberations continued on the best way to provide a permanent new facility. This is where north coast property developer Seymour Sweeney and his company Seaport Investments entered the picture.

Sweeney had been amassing a landholding in the area above the

Causeway and had tabled plans to build a hotel, an arts and crafts centre and a tea room. He also secured planning approval to turn a listed building close to the Causeway car park—called the Nook—into a pub and restaurant.

Instead of building a replacement for the burnt-out visitor facility itself, Moyle Council decided to invite expressions of interest from potential developers. Sweeney put together a multi-million-pound proposal, involving an underground centre housed in a grassed dome. He was strongly opposed by the National Trust, which submitted an alternative blueprint to the council. The Trust was deeply suspicious of Sweeney's intentions for the surrounding area, in light of his previous proposals. It had fought unsuccessfully against planning approval for the Nook, and even went to the lengths of buying the ageing Causeway Hotel on the headland to prevent it falling into his hands.

In early 2002, the council decided after some heart-searching to abandon its plans to make its land available to an outside developer. It seemed content at this stage to rebuild a modest new visitor facility itself. Sweeney countered by applying in February 2002 for outline planning permission for a grassed dome visitor centre on his own land nearby. The following year, with the Assembly by now suspended, Direct Rule ministers effectively overruled the council's intention to go it alone. The ministers declared that a 'world class' public sector building was required and unveiled plans for an international architectural design competition. It took more than two years to complete this process.

In October 2005, Secretary of State Peter Hain announced that the winning design had been provided by Roisin Heneghan of Heneghan Peng Architects, based in Dublin. Mr Hain commented: 'This project involves a number of organisations working together as partners—Moyle District Council, the National Trust, the Northern Ireland Tourist Board and government. I congratulate everyone involved in taking the project to this stage and look forward very much to its realisation.'[3]

But the scheme was still some distance off fruition when devolution returned in 2007. There had been detailed negotiations on how the centre would be run, and how its proceeds would be shared out. Strict planning conditions had also complicated the goal of finding additional car parking space, as surrounding protected greenfield land was ruled off limits. It had been decided to seek full planning permission for the Heneghan-designed centre, rather than outline approval. But an application had still to be submitted when the Stormont Executive was formed in May 2007.

Sweeney's rival visitor centre planning application had meanwhile been stuck in the system since 2002, without a verdict having been reached by the Department of the Environment (DOE). Long delays in major cases had become a feature of Northern Ireland's planning process. A major upsurge in applications had left the Planning Service struggling to cope, and it was also being hampered by the loss of experienced staff to better paid jobs in an expanding private sector consultancy scene. There was an expectation that Sweeney's application would be turned down, not least because it would involve greenfield development in the immediate vicinity of the Causeway. DOE Planning Service officials had even begun drafting official grounds for a refusal. Then two new DUP ministers moved in and turned everything on its head.

The two departments involved with the Causeway had both come under DUP control—senior party figure Nigel Dodds was the new Minister for Enterprise and Fermanagh MLA Arlene Foster was Minister for the Environment. The party's decision to take the DOE portfolio had caused some surprise, as it had little apparent affinity with environmental causes. Some cynics even joked about DUP standing for the Developers' Unionist Party. The party was openly sceptical about proposals to set up an independent environmental protection agency in Northern Ireland. All the other main parties at Stormont backed this suggested reform, which would have brought the province into line with the rest of the UK and the Republic. But when an expert panel was appointed under Direct Rule to examine the issue, the DUP failed to show up for scheduled evidence sessions, and did not even make a written submission.

Taking the environment portfolio in government did, though,

fit in with the party's wider objectives. The DUP fancied shaking up and speeding up the planning system, as part of its vision of boosting business. A month into their new jobs, Foster and Dodds met to discuss mutual issues of concern between their departments, including the Giant's Causeway. Sweeney's private sector alternative to the government-backed visitor centre scheme was about to get a boost. The Department of Enterprise's official record of their 7 June 2007 meeting states:

> Both Ministers agreed that private sector development of visitor facilities was more desirable and that agreement between the developer and local stakeholders, primarily Moyle Council and the National Trust, would represent the ideal scenario. Minister Foster indicated her intention to receive papers and visit the site re the private sector application in the near future.[4]

The DUP's enthusiasm for the private sector was already making a difference. But there was a problem with the intention of moving ahead on the basis of Sweeney's blueprint. A report on his application by the Planning Service chiefs had just been submitted to the Minister. Its conclusion could not have been clearer: 'Planning Service has fully assessed the proposal and is of the opinion that the application should be refused.'

This document was dated 1 June 2007—just six days before Foster met Dodds and 'agreed that private sector development of visitor facilities was more desirable'. The top planners spelt out six separate grounds for refusing Sweeney permission, based on a series of existing policies and guidelines. Their report also cited expert views from elsewhere in the DOE. It said Landscape Architects Branch officials were 'concerned about the cumulative impact of development in this area over time, and are of the opinion that given the sensitivity of the landscape its capacity to take any more development is limited'. The report to the Minister also made clear that colleagues within the Department's Environment and Heritage Service were equally forthright.

They are of the opinion the development proposal would result in a significant expansion of the developed area at the Causeway head and would therefore have a major adverse impact on the landscape character, and quality of the approach to the world heritage site. As a consequence, the visitor experience to this natural phenomenon would be markedly devalued. Planning Service agrees with this view.

Foster, presumably unconvinced by this clear verdict, visited the Causeway area over the summer.

Matters were brought to a head by an Assembly debate scheduled for 11 September. It had been triggered by the SDLP, and the Department of Enterprise was expected to come in for heavy criticism over the time taken to deliver on the public sector visitor centre plan. On 10 September 2007, Foster and Dodds radically altered the terms of that debate. The Environment Minister issued a press release, announcing that she was proposing to grant approval to the Sweeney application. Foster said she had visited the site and given fullest 'consideration' to the report she had received from the Planning Service. This was the 1 June report quoted above, which unequivocally recommended refusal. The Minister continued: 'Having done so, I have concluded that there is considerable merit in what is proposed and I am of a mind to approve it.'[5] Within the hour, Dodds had responded with an official announcement of his own, effectively shelving the £21 million public sector scheme his department had been working on since 2003.

The DUP was well pleased with itself, as the Assembly debate the following day showed.[6] Ian Paisley Jnr, a long-time advocate of the Sweeney plans, told fellow MLAs: 'With this project, as with many others, the Government have cleverly transferred the risk to the private sector but ensured that taxpayers—the people who really matter—continue to benefit from having a centre that has been paid for by private money.' In his contribution, Sammy Wilson said: 'Using private money is one of the new ways of doing things.' Wilson also stated:

Let me make it clear that when the Minister was considering the planning application she would have had to consider the views of the Environment and Heritage Service, for example, and if there was an element of doubt at all about the impact on the environment, I know what the decision of the Environment and Heritage Service would be. It would tell the Minister to have nothing to do with the application; and I speak as someone who has criticised the Environment and Heritage Service and the Planning Service on many occasions.

Wilson was clearly unaware at this stage that the Environment and Heritage Service had recommended a refusal of Sweeney's application. That only became public knowledge later that month.[7]

Winding up the Assembly debate, Enterprise Minister Nigel Dodds stated: 'If Members really had taxpayers' interests at heart, they should not decry our efforts or take a dogmatic Marxist approach, which says that only the public sector can deliver.' A press statement posted on Junior Minister Ian Paisley Jnr's website the following week took up the same pro-private theme in relation to the Causeway. 'Politicians need to learn that the private sector is not a dirty word,' it declared. The statement also said: 'The private sector obviously isn't always the answer but it always ought to be considered as an option for service delivery.' Whether this privatising zeal extended in Paisley Jnr's mind to the health service, public transport and the education system was not explained.

The press statement also said: 'Despite the fact that a private developer is willing to shoulder the risk involved in constructing and running a visitor centre worthy of a World Heritage Site and save the public purse in excess of £20m in the process, economic Neanderthals are insisting that such a centre must be in public hands.'

There were a few problems with the claim that the Sweeney scheme would save the public purse £21 million. For a start, it was by no means clear at this point what the actual contribution funded by the Department of Enterprise, Trade and Investment would be to the National Trust–Moyle Council alternative to Sweeney. Various funding options were being explored under this scheme, and there was an expectation that the Trust itself would provide some of the investment. More importantly, Minister Dodds had been told by his own department to expect a grant bid from Sweeney's Seaport company for his proposed centre. That advice came in a memo from an official on 7 September 2007—just before Sweeney's plans had been placed in pole position by DUP ministers. This Department of Enterprise ministerial briefing document said:

> A private sector led solution would negate the need for the planned Government investment of up to £21m. However, it is likely that Seaport Investments will seek grant aid for its proposal. This application could be for as much as 50% of the total build cost which, given the proposed scale and size, could be anything from £15–£20 million.

In other words, don't bank on the private option coming without a cost for your department. Talk then of £21 million being saved for taxpayers was somewhat misleading. As will be shown in the next chapter, Sweeney had already explored other potential grant sources—with support from Paisley Jnr. It was Thatcher herself who famously declared: 'There's no such thing as a free lunch.' That pearl of wisdom was certainly true in regard to letting the private sector deliver the Causeway centre. There would be a cost to the public interest. It would mean, for example, the public sector losing long-term proceeds from car parking and other revenue-raising activities at the site. There was also the wider issue of granting a single businessman prime control at the entrance to Northern Ireland's top tourist attraction. Also, excessive commercial development in the vicinity could bring economic loss by eventually diminishing its attractiveness to tourists. Such considerations held little sway in the mindset that viewed the private sector with something close to awe. These views extended well beyond the DUP. It was pretty much the orthodoxy of the day in Northern Ireland.

Sweeney's plans received timely support in late September from University of Ulster economist Michael Smyth. Smyth's name has cropped up a few times already in this book, as an adviser to the Assembly on business matters, and a commentator on economic affairs in the province. His intervention in the Causeway debate was therefore not insignificant. It came in the shape of an aggressive newspaper article, co-written with University colleague Professor David Carson. Carson, a professor of marketing, had accompanied Sweeney and Paisley Jnr to a meeting on the Causeway with a Direct Rule minister a few years earlier. The article by the two academics slammed the 'current yah boo media debate' on the visitor centre issue, and described the public sector option as 'fundamentally flawed' in terms of its size and scope. They also claimed the world was 'littered with cost-draining visitor centres which, because they are owned and operated by public sector organisations, cannot bring a business acumen to creating a successful business'. And they concluded:

It has taken seven (repeat seven) years for the public bodies concerned to reach agreement on a proposal. What other country in the free world would take this long to make a decision on a replacement building at its most important tourism destination? The fundamental question is: are we prepared to allow the same dilatory public bodies to oversee the construction and operation of our most important visitor centre? If the answer is yes, then let us stop whining about the size of the Northern Ireland public sector because it is about to get even bigger.[8]

The National Trust had taken the tactical decision not to get dragged into a media scrum by responding to every criticism hurled its way. But it could have retorted that the chief responsibility for the stalled public sector scheme had rested with the Department of Enterprise since 2003, and not itself or Moyle Council. Had it wanted to, the Trust could also have pointed to its portfolio of visitor attractions across the UK, and politely suggested that it had much more experience of running successful tourism centres than a north coast house-builder.

It was fairly clear by the time the Smyth and Carson article appeared that Arlene Foster had unleashed a political controversy far deeper than she could ever have expected. Part of that was down to the involvement of Sweeney, rather than a less contentious businessman. The plain truth was that he did not make a great poster boy for the resurgence of Northern Ireland's private sector. An intelligent man, Sweeney can be humorous and indeed charming at times. But he also has a belligerent side and has never seemed to worry too much about being unpopular. That is probably just as well, given the way many people regarded him.

Property development has been a controversial subject on the north coast for many years. There have been long-standing fears about seaside towns and villages being blighted by the expansion of holiday homes, which are only occupied for a short period of the year. Concerns were also growing by this stage about the impact of property development in non-coastal districts, involving large numbers of townhouses and apartments. It was no great surprise that Sweeney's Causeway centre planning application was the subject of 98 objections to the DOE. Organisations in the anti camp included a residents' association from the north coast village of Portballintrae, and a wider grouping called the Causeway Coast Community Consortium. There were only two letters of support for Sweeney.[9] Clearly, he was not going to be cheered to the echo in his own community if he succeeded with his Causeway project.

Suspicions lingered that Sweeney would follow up a visitor centre planning approval by dusting down past proposals for a hotel and other commercial developments in the vicinity. When asked if he could give a guarantee that there would be no further large-scale buildings on the landscape, he said: 'I can't give any guarantee about anything other than I hope that I'll be having a cup of tea at home tonight at seven o'clock.' And he continued: 'If there is a commercial case that is supported by tourist planning policies and prevailing planning policies that allows something to be built in Northern Ireland, no matter where it is, then that is the right of every citizen to apply for that permission.'[10]

Sweeney also had a habit of going to the courts in pursuit of his business interests. He had taken a judicial review case against the DOE's draft Northern Area Plan, a document which set out zoning—and limits—for future development on the north coast. He also called in his lawyers when a local councillor staged a protest in 2003 at one of his contentious development sites in the north coast seaside town of Portrush. Christine Alexander had stood in the way of a digger, and ended up with a £7,500 bill for damages and costs after being sued by Sweeney for trespass and nuisance. When asked about the case a few years later by a journalist, the developer declined to comment, adding: 'If you run a story that is inaccurate then I will have to take action.'[11]

It would be naïve to criticise Sweeney for his hard-headed approach to planning issues, or indeed for making himself unpopular. Developers by their nature seek to maximise profit opportunities from available land holdings. And Sweeney was very good at aggressively pursuing his interests. But business prowess is one thing. It did not necessarily mean he should be entrusted with the gateway to Northern Ireland's most famous natural attraction.

While Paisley Jnr had no qualms about enthusiastically supporting Sweeney, his DUP Assembly colleague Gregory Campbell took a different view. He represents east Londonderry, a neighbouring constituency to north Antrim, and one where Sweeney had made his presence felt. Campbell's constituency office workload had been increased as a result of local objections to proposed Sweeney developments. In the summer of 2007, he took a delegation to meet Foster to voice concerns on a number of planning matters. Among them was a Sweeney scheme for the town of Coleraine. Campbell hinted at being uncomfortable on the Causeway question during the Assembly debate following Foster's 'minded to' announcement. He told MLAs that 'planning applications submitted by the developer in question have caused difficulties for many people in the past', adding:

Many of them have been in my constituency, and I have represented constituents in opposition to some of those applications. However, this planning application is completely separate and different to any of those. I have never come across any planning application, either from this applicant or anyone else, of this nature. There are no similarities in that respect. Given that background and that context, however, this entire process, from today, must be subjected to the closest possible scrutiny. If it were not, I would totally and unequivocally oppose it without reservation.[12]

It was not a ringing endorsement of Sweeney.

The row about the developer's designs on the land above the Causeway was fuelled by more than just his business activities. The fact that Sweeney was a member of the DUP was publicly confirmed in response to media inquiries on 11 September. It prompted Foster, a solicitor by trade, to issue a swift warning:

Today there have been reports, in some sections of the media, which might have implied to some, that I may have allowed other extraneous factors, ie the party political membership of the applicant, to affect my views on this application. I totally reject any such implications. I regard them as baseless and scurrilous. A minister, when making decisions, cannot and should not investigate party affiliations of applicants, and I did not do so in this case. I do not know the applicant, have never met him, and know nothing about him. If anyone impugns my integrity in this matter I will be seeking legal advice and will act accordingly.[13]

Foster also repeatedly made clear that she had not been lobbied by anyone on the visitor centre application. She told the Assembly, for example on 24 September 2007, that there had been 'absolutely no representation' from the Junior Minister Ian Paisley Jnr 'or anybody else, for or against the application'.[14] And she added for good measure: 'I am happy to put that on the record.' In a subsequent newspaper interview, she said she had been unaware that either Ian Paisley Snr or Ian Paisley Jnr had been long-time supporters of Sweeney's scheme. 'Why would I know what a constituency's MP and MLAS were pushing for?' she asked. 'I wouldn't have a clue, for example, what other MPs and MLAS are pushing for in other areas.'[15]

There is no reason to disbelieve this statement by Foster, and there is no evidence that she was lobbied by either of the Paisleys. Paisley Jnr had lobbied strongly for Sweeney under Direct Rule— both to government ministers and officials. Quite why he stopped these efforts when devolution arrived in May 2007 is a matter for him. He did raise it with the new DUP Environment Minister in an Assembly debate on planning held just a fortnight into the new Stormont era. In this debate—on 21 May 2007—Paisley Jnr complained about business opportunities being 'slowed down by the planning process'. He continued:

> I can mention numerous such projects in my constituency, such as that of a new tourism facility at the Giant's Causeway; a new golf facility at Bushmills; and the restoration of Galgorm Castle. Those projects received widespread support from the councils and the community. Unfortunately, two of those cases have been slowed down by five years, and the other by six years, while the developers wait to be allowed a proper hearing and to be given either an approval or a refusal. Those delays are not acceptable.

The 'new tourism facility at the Giant's Causeway' he referred to can only have been the Sweeney scheme—there was no other visitor centre planning application in the system. Replying to him as she concluded this debate, Foster said: 'Mr Paisley Jnr mentioned three specific cases. I am fully aware of the issues that surround those three matters, and I will advise him and other Members on those in due course.'[16] Paisley Jnr should have been secretly pleased that a decision had not previously been issued on Sweeney's centre application. If it had been reached in previous years it would more than likely have been a refusal—unless a Direct Rule minister opted to overrule the Planning Service.

The report from planners that Foster received in June 2007 remained under wraps for the rest of the year, despite demands from the cross-party Assembly Committee to see it. The views of the DOE's Environment and Heritage Service were, however, prominently reported in the press. They entered the public domain because they were included in the DOE's open file on the planning application. This prompted more criticism of Foster. Her handling of the controversy was helped by the inability of most of her critics to land a glove on her in any public debates or discussions. Foster kept repeating that she had not actually made a final decision, and that there were still some outstanding issues on the visitor centre application to be addressed. Her emphasis on a decision not having been taken did not penetrate through her entire party. When the Minister appeared before the Assembly Environment Committee to give evidence on the Causeway, DUP backbencher Trevor Clarke enthusiastically told her: 'Minister, could I congratulate you on the decision that you made?'[17]

Foster also sought to calm the row by emphasising that she would be governed solely by planning considerations when reaching her eventual verdict. That did not augur well for Sweeney's chances. The advice given to Foster by the Planning Service could not have been clearer. Environment ministers have the right to overrule their officials. But this would not have been a case of a Minister simply imposing her will on her department and getting on with it. For a start, Foster must have been conscious from an early stage that a court challenge was likely.

The National Trust as a leading UK charity had the resources for a judicial review on a Sweeney approval. This option was hinted at in an early press release by the charity, which said it would be 'astounded' if full permission was actually granted to the businessman. The Trust's director for Northern Ireland, Hilary McGrady, commented: 'Given our conviction that a second visitor facility, on a greenfield site, would be wrong and would set a disastrous precedent for development so close to the World Heritage Site, we will now be seeking advice on all our options.'[18]

Foster also had to face the fact that she was treading in national and international waters. The Causeway's cherished status as a World Heritage Site meant that a UK government department and the United Nations body UNESCO both had a role to play. UNESCO does not just designate World Heritage Sites. It also monitors their condition and management, and can formally declare them in danger. Formal responsibility for reporting to UNESCO on all the UK's World Heritage Sites rests with the Department of Culture, Media and Sport (DCMS) in London. The National Trust did not take long to make representations to the Department. The charity's overall UK chief, director general Fiona Reynolds, wrote a strongly worded letter to DCMS Minister Margaret Hodge in September 2007 on the provisional Sweeney approval. Reynolds stated: 'I recognise that you will be sensitive to the responsibilities of the newly reconstituted Northern Ireland Assembly, but responsibility for protecting the integrity of world heritage sites lies firmly with the UK government and the situation needs your intervention.'[19]

The DCMS did become involved behind the scenes. Its officials briefed UNESCO on the Causeway situation in October, and agreed to provide a formal report to the UN body's World Heritage Committee by the end of January 2008. Hodge herself met with Foster in London in December 2007. Northern Ireland's Environment Minister—some seven months into her job by then—must have been very well aware at this point just how high the stakes were.

This was not the first time that the DCMS had taken an interest in decisions relating to Northern Ireland's only World Heritage Site. In 2001, another Minister from the London Department, Baroness Blackstone, wrote to the then Ulster Unionist Environment Minister Sam Foster to voice concerns on two Causeway-related issues. One was the proposed sale at that time of Moyle Council's visitor centre site, while the other was the planning approval being issued to Sweeney for the Nook pub/restaurant development. Blackstone warned Foster that the National Trust could request UNESCO to add the Causeway to its 'at risk' register. Her letter added: 'I need not tell you that the prospect of having one of our world heritage sites placed on the "In Danger" list would be a severe embarrassment for the UK.'[20] UNESCO had itself given unfavourable signals on the Sweeney scheme in 2003, when spelling out ground rules for a new Causeway centre.

A UNESCO 'mission team' visited the north Antrim site in February that year, and produced a detailed report. With a view to protecting the surrounding landscape, the report concluded that a new centre should be no larger than the one burnt down in 2000. It said a new facility could be built on the existing Moyle Council site 'without any extension in size and height to provide the basic and necessary visitor information and interpretation at the entrance to the World Heritage site'.[21] Sweeney's proposals involved a much larger-scale building. Significantly, the UNESCO report also stated: 'The mission concludes that no additional development at the existing visitor information site and in the vicinity of the main entrance (outside the World Heritage site) should take place.' This effectively ruled out the Sweeney scheme, given its proximity to the main entrance to the Causeway site.

UNESCO's World Heritage Committee formally approved the mission team's findings in a Paris conference in the summer of 2003. Arlene Foster was therefore faced with firm recommendations against the Sweeney blueprint from her department, plus the prospect of seriously irking UNESCO. The odds seemed stacked against a sustainable and valid approval decision. In line with Foster's wishes, Planning Service officials held a series of separate discussions towards the end of 2002 with Sweeney's Seaport company, the National Trust and Moyle Council. The hope was that some kind of compromise could be reached between the groupings, paving the way for an agreed approach. It was optimistic to say the least. There had been a previous attempt at a talks process back in 2002, involving the Assembly Enterprise Committee. Nothing came of it. The chances of a meeting of minds between a property developer and a conservation charity always seemed slim—so it proved in the discussions held by the Planning Service in late 2007.

Any deal would presumably have had to be based on an

approval for Sweeney, with the Trust and Moyle Council agreeing to come onboard with his scheme. He did make an offer of compensation to the council for loss of revenue from the car park—in return for it vacating the area. And there was also some talk of the Trust renting space in his new centre and receiving an undefined contribution towards the upkeep of the Causeway. There were no takers for his offers.

Instead, the Trust and council decided to take control of the plan that had been fronted by the Department of Enterprise since 2003. This involved reviving the award-winning design from the international competition, and pressing ahead with a planning application. The two organisations reached an agreement on this basis in late 2007, with the council agreeing to lease its land to the Trust. Enterprise Minister Nigel Dodds met both bodies, and issued a press release afterwards saying: 'I welcome the National Trust and Moyle District Council's plans to work together to find a solution to deliver a visitor facility worthy of the world heritage site at the Giant's Causeway.'[22] This was a very public sign that DUP ministers were not going to die in a ditch trying to save Sweeney's dream.

Foster, meanwhile, had the small matter of a planning decision to reach on the businessman's application. On 11 January 2008, the Minister received another report from the Planning Service, a companion volume to the June 2007 report that she had been prepared to overrule. The new document explained that there was no evidence that any 'mutual agreement or accommodation' was possible between the different sides. 'Planning Service engagement with the applicant and key stakeholders has not provided any new information that would overcome the serious planning policy failures identified in the original report,' it said. It also stated bluntly that Sweeney's plan would involve a 'significant expansion' of the developed area at the Causeway, with an adverse impact on the landscape. 'Although the proposal is below the ridgeline and is designed as a grassed dome it would still represent an alien feature in the landscape,' the Planning Service added.

It was also made clear that approval would create 'duplication of many of the facilities provided by the existing visitor centre'. That was because there was no reason for Moyle Council or the National Trust to vacate their sites. Sweeney had argued that a legal 'discontinuance' order could be issued under planning law, requiring removal of the existing premises. But the January 2008 Planning Service report said the Department could not 'properly exercise' this power 'to facilitate a proposal that is contrary to several planning policies'. It also said: 'Even if the existing centre were to be removed the proposal would still result in significant expansion of development into a green field area adjacent to the WHS [World Heritage site] and within the AONB [Area Of Outstanding Natural Beauty].' UNESCO's requirements on a new Causeway centre were not a focal point of the June 2007 report to the Minister. But they were addressed in detail in the January 2008 follow-up. The Department's Environment and Heritage Service expressed the view that the Sweeney scheme represented a 'significant departure' from UNESCO's position. And it concluded that approval would bring a 'high risk' of the Causeway being placed on the official list of World Heritage Sites in danger.

This reflected thinking at a senior level across the water. In an internal email sent on 25 September 2007, a senior DCMS civil servant referred to the 2003 UNESCO mission report as 'not favourable' to the Sweeney proposal. The London government official further stated that there was a 'real risk' that planning approval would lead to UNESCO considering 'in danger listing' for the Causeway.[23]

All the advice before Foster was clear. The Minister had vowed to reach her final verdict on planning grounds alone. It was difficult to see any planning basis for granting Sweeney permission. Her 'minded to approve' approach had left her driving down a one-way street at speed. The two choices before her were to plough on, regardless of the wreckage, or change direction. There was no real decision to take.

Foster formally announced her U-turn to the Assembly on 29 January 2008. Informing MLAs that the developer's application was being turned down, she stated: 'I am convinced that the proposal, as it stands, would have an adverse impact on the world heritage site, as I believe that it could adversely affect the character of the area.' Sitting beside her on the front bench as she revealed her decision was party and ministerial colleague Ian Paisley Jnr. He had rubbished the notion of a threat to the World Heritage status in the Assembly debate on the Causeway the previous autumn, saying: 'I hope that the organisations and individuals who are making that threat will withdraw it and recognise that this is an opportunity for Northern Ireland to get a world-class visitors' centre urgently, expeditiously, practically and legally.' By January 2008, the organisations 'making that threat' included Arlene Foster's department and the Department of Culture, Media and Sport in London. The Environment Minister sided with the officials, and not Paisley Jnr.

A few weeks later, Sweeney announced that he would be challenging the refusal decision through the planning appeals process. The ever-faithful Paisley Jnr issued a statement backing the businessman's move. By that stage, he was no longer a junior minister.

That is another story, and it's time to start telling it.

Chapter 6
Junior in Bother

'I have a sentimental weakness for my children, and I spoil them as you can see; they talk when they should listen.'

DON CORLEONE referring to his son Santino, in the movie *The Godfather*

How pleased must Ian Paisley Jnr have been in early September 2007, when Seymour Sweeney was given preliminary approval for his Causeway plans? The DUP was in power. Junior was a minister, with civil servants at his beck and call and a government car to ferry him about. And, since you ask, a salary of about £70,000 a year all told. Not just any ministry either, but working directly for his father, the First Minister of Northern Ireland. Who would have guessed it? All the years as an outsider and now the big man was top of the heap. His dad, his friend, his hero. The First Minister. After all those years of sneers. He had been reviled and condemned countless times. Now he was being lauded around the world.

The new Stormont power-sharing deal was already well bedded down by now. It had all been brilliantly managed, leaving unionist hardliners out in the cold. Some day, the truth about Junior's central role in the deal-making would have to be told. Junior, letting the British government know he was the gatekeeper to his dad, a man to have onboard if they knew what was good for them. The discussions with Peter Hain and his people, even Tony Blair. Was there another 41-year-old anywhere on these islands with such access and influence?

Now the DUP could start to make a real difference, get rid of all that wishy-washy, politically correct liberal thinking. Put the tree-hugging environmentalists in their place. Take the regulatory burdens off the backs of businessmen. Set them free for the task of building a dynamic new Ulster. People like Seymour Sweeney.

Seymour, Paisley Junior's ally, associate or friend—call him what you will. Seymour the DUP member, one of us. All those years of bending the ears of ministers and officials on his behalf. Let him build the new Causeway centre. But they wouldn't listen. Too heavily influenced by the National Trust, the great and the good.

But things had changed now. The DUP was running the show now. And Seymour was going to get approval. Of course, there was a row about it. It wouldn't be Northern Ireland if there wasn't. It wouldn't be as much fun if there wasn't. And who better than Ian Jnr to go on the offensive? Seeing off Seymour's enemies on the airwaves would be a breeze.

So now Junior's on the Nolan radio show, defending the Causeway plan. Not a problem. Was never going to be. The interview is nearly over.

'Tell me this, Ian Paisley Jnr, the developer Seymour Sweeney and his company, do you know him?'

'He happens to be a constituent. He lives in north Antrim.'

'He's one of your constituents, is he?'

You can almost hear the Junior Minister laugh as he replies: 'He's a constituent of all six MLAs. He lives in north Antrim, that's correct.'

'And you support him?'

'I know of him, yes.'[1]

In those seconds, Paisley Jnr's ministerial career went into a nosedive. This chapter explains how and why.

MIXING WITH THE RICH

It's a natural and necessary part of any politician's job to interact with wealthy businesspeople. Sometimes that can mean speaking up on their behalf, for instance by backing constituency-based projects. Politicians with influence will also find no shortage of businesspeople wanting to make their acquaintance. That is also entirely normal. But the situation can often be delicate for those in government.

It's best for all concerned to maintain a certain distance and reserve, ensure protocols are observed. Ministers need to be vigilant, not just on the propriety of any engagement with business interests, but also on how it would appear to voters. That's because government decisions can be priceless in the world of commerce. Verdicts on grants, public sector contracts and regulatory controls can make or break companies overnight.

It was often said that the infatuation of Tony Blair's new Labour regime with super-rich entrepreneurs was one of its greatest weaknesses. It was barely in office, having promised to be whiter than white, when it was rocked by the Bernie Ecclestone affair. That involved accepting a £1 million donation from Ecclestone, a big noise in the world of Formula One racing, and later agreeing to exempt his sport from a tobacco advertising ban. How did it think that would look to the public?

The 'cash for honours' inquiry was another example of the Blair government getting into trouble for courting the largesse of the wealthy. Peter Mandelson's turbulent ministerial career provides a further salutary lesson. Rupert Murdoch is reported to have decided very early on that Mandelson would be a pushover. The press baron—or one of his associates—allegedly dubbed him a 'starf*****'—put more politely, someone who goes star-struck in the presence of the rich and powerful. Mandelson later lost his Cabinet job as Northern Ireland Secretary of State over the Hinduja affair. It was discovered that he had contacted a fellow minister over a passport application by Srichand Hinduja, an Indian billionaire. Hinduja was also a major sponsor of the government's Millennium Dome project, which Mandelson had been involved with as a Minister. Mandelson was later cleared of any wrongdoing by a Cabinet Office inquiry. There are different views on that verdict. But there's little doubt that he had been foolish to get himself into the situation in the first place. He also compounded the situation by forgetting whether or not he had personally made the passport-related phone call.

It is entirely right for the media to keep a watchful eye over the interaction between politicians and the business world. That applies in a relative backwater like Northern Ireland just as much as it does in the Westminster political village. Basic rules of public life like propriety, openness and transparency apply to mini-Masters of the Universe like Ian Paisley Jnr and their small-time operations, as well as more major players like Mandelson.

When it came to his relationship with property developer Seymour Sweeney, Junior Minister Ian Paisley Jnr did not make a good start on the Nolan radio show. The phrase 'I know of him' haunted him for months.

YOU'VE GOT A FRIEND IN ME

Along the north coast, Paisley Jnr's long-time connections with the businessman were very well known. In fact, a nationalist politician had phoned the Nolan show during that morning's on-air discussion, urging it to quiz the Junior Minister about his Sweeney links. John Dallat, an SDLP MLA for a constituency neighbouring Paisley Jnr's, had tuned into the show from his car. He was among the many listeners to later splutter in disbelief at the 'I know of him' reply. It gave the impression of something even vaguer than an acquaintance, as if Junior had just heard Sweeney's name mentioned in casual conversation occasionally. He might have thought he was being clever at the time, avoiding being drawn into personal territory. His words had the opposite effect.

Having appeared less than open, Paisley Jnr faced immediate questions about the extent of his involvement with Sweeney. The media scented a story. But there were in fact a string of stories. The immediate context was the announcement by DUP Minister Arlene Foster on being minded to approve Sweeney's Causeway application. But the revelations soon fanned out to include everything from holiday homes to lobster fishing.

HOUSE AT THE COAST

In the first flush of the Causeway centre planning application row, Sweeney's firm Seaport issued a press release detailing his links to the DUP and the Paisleys. It was an attempt to counter growing media speculation, through an upfront statement of the facts. The statement confirmed that Sweeney was a DUP member 'and like all members pays his annual subscription at the usual rates'. It also stated: 'Neither he nor any of his companies have now, or ever, been a donor to the party. Mr Sweeney has no other links to the DUP either personally or through family connections.'[2]

The developer went further than he had to here. Donations to political parties were still a private affair in Northern Ireland—unlike in the rest of the UK or the Republic. The statement continued:

> He can confirm that many years ago at one of Seaport's developments, namely Ballyallaght Farmyard Cottages outside Bushmills, a property was purchased by Ian Paisley Jnr in the normal way through sales agents and solicitors. Ian Paisley Jnr paid the full market sales price which was more expensive than the house neighbouring his property by virtue of the fact that the house he bought was slightly larger.

This confirmation did not bring closure over the Ballyallaght holiday home on the north coast. In common with similar developments, a management company had been formed for Ballyallaght with Sweeney and his wife Carol as directors. The individual property owners at the small site were listed in the company's official returns as members, all of them with one share each. Paisley Jnr and his wife Fiona jointly held one share. The company's role involved provision of communal facilities and services at the development.

Similar arrangements are often put in place for apartment blocks, with a management company receiving payments from individual unit owners for shared services. Paisley Jnr was relaxed about details of his holiday home purchase in 2004 coming to light, saying: 'I have no questions to answer on this. I believe it's all open and above board. The property was bought a number of years ago through normal channels.'[3] The management company did mean, however, that there was an ongoing formal legal and financial link between the Junior Minister and Sweeney.

As well as doubtless providing a comfortable retreat for the family, the Ballyallaght holiday home was listed as Paisley Jnr's address in his nomination papers for the 2007 Assembly elections. It was in his north Antrim constituency—unlike his main family home between Lisburn and Moira, some 60 miles away in County Down.

Another family link to Ballyallaght was soon confirmed. Paisley Jnr's in-laws—his wife Fiona's parents—also owned one of the holiday homes. It was stressed once again by Sweeney that the sale had been at full market value. This would not be the last time that Paisley Jnr's father-in-law, retired Lisburn businessman James Currie, would find his name being dragged into the media. His daughter Fiona took great offence at a media report about her parents owning a holiday home. She rang the author to denounce him personally for daring to write about the matter. It was understandable for her to be annoyed at family business being pored over in the press.

Worse embarrassment was to come. It was revealed that Paisley Jnr's holiday home was officially registered in the name of Sweeney's wife and business partner, Carol.[4] A transfer of ownership had not been recorded at Land Registers of Northern Ireland (LRNI), the government's registration agency for land and property. In a strict legal sense, this meant that ownership still rested with Carol Sweeney, despite payments having been made by the Paisleys for the property. Paisley and Sweeney both blamed the situation on an 'administrative hiccup'.

Fiona Paisley caused general bemusement by taking to the airwaves herself on the subject. After a documentary had highlighted the house registration details, she invited a broadcaster out to her home to view mortgage documentation. The aim was to prove that they had been paying for the property. She also took the opportunity to hit out at her husband's critics and to air a conspiracy theory about the pressure he was under. 'I think it's a witchhunt for Ian,' she said. 'I think somebody's out to get him. They don't like that he's doing a good job up there and they don't like that he gets the votes up there and that's all it is.' The loyal wife also expressed the hope that her husband would be 'left to get on with the job that he's been elected to do'.[5] Alas, it was not to be.

The 'administrative hiccup' explanation for the holiday home registration was subsequently vindicated in an investigation by Assembly Standards Commissioner Tom Frawley. But the registration oversight was still an embarrassment for Paisley Jnr. He also managed to compound it with an attempt to place the blame on LRNI. He told a TV interviewer: 'I am aware that there is some sort of administrative hiccup in Land Registry. It is legally in my name. I can assure you it is mine.'[6] The next day, when the matter was again aired on the airwaves, Paisley Jnr said: 'I did come on to your programme this morning and I heard a number of your callers ringing in and saying no surprise at Land Registry on this one.'[7]

By happy coincidence, LRNI was an agency of the Department of Finance. And its Minister at this time was Peter Robinson, DUP deputy leader. The SDLP's John Dallat tabled a timely Assembly question, asking Robinson for his assessment of the situation. The Finance Minister replied: 'I can confirm that Land Registers NI is not responsible for any administrative irregularities at Ballyallaght Farm Cottages, Bushmills.'[8]

The registration of the home was finally transferred to Paisley Jnr in late 2007, some three years after it had been purchased. By this stage, there were yet more questions about the holiday home development itself and the process by which it had been granted planning permission. Paisley Jnr confirmed that he had lobbied the Department of the Environment in support of Sweeney's Ballyallaght planning application in 2002. He stated that he had not known at the time of his lobbying that he was going to end up making a purchase himself, adding: 'And I bought it at the full market value and I wasn't advanced in any way or advantaged in any way by supporting the application.'[9]

It is a distinct possibility that Sweeney's Ballyallaght application might not have received permission had political pressure not been brought to bear. Lobbying by MPs, MLAs and councillors on planning decisions is an everyday occurrence in Northern Ireland. Whether this kind of pressure helps produce a rational, coherent system of development control is a matter for debate.

The Ballyallaght approval decision was taken by the then Ulster Unionist Environment Minister Dermot Nesbitt, against advice from a senior level within his department. It was made in October 2002, just days before Nesbitt vacated his office due to a collapse of power-sharing devolution at that time.

The DOE's Environment and Heritage Service (EHS) recommended refusal for the Ballyallaght holiday homes, citing concerns about the scale of the proposed Sweeney development. A key EHS consideration was that the location was in the wider setting of the Giant's Causeway World Heritage Site.

The Planning Service Management Board met in July 2002 to discuss the proposed Sweeney holiday home development. According to the official note of the meeting, the senior planners present agreed that they had to 'accept EHS's assessment' and attach 'considerable weight' to their views. They also accepted that there were no 'exceptional circumstances', as required under planning policy, to merit setting aside EHS's view.[10]

An insight into the influence of lobbying can be gleaned from another internal Planning Service document from later in July 2002.(11) In it, an official recorded details of a phone call she had received from Sweeney about his Ballyallaght application. According to her typed note, Sweeney said it was his understanding that the meeting between EHS and the Planning Service 'had taken place and as EHS were refusing to alter their view, the file would be pushed up to the Minister to take the final decision'. The developer also stated that his 'contacts' were keeping in touch with the Minister's office and had 'stated categorically that the Minister had seen no papers, had no files and had not been briefed'. Minister Nesbitt made a visit to the site on 10 October 2002 and ruled at a meeting the following day that the scale of Sweeney's development was acceptable, despite EHS's objections. Permission was granted for 14 homes. Within two years, Paisley Jnr was the proud owner of one of them and his father-in-law of another.

By late 2007, the number of approved dwellings on the site had grown to 18. By this stage the Department of the Environment had effectively admitted that Nesbitt's 2002 approval decision had not been its finest hour. This came during a Planning Appeals Commission hearing in April 2007 on another proposed holiday home development on a site adjoining Ballyallaght.[12] The applicant behind this scheme not unreasonably pointed to the approval granted to Sweeney a few years earlier. In its submission to the appeal hearing, the Department said of Sweeney's Ballyallaght site: 'It is accepted that the scheme is not a particularly good example of development and the same density should not be perpetuated.' In its subsequent report issued in August 2007, the Appeals Commission threw out the bid for the further holiday home development. It criticised the Sweeney Ballyallaght scheme as having 'a material effect on the integrity of the world heritage site setting over a wide area' and said it was 'difficult to understand' how it had been approved.

The Appeals Commission also called Minister Nesbitt's 2002 Ballyallaght ruling into question, saying: 'The rationale behind the Ministerial approval of the adjoining development is not clear in relation to whether exceptional circumstances were put forward. However, a poor planning decision which clearly affects the setting of such an environmental asset does not justify a further approval.'

There was detailed media scrutiny in late 2007 of the Sweeney holiday home development. This succeeded in shining a light on the workings of Northern Ireland's less than perfect planning system. It also raised questions for the Junior Minister over his decision to buy a property in a development he had helped bring about through lobbying. This left him open to the charge of blurring the important boundary between public and private interests.

GONE FISHING

The media investigations of Paisley Jnr's links to Sweeney quickly turned up the fact that the pair had gone lobster fishing together.[13] This would not have been much of a revelation had it not come a few days after the 'I know of him' remark by the Junior Minister about the developer.

Of more significance was the fact that both Paisley Jnr and Paisley Snr had lobbied in 2005 on a sea fishing licence issue linked to Sweeney. A prominent north coast fisherman had died, and a dispute developed over who would succeed him as holder of a drift-net salmon fishing licence. The two Paisleys intervened on behalf of a member of the late fisherman's crew, Stephen McLaughlin, backing his case for a licence. The efforts proved successful, and McLaughlin was issued with a licence in June 2005 by the Fisheries Conservancy Board, the relevant government body. His no doubt delighted crew included none other than Seymour Sweeney.

Paisley Jnr had written to McLaughlin personally on his case against the rival licence bidder. Paisley Snr's contribution involved sending a sternly worded letter to the Fisheries Conservancy Board in April 2005. The letter, which may have been signed on his behalf by Ian Jnr, called for McLaughlin's application to be urgently processed 'so that he can continue to fish Portballintrae and Bushmills'. It concluded with the hint of a threat: 'I trust that you could urgently consider this matter which my colleague Mr Desmond Stewart raised with [the] Board upon my request a few days ago. I do not want to have to raise this matter at Parliament, but I believe that my constituent's needs do require urgent consideration.'[14] In other words, I'll start making a fuss about you to the government if you don't sort this out.

After all these efforts, McLaughlin ceased to be a licence holder on 31 December 2005—just six months after being granted it. On 10 January 2006, a licence was issued to a member of his crew—a well-known property developer called Seymour Sweeney.[15]

Incidentally, the Desmond Stewart referred to in Paisley Snr's April 2005 letter to the Fisheries Conservancy Board was a DUP councillor. He served on the fisheries body and had presumably been supportive of the successful McLaughlin bid for a licence. Stewart was also mayor of Coleraine on the north coast for a period. But his local government career took a bit of a hit in 2006 when he received a four-month jail term for electoral fraud. His offences involved using the postal votes of residents in a nursing home in Portrush. On his way in to be sentenced, Stewart struck a press photographer, earning him a subsequent fine for assault.

The lobster fishing connection between Paisley Jnr and Sweeney was reported in mid-September 2007, in the early days of the Causeway visitor centre row. At the same time, a photograph was unearthed showing the two Paisleys and Sweeney together. Also in the picture was Moyle DUP councillor David McAllister. He had a bit part role in the controversy over links between his party and Sweeney, as the developer had signed his nomination papers for the 2005 local government elections. McAllister explained: 'I know him as a personal friend. I've known him all my life.'[16]

In a TV interview broadcast in October 2007, Sweeney said he had no regrets about signing the papers, as McAllister was 'suited for the job'.[17] The Moyle councillor had been fined £200 the previous year for benefit fraud worth £17,744.[18] McAllister denied any wrongdoing and said the prosecution was in connection with council allowances paid while he claimed benefit. Records from the Social Security Agency showed that a complaint about its investigation into McAllister had been received from one of the Paisleys.[19] Documents relating to the written representation had been destroyed, so the Agency was unable to say if it had come from Senior or Junior.

McAllister, by this stage a part-time worker in Paisley Jnr's Bushmills constituency office, was back in court in 2008, this time for waste offences. He was fined £3,000 for unlawful in-filling activities at a building site.[20] It was later revealed that he had attended just three Moyle Council meetings in the financial year 2007/08, while receiving a councillor's allowance of £9,499.[21]

Two of the meetings, according to official records, were special sessions to discuss Giant's Causeway visitor centre issues.

CRONYISM AND THE CAUSEWAY

There is nothing wrong with politicians lobbying for business-people in their constituency. Indeed, it is a normal part of a constituency representative's role. But it is also entirely legitimate for others to examine the nature and scale of any such lobbying, and the motives behind it. That is particularly the case when there has been sustained and heavy lobbying over the years for one businessman, who just happens to belong to the politician's party. That can lead to accusations of cronyism, plus questions as to whether the elected representative has become too closely allied with a particular commercial interest. That is what happened to Ian Paisley Jnr in relation to the Giant's Causeway.

Once again, the initial focus involved contrasting work conducted behind the scenes for Sweeney with the 'I know of him' remark. But the scrutiny soon brought out further details about his long-term dedicated lobbying efforts. There were, for example, Paisley Jnr's attacks on the DOE's attempt to establish a new development framework for the north coast through a Northern Area Plan. Paisley Jnr argued aggressively that not enough land was being zoned for housing. And when Sweeney launched a judicial review against the Northern Area Plan in December 2005, the DUP MLA was quick to welcome the move.[22] That judicial review case continued, presumably with Paisley Jnr's ongoing support, after devolution returned. That meant Sweeney was taking the Department headed by Junior's fellow DUP Minister Arlene Foster to court.

Although it was not the subject of the legal challenge, the Northern Area Plan had implications for the Giant's Causeway visitor centre debate. It said only 'exceptionally modest' developments should be permitted in the vicinity of the World Heritage Site to meet the 'direct needs of visitors'. Sweeney's large-scale Causeway centre blueprint was hardly modest.

On another front, Paisley Jnr had also taken an interest in a steam train tourism service between Bushmills and the Giant's Causeway. This initiative was established as a charitable venture in 2002, but subsequently ran into financial troubles. Paisley Jnr had voiced concern in relation to public funding for the scheme and was prepared to comment publicly on financial difficulties when they arose. In March 2003, he spoke to the *Belfast Telegraph* about recent discussions at Moyle Council in relation to the railway's cash flow problems. 'Two years ago, I met the local government auditor about this project and pointed out then the very problems the railway would face if it was not properly financed,' he said. 'It appears that this is now coming to fruition.'[23] The following year, Sweeney stepped in and bought the rail link service. The purchase served to enhance Sweeney's landholding around the Causeway.

Paisley Jnr also sided with the developer in a 2004 planning battle over a proposed new housing site in Bushmills. The DOE had backed objectors and cited concern about the location within the Causeway Coast Area of Outstanding Natural Beauty. Sweeney won approval through a planning appeal process, with both Paisley Jnr and Moyle councillor David McAllister appearing as witnesses for him at the hearing.[24]

These lobbying examples were largely matters of public record. They could be defended on the basis that politicians have every right to speak up for companies bringing jobs and investment to their area. But more controversial examples of pro-Sweeney pressure soon emerged. That was due to the Freedom of Information (FOI) Act.

It was firstly confirmed that Sweeney had made an unsuccessful bid for grant-aid for his Causeway centre in 2002.[25] The application was to a public body called the Heritage Lottery Fund, which distributes a portion of the money raised from the UK's National Lottery. This revelation, in late September 2007, was not without significance by itself. After all, proponents of a private sector Causeway centre had just been claiming that it would save the public purse £21 million. Yet here was concrete evidence that the developer had already sought public money to help fund his project.

Details of the failed grant application disclosed from the Heritage Lottery Fund under FOI showed that Sweeney's formal application had named Ian Paisley Snr as a prospective trustee of the proposed visitor centre. The papers stated that a charitable body, the Giant's Causeway World Heritage Trust, would be set up to oversee the new enterprise. Four people were named as confirmed trustees—Sweeney, his wife Carol and two solicitors. It then stated that three further people would 'shortly be trustees'— including Ian Paisley MP.

The fact that Paisley Snr's name had been officially used in support of the grant bid intensified the cronyism allegations. It also introduced a note of irony. The Free Presbyterian Church regarded the National Lottery as a sinful form of gambling, yet here was its Moderator linked to a bid for some of its proceeds.

Sweeney has stated that Paisley Snr's name was used without his knowledge in the paperwork sent to the Heritage Lottery Fund.[26] Using a senior MP's name without consent in pursuit of public funds would seem to some to be quite a serious matter. But the Paisleys do not appear to have held it against the developer.

Then came a much more serious discovery. A further FOI request to the Heritage Lottery Fund yielded an angry letter sent to the body's London-based chief executive in January 2003 by Paisley Snr.[27] Typed on House of Commons headed paper, the letter appeared to have been signed on Paisley Snr's behalf by his politician son. It condemned the decision to turn down Sweeney's Causeway centre grant bid. It twice claimed that the businessman's plans had the support of world heritage body UNESCO. Quite simply, this was not true.

It stated: 'The application as presented has UNESCO approval and, more importantly, it was a multi-million pound scheme which ought to have attracted Heritage Lottery Fund support.' With that sentence, the letter suggested that UNESCO was not only onboard with Sweeney's development proposal, but had also approved his grant application.

There was more. Grant refusal grounds given by the Heritage Lottery Fund were described as 'absolute rubbish'. Paisley Snr continued: 'UNESCO saw and approved the plans and they were actually very impressed by the proposal.' The letter concluded with a hint of menace, similar to the fishing licence correspondence quoted above. It told the Heritage Lottery Fund:

Either you are completely detached from what is happening on the ground in Northern Ireland, have been poorly advised or are pursuing an agenda to ensure that a rival bid receives Heritage and Lottery funding. If that is the case I will, of course, have to raise this matter of fraudulent application of funding in my constituency at Westminster.

Here was one of Northern Ireland's most senior politicians issuing a veiled threat to a public official. More seriously, he did so on the basis of incorrect information about the policy of an international authority. This was inappropriate lobbying.

In October 2007, senior UNESCO heritage official Dr Mechtild Rössler refuted any suggestion that her organisation had been backing Sweeney. She explained that UNESCO's role precluded it from giving any verdict on private sector proposals, as it only dealt with governments.

The Paisleys had clearly made a mistake while pressing for a grant for Sweeney. They could have backtracked graciously and admitted to a misunderstanding. But Paisley Jnr instead sought to defend the Heritage Lottery letter, saying:

> The characterisation that it was supported or approved in a general way, I think, was a fair characterisation, because anyone who knows how UNESCO works knows that they do not have a formal approval route, that it can only be a general approval. And I think that that was fair and for it now to be characterised as something stronger than that general note of support, I think, is grossly unfair to Dr Paisley, grossly unfair to me and grossly unfair to the Democratic Unionist Party.[28]

The notion that a United Nations body like UNESCO had some kind of vague 'general approval' procedure is frankly ridiculous. It is not being suggested here that the Paisleys had sought to deliberately misrepresent the situation. What they did was get their facts wrong and then compound their error by failing to own up to it.

The misunderstanding appears to have stemmed from a meeting Sweeney and his advisers had held with UNESCO officials in Paris in 2001. He was presumably received courteously rather than with unbounded enthusiasm. But even if anyone at the UN organisation had been bowled over by his ideas, there would have been no authority whatsoever for any individuals to issue 'approval'. That is not what UNESCO is about. As Rössler herself put it, when the Paisley letter to the Heritage Lottery Fund became public:

> There is no UNESCO approval, that cannot be. I mean you cannot just come to an office and say here is a plan, and I'm asking for your approval. I mean, what is this? There are official procedures. This is an international legal instrument signed by 185 countries on this earth. Do you think we can deviate from procedures under these circumstances? I don't think so.[29]

Sweeney himself had made similar claims about UNESCO support at one stage. A press release issued by his company Seaport in May 2002 referred to having received 'wholehearted approval' from the UN body the previous year. But by the autumn of 2007, he had backed away from this suggestion. Sweeney told a press conference held in Belfast in October 2007: 'It is very important to clear this up. I have never said that we had UNESCO approval for the scheme.' When later challenged about the press release issued by his company some five years earlier, he said: 'You can put that to me and if I said that, that's fine, but it's not correct. I'm happy to retract that.'[30]

UNESCO had by that stage privately underlined its position to Sweeney's team of advisers. A planning consultant working for the developer had emailed Rössler in autumn 2007, seeking another meeting in Paris. Rössler had by then been alerted to media reports on UNESCO's stance. Replying to the consultant's email, she stated: 'Kindly note that the recent statements in the press on this matter are not accurate. 'UNESCO has not given any favourable consideration to a specific project.'[31] This email was copied to a senior official at the London-based Department of Culture, Media and Sport, due to its overall responsibility for UK World Heritage Sites.

The request from Sweeney's consultant for another Paris meeting was turned down. It is not surprising in these circumstances that Sweeney felt the need to distance himself from suggestions that he had the UN body onboard.

But the Paisleys did not follow his example. Instead they went on the attack.

LAZY JOURNALISTS

Paisley Snr had a long history of lambasting journalists. One of the most notorious outbursts came after press reports about health problems he had been suffering in 2004. His family kept the nature of his illness a secret, but the DUP leader's haggard appearance inevitably prompted media speculation. Hitting out at the coverage, he declared: 'I would say it's just because I happen to be a Protestant and journalists happen to be Romanists that they think they can take it out on me.'[32]

The press coverage of the 'Causeway cronyism' story was pretty intense by October 2007. First Minister Paisley launched what looked very much like an attempt at retaliation. During question time at the Assembly, a DUP backbencher asked him: 'Does the Office of the First Minister and deputy First Minister have any plans to consider reform of FOI?'

Paisley replied:

There is no doubt that the evidence thus far already suggests that dealing with FOI requests takes up a considerable amount of staff time. On occasions, the requests are of a wide-ranging and detailed nature that require many hours of research, and are sent in by lazy journalists, who will not do any work, but who think that we should pay them and give them the information that they want. That, inevitably, adds time and resource pressures onto the Departments. If, in collating evidence on how the current procedures are working, the Departments discover that reform is needed—and I think they will—it will have to take place.[33]

This 'lazy journalists' attack was just four days after Paisley Snr's Heritage Lottery Fund letter had been revealed in the press through FOI. If it was meant to cow uppity hacks into submission, it failed miserably. The *Belfast Telegraph* featured the attack under the heading: 'Is something troubling you, First Minister?'[34] It contrasted the Paisley comments with a 'glowing' press release on government FOI disclosures issued in July 2007. Paisley had stated in that release: 'In response to requests concerning a wide range of issues of public interest, our departments have disclosed significant amounts of information never released previously. They are making considerable strides towards achieving our goal of more open government.'

The fact was that Stormont had no power to amend the FOI Act, as it also applied to England and Wales. It was just an example of old-style Paisley sabre-rattling. There had been similar anti-FOI talk in government circles at Westminster earlier that year. But that was during the dying days of the Blair regime, and the idea of curtailing the Act faded after Gordon Brown took over as Prime Minister.

Paisley's attack did suggest a worrying attitude to accountability issues in Stormont. A veteran UK campaigner for open government, Maurice Frankel, reacted to his comments with some wise words of advice. Frankel pointed out that any move to restrict scrutiny of politicians was the last thing the Stormont system needed. 'Above everything else, it needs openness and higher standards of scrutiny to demonstrate that the political system is functioning in an open and accountable way and is doing the job that people expect of it,' he warned. 'For it to go in the opposite direction would undermine public confidence in what politicians were doing—at a time when they most need public confidence.'[35]

MORE LOBBYING SECRETS

By happy coincidence, another significant FOI disclosure soon came along to shed further light on the pro-Sweeney lobbying activities that had been going on. It showed that Paisley Jnr had made 13 different contacts with one government department in the space of five years in support of the developer's Causeway plans.[36] These involved letters to ministers, meetings with ministers and officials, and phone calls to senior civil servants. It was yet more evidence of the amount of time and effort that had been expended by a busy politician in support of just one businessman and one business project.

There was also further proof of contentious claims being made behind the scenes. The FOI disclosure was issued by the Department of Enterprise, Trade and Investment (DETI) and the 13 examples of lobbying it revealed spanned the period 2001 to 2006. They included letters from Paisley Jnr to the DETI's then Ulster Unionist Minister Sir Reg Empey in August and November 2001. These expressed support for a Sweeney plan for a major arts and crafts centre on his land near the Giant's Causeway. The possibility of grant-aid was floated, with Paisley Jnr stating: 'I trust that you will look favourably at my constituent's request for advice and guidance from centre government for the development of this proposal and what assistance may be available to him if his planning application is successful.' Correspondence from Sweeney was attached, showing that he was planning an arts and crafts centre at that point as well as a visitor centre. Put another way, he wanted to build two new Causeway developments.

The arts and crafts centre proposal was aborted the following year, when the Planning Appeals Commission ruled against the scheme.[37] Among the grounds for this refusal was the impact on the setting of the Causeway World Heritage Site.

The FOI disclosure also included details of a November 2004 meeting with Direct Rule DETI Minister Barry Gardiner. If the Department's official record is to be believed—and Paisley Jnr did not challenge its details when it was made public—then he made some quite startling suggestions at these discussions. It quoted him, for example, displaying almost childlike enthusiasm for the private sector. According to the DETI's account, Paisley Jnr 'noted the successful turnaround in fortunes of the Royal Victoria Hospital car park' as an example of 'successful private sector involvement'. The car park at the Belfast hospital had in fact been a disaster of a privatised project. The scheme had been widely criticised earlier that year after a Northern Ireland Audit Office report.[38] It showed that the developer had been effectively handed years of easy profits, while the hospital was forking out large sums in subsidising users.

The DETI's official note of Paisley Jnr's November 2004 meeting with Minister Gardiner also recorded an audacious attempt to sideline Moyle Council and the National Trust, the key stakeholders on the Causeway centre. It stated: 'Ian Paisley suggested that the project could move forward without the stakeholders as the access to the 'stones' was a right of way and that the land for the facilities could be vested.' The note further said: 'He also stated his belief that now was the optimum time to get new facilities in place, as a return to devolution would attract too many "new players" to the project.'

This would mean a Direct Rule government using compulsory purchase powers to vest land from Moyle Council, a public authority in Paisley Jnr's constituency. And it was being argued that it should be done right away, before devolution brought 'new players' into the situation.

One other document is particularly worth noting from the DETI FOI disclosure. It was a file note of a phone call made by Paisley Jnr on 30 September 2005 to a senior tourism official within the Department. That date is significant, because it was the day of a key Moyle Council meeting. On the council's agenda was a formal decision to move ahead with the public sector Causeway centre project in conjunction with the National Trust.

Paisley Jnr made a last ditch bid to block this agreement. He told the DETI civil servant that the DUP 'had a number of real concerns' and did not consider the visitor centre deal 'to be in the best interests of ratepayers'. The civil servant's file note on his conversation with Paisley Jnr concluded: 'I got the impression that my responses gave him little leverage and so his only hope now is to appeal directly to Ministers in which case we need to be steadfast in resisting any attempt to delay our planned announcement.'

The DETI did indeed remain 'steadfast' at this point, and the winner of the international competition was announced. It was only after devolution returned that the Department's approach changed.

A document which came to light separately from the DETI FOI disclosure exposed just how active the Paisleys were on 30

September 2005.[39] The efforts to halt the imminent decision by Moyle Council to move ahead with the National Trust went beyond a forceful phone call to a civil servant. That same morning, a letter on House of Commons headed paper from Paisley Snr was faxed to Moyle Council's chief executive. It requested a deferral of a decision to allow for further consideration of the visitor centre deal on the table. The letter claimed taking a binding decision 'without first exploring all of the options' would constitute 'negligence' by the council. It would also, he did not add, have been contrary to the interests of Seymour Sweeney.

Paisley Snr's intervention did not sway Moyle Council, however. It continued to stick with the Trust, even when Sweeney seemed poised to win the battle by 2007.

LIMITED DAMAGE

All the lobbying details outlined above—and more—entered the public domain in the last four months of 2007. They exposed the hardball tactics sometimes employed by the Paisleys.

There was an embarrassment factor, and not just because it all made a nonsense of the 'I know of him' comment by Junior on the radio. This was not a pleasant picture overall. Paisley Snr had been shoving his righteous morality down people's throats for years. He and his son were now caught up in a lingering cronyism controversy.

Public officials had been given robust treatment, the position of a United Nations organisation had been inaccurately represented, and an incredible level of effort had been expended. It had all been for the sake of one developer. Discontented members of Paisley's Free Presbyterian Church noted that Seymour Sweeney was a pub owner, as well as a property tycoon. The bid to get him money from the sinful National Lottery also did not go unnoticed.

It is not that easy to make a public interest defence for all the pro-Sweeney lobbying. If the businessman's visitor centre scheme had gone ahead, how much difference would this have made to the lives of north Antrim constituents? The public sector alternative had the virtue of bringing long-term revenue to Moyle Council, as well as ongoing funding for the National Trust's job of looking after the famous stones.

There is no doubt that the Causeway-related lobbying revelations of late 2007 were damaging. But the indications at that time were that the Paisleys would be able to shrug off the controversy sooner or later. This was partly due to the fact that no evidence existed of them receiving anything from Sweeney. The developer had stated categorically that he had given no money to the DUP—apart from his membership fees.

What was unknown at this time was that Sweeney had come to the Paisleys' assistance during 2007, in a property deal that provided them with a shiny new constituency office. The facts of that case would not emerge until February 2008—with devastating consequences for Junior's ministerial career. Such a dramatic outcome looked highly unlikely even at the peak of the Causeway row.

Chapter 7
Senior in Bother

'We are not expecting anything untoward'
Paisley supporter talking ahead of the Free Presbyterian
Church meeting that resulted in Ian Paisley standing down
as Moderator

The autumn of 2007 did not go well for the Paisleys. If the House of Paisley had actually been a physical building, this was the time the surveyors delivered disturbing news. It wasn't just a touch of rising damp in the bathroom, rodents in the attic or dry rot in a storeroom. Big cracks in the walls had started to appear, indicating some serious structural damage.

As the previous chapter has detailed, 11 September 2007 was when Ian Junior landed himself in trouble with his 'I know of him' gaffe about Seymour Sweeney. Just a few days before that, Paisley Snr had suffered a previously unthinkable reverse in his church. Faced with a determined rebellion in Free Presbyterian ranks over his role in the power-sharing government, Paisley agreed to step down as its Moderator. Had the question of his leadership been pushed to a vote, he might very well have suffered a humiliating defeat. At the very least, his small denomination would have been left very badly divided, perhaps even irreparably split.

The lengthy meeting of the ruling Free Presbyterian Presbytery which triggered his decision was held behind doors on 7 September. It was picketed by anti-power-sharing protestors, who handed out leaflets saying: 'Ian Paisley's own words stand as a condemnation to him. He is guilty of all that he accused others of being guilty of. There's only one thing left for Ian Paisley to do: repent.'[1] The tactics and rhetoric he had used in the past were now being deployed against him.

Different accounts and interpretations of what went on in the private Presbytery gathering have emerged. Paisley's loyal supporters have tried to counter suggestions that he was forced out. One unnamed 'senior church figure' commented later that particular weekend: 'This was his decision to step down. It was a voluntary decision, he had even talked about this some months ago. It was not on the strength of this meeting that the decision was made.' But the same person also described the situation as 'very sad'.[2] That gave a clue to the downbeat mood of the pro-Paisley camp. They had not envisaged it unfolding in this way, and had been predicting that the Presbytery meeting would not lead to any changes in leadership.

Instead, a different outcome was announced, with Paisley only staying on as Moderator until January, and then not seeking re-election to the post. A *News Letter* editorial commented: 'Although it was well-known that there was disquiet in some of his congregations about recent political developments, few believed that the murmurings of discontent would lead to any change in the status of Mr Paisley.' It continued:

> It is clear from what has emerged since that Mr Paisley's primary motivation was to avoid a damaging internal conflict. The outcome that was agreed—that he would stand down and elections would be delayed until January—was a dignified way of resolving the situation, but one which will surely have hurt a man who has devoted a large part of his life to this institution.[3]

It was not just a question of him being personally hurt. The development was also a blow to his authority and it left him weakened in political terms. The man with a reputation for confrontation was in retreat.

Furthermore, the unexpected church development also sent thoughts running in a section of the DUP about a leadership handover, and a complete end of the Paisley era. A *Belfast Telegraph* editorial took the view that the First Minister had 'lost an important battle' and warned:

Not everyone, within a religious community that has suffered from IRA violence, was going to approve the DUP–Sinn Féin deal, and the surprise is that Mr Paisley and his supporters seem to have underestimated the opposition. They failed to prepare their believers for the political transformation that was necessary, and they are paying the price—as Mr Paisley's opponents have paid in the past.[4]

Attempts were made to put the best interpretation on his exit plan as Moderator. A spokesperson for Paisley told one newspaper: 'It was his decision and he is very happy.'[5] The decision has been defended on the grounds of the need to preserve unity in the Free Presbyterian Church. That in itself is an indication of the divisions among members about Paisley's dual role as Moderator and First Minister.

Paisley publicly described the Presbytery meeting as 'wonderful'.[6] But his sermon to worshippers at his church that Sunday morning revealed just how serious the situation could have become. 'At our annual Presbytery meeting held here on Friday night, 7 September, the Free Presbyterian Church was facing a very real crisis,' Paisley admitted to his congregation. 'By what that I can only describe as Christ's intervention, the atmosphere of that meeting suddenly changed and the entire Presbytery knew it, and the meeting ended with the giving of this preacher a round of acclamation. It was a melting, holy time. We wept and we rejoiced.'[7]

The Free Presbyterian Church is never going to release a transcript or minutes of the famous Presbytery showdown. But the key details of what went on are fairly clear. While international statesmen were applauding Paisley's devolution deal with Sinn Féin in the spring of 2007, a section of his church was somewhere between heartbroken and furious. All they had been taught over the years had been turned on its head. Against this, other members remained true to the man who had led them for decades. They argued that the church had given him permission to enter Parliament many years earlier, and his elevation to high office was a matter for the electorate.

The internal friction had spilled into Presbytery proceedings prior to the September showdown. Chief Paisley critic Rev. Ivan Foster was even heckled at one meeting. Amidst these conflicting views, it was decided within the church leadership to establish a commission. Its remit involved reviewing Paisley's dual role as Moderator and First Minister.

Attempts were meanwhile made to play down the significance of the tensions. One of Paisley's most trusted lieutenants publicly claimed the situation was becoming calmer within weeks of the new power-sharing government being established. Rev. David McIlveen, an official spokesman for the church, said he was not aware of any looming challenge to Paisley. 'My own feeling as time has gone on is that things are settling down,' he said. 'Certainly we are not going to allow the church to be dragged into the mire of politics.'[8]

The scale of the bitterness, however, was illustrated by Paisley himself through the pages of the church magazine *The Revivalist*— a trusted method of conveying messages to the flock. In an editorial in the spring of 2007, he portrayed himself as God's anointed leader and suggested church members who criticised him were doing the devil's work.[9] 'There are ways to deal with disputes in the church and that way is clearly not the way of slandering God's leadership,' the article stated. It also said that Satan 'especially hates the man whom God anoints and appoints', and cited examples from the Bible. 'The tactics of Satan have not changed and the Bible was written that we might be prepared for similar satanic attacks upon the leaders of God's work today,' he added.

Wife Baroness Paisley joined the battle in the same issue of *The Revivalist*, writing:

Today there are those in church and state whose vision is so distorted by self-righteousness they are of the opinion that they couldn't possibly be wrong and so they go around criticising those to whom under God they owe their very salvation, their positions, their churches. Like the Israelites of old treated Moses so they treat today's God-anointed leader.

Such strong words might have been enough to quell a revolt in the past. Not this time. Even being linked to the Devil himself by their church leader did not silence the detractors.

There were different facets to the unrest within Free Presbyterianism. At the heart of it was revulsion at the sight of the Moderator standing beside Martin McGuinness in government. Paisley and his church had taught that such an alliance with 'men of violence' was morally wrong. There was also a more theoretical debate about a church leader simultaneously holding the highest political office in the land. As one Free Presbyterian source puts it: 'A Government is usually pragmatic and tries to maximise support, whereas a church should be strongly tied to the teaching of the word of God.' The First Minister was not just any church leader either, but the head of one of the most uncompromising denominations in the British Isles.

As previously detailed in this book, Paisley's two roles created various conflicts and contradictions. The funding from his OFMDFM department to gay groups was not the only example, but it was the most wounding. Apparently, there were even tears shed by some members over the issue. One church source talks of extreme distaste being felt at the idea of showing 'even the slightest degree of empathy with sodomy'. He also says: 'There is an abhorrence linked to that. It is more nauseating than the moral implications of standing shoulder to shoulder with Sinn Féin.' Outside the narrow confines of Free Presbyterianism, that seems like a shockingly extreme statement. But there are nevertheless strong grounds for viewing it as an accurate reflection of how church members feel. The hardline sentiment is also clearly shared by senior figures in the DUP, who continued speaking out about homosexuality long after the devolution pact with Sinn Féin was agreed.

A more minor clash between religious purity and government was exploited by Rev. Ivan Foster just before the all-important September 2007 Presbytery meeting. DUP Culture Minister Edwin Poots, a Free Presbyterian, had visited a Belfast project for aspiring rock musicians. The Oh Yeah Centre was located in Belfast's

Cathedral Quarter, a burgeoning area for night life, tourism and cultural pursuits. Its creation had the backing of Gary Lightbody, lead singer of Northern Ireland's most successful band for a generation, Snow Patrol. That helped to make it just the sort of project a politician and a government would want to be associated with in normal circumstances.

But words of encouragement for the initiative from Minster Poots were met with outrage from Foster. The County Tyrone clergyman branded Oh Yeah a 'blasphemous enterprise' and said that the DUP Minister's stance was 'unchristian and contrary to the standards set forth in Holy Scripture'.[10] This would be very much a minority view in Ulster Protestant circles. Yet it was in line with Free Presbyterian and Paisleyite teaching. His church had indeed maintained for years that rock music was evil.

The story of the Oh Yeah row broke in the media on 6 September 2007—the day before the big Presbytery meeting. That same week, however, 'senior church sources' were quoted in the press saying it was 'extremely likely' that Paisley would be re-elected as Moderator once again. One unnamed member of the church leadership also said: 'We are not expecting anything untoward.' Another source added: 'The overwhelming feeling is that the church should not be dragged into the mire of politics.'[11]

However, the Free Presbyterian Commission that had been set up to examine Paisley's roles as Moderator and First Minister found itself unable to speak with a single voice. A narrow majority on the panel reached the conclusion that the two positions should not be jointly held. That came before the September Presbytery meeting for discussion. The crunch in its private discussions followed a procedural vote. A Paisley supporter proposed that the meeting move to the next item of business, which was to have been the re-election of the Moderator. This move was defeated. One church member present, who would not be regarded as anti-Paisley, recalls: 'It was clear that there was a division and that the division was clearly not in his favour.'

A break was called, during which Paisley conferred privately with key individuals. Foster, who had wanted the meeting to vote

Paisley out of the Moderator's position, was brought into the discussions. It was put to him that Paisley would agree to stand down in January. Foster concurred and the two former close allies shook hands in what must have been a poignant moment. A showdown vote was avoided.

It will never be known for certain what would have happened if Paisley had stood his ground and the meeting had proceeded towards a vote. He could have rallied support with an emotional plea, recalling all the years he had devoted to the church. It is one thing to rebel on a procedural matter, and quite another to look into your leader's tearful eyes and vote him out. Paisley chose to take another course which avoided this possibility.

Paisley's supporters have pointed out that he had been talking about bowing out for some time. It has also been suggested that he might very well have vacated the Moderator's role of his own volition early in 2008. In other words, if the September Presbytery meeting had re-elected him as normal, he would have stood down a few months later. He was robbed of such a smooth transition by the way things turned out at the Presbytery. The anti-Agreement rebels within his church therefore scored a direct and unpredicted hit.

During his Sunday sermon after suffering the Presbytery blow, Paisley sought to lift the spirits of his Memorial congregation. He also voiced some regret for what they had been through. Pledging to continue his ministry, he told the service:

God has given me a good body, He's given me a loud voice, He's given me a great wife and He's given me a great family, and great children. But He's done more than that. He's given me a great people and I regret that they have had to pass through a time of deep trouble for them. And I know how you feel and I will not tell you how I feel. But this I want to say to you today that God is at work and we will see Him perfect that which concerneth Him.

He concluded his address with what sounded like defiance:

Do not despair. A man rang me last night and he said to me: 'I despair for you, Ian.' Well, I'm not despairing. I am happy in the Lord. And the greater the hole the devil digs, the mightier will be our deliverance by the power of Christ. So let the devil over strain himself, let him rupture himself by trying to dig a mine pit for God's people. That mine pit can never be dug successfully.

He still seemed to believe that those lined up against him were doing Satan's work. It was like a DUP version of the 'divine right of kings'. Paisley was doing God's work during all those years when he was denouncing the politics of compromise. Happily, the Almighty was also on his side when he finally decided to compromise himself. Those who dared to criticise him, meanwhile, were working for the Devil. A temporary truce of sorts was declared within Free Presbyterianism as a result of the September Presbytery. Internal opponents of the departing Moderator agreed to remove comments from the internet.

New Secretary of State Shaun Woodward, who had succeeded Peter Hain in June 2007, did his bit. He spoke of the importance of keeping church and state separate, while recognising Paisley's long period as Moderator. 'But the emphasis now for him is as First Minister of Northern Ireland,' Woodward argued. 'That is a job he is doing incredibly well.'[12]

There were signs during that month that not everybody agreed with this glowing assessment. Rumours were circulating at Stormont over plans to cut down on the joint engagements for the First and Deputy First Ministers. It was an early sign that the Paisley and McGuinness Chuckle Brothers routine—and the smiling photographs that went with it—were playing badly at grass-roots level.

As the Assembly reconvened in September after its summer break, senior DUP politician Gregory Campbell issued what was a barely coded message. The MP and MLA effectively called for a more frosty working relationship between his party and Sinn Féin. 'Republicans have begun to believe their own rhetoric and are still floating on a bubble of banality as a result of puerile photographs which they think are going to represent the future,' Campbell claimed.[13]

Whispers about Paisley's age and the demands of his office also started to become louder. The imminent loss of his church leadership role left him looking less secure. Surveying his position, columnist Susan McKay concluded:

> He has done the right thing at long bloody last for this country. But he is old now. He mutters, gets things wrong, can't think on his feet. It is no shame at 81. He is increasingly reliant on the charmless Junior, who showed himself to be a liability to his ministerial colleagues over the Causeway fiasco. Paisley has got all the snaps to put on the sideboard. Smiling with the prime minister. Smiling with the Taoiseach. Smiling with the Irish president. Smiling with the unrepentant terrorist—sorry, with Martin. It is time to go.[14]

SENIOR MOMENTS

The reference to getting things wrong had become a talking point within DUP circles. They are unlikely to get any thanks for it, but the media—and rival politicians—were quite reserved about the verbal stumbles of the elderly First Minister.

Age was a major topic for discussion in British politics that autumn. Sir Menzies Campbell resigned as Liberal Democrat leader in October 2007 after months of speculation about him being too old for the post. He was 66. First Minister Paisley was 15 years older and was an MP as well as First Minister. Yet his age never became a major political issue in the public sphere.

Opportunities for critics to highlight the subject certainly arose. Just a month into his job, Paisley embarrassingly gave the wrong answer to an Assembly question. SDLP MLA Thomas Burns asked him about a 1999 comment by Ian Paisley Jnr, criticising the creation of junior minister posts at Stormont. This was a timely point to recall Junior's words, given that he had just taken one of the revived junior minister posts himself.

Replying to Burns, the First Minister said:

> The Deputy First Minister and I have made it clear that the Office of the First Minister and the Deputy First Minister is totally committed to promoting equality and human rights. The First Minister and the Deputy First Minister are completely opposed to any form of discrimination and harassment against any citizen.[15]

Paisley was answering a question he had not been asked—on his son's controversial comment about being 'repulsed' by homosexuality.

In September 2007, DUP Assemblyman Ian McCrea asked about progress towards mutual recognition of driving bans on both sides of the border. Again, the First Minister seemed to give a reply to an entirely different question, saying: 'I would like to see a good relationship between both parts of this island without any political claims of jurisdiction by either one.'[16]

The following month, Paisley appeared to answer a question from Sinn Féin member Martina Anderson before it had been put to him. This prompted SDLP MLA Alban Maginness to comment: 'I do not know whether I am more confused than the First Minister.'[17] And in December 2007, in answer to a question about Northern Ireland's Equality Commission, Paisley said: 'I am glad that the Member has raised this matter. I will take it up with the chief commissioner, and we will test it out with her.' Ulster Unionist Danny Kennedy interjected to point out that the chief commissioner was, in fact, a man.[18]

The occasional signs of apparent bewilderment in the Assembly led to speculation about how Paisley was coping with the workload of being a minister. The endless rounds of meetings, the paperwork, the constant engagements and all the bureaucratic burdens of government would be a challenge for any senior citizen. One government official has summed up the reality with a diplomatic off-the-record comment: 'Let's just put it like this—there were good days and bad days.'

Paisley could still be capable of a nasty aside or two in the Assembly, indicating that his old fighting days were not completely behind him. Some of his most venomous barbs were not aimed at Sinn Féin, the enemy turned partner-in-government, but the middle-of-the-road Alliance Party. Alliance leader David Ford remarked in the house at one point about 'laying oneself open to abuse' by merely asking questions. Paisley snapped back: 'I am sorry that when he does not get it the way he likes it, he considers it abuse. I have never abused the honourable Member; if I had, he would not be sitting in his place today.'

Quite how the First Minister would have had the power to eject Ford from 'his place' was not explained. Nevertheless, Paisley's incoherent quip was met by 'laughter' according to the Assembly record of the debate.[19]

In another Stormont exchange, Alliance deputy Naomi Long asked the First Minister how long he and McGuinness intended to 'dine out' on the feelgood factor created by their power-sharing deal. Paisley replied with a jibe about Long's appearance: 'I am sure that the honourable lady enjoys dining out herself.'[20] Making a personal remark like that at Westminster or in the Dáil could land a government minister in bother. Not in Stormont. The retort was also somewhat rich coming from Paisley, given his less than slight frame and his notorious appetite.

Meanwhile there was defiant talk from the First Minister whenever his future was mentioned. In April 2007, even before the new power-sharing government had been formed, Paisley gave a forthright answer when asked how long he planned to stay in power. 'I am pleased you asked me that question. I will serve the full four years. I will not be resigning.'[21] Speaking during a visit to the Labour Party conference in late September 2007, he insisted that he intended to both serve his full term as First Minister and stand again for the House of Commons. 'My voice needs to be heard in Westminster and especially with the good rapport I get now, I might as well make hay while the sun shines,' he said.[22]

Similarly, in a special UTV interview in November to mark his first six months in office, he was asked if was still determined to see out all four years as First Minister.

> Oh yes, indeed I am. I feel well. I am very well received
> everywhere I go. I have sought to show a human face amidst all
> the troubles. I have never met a prime minister who has been
> accused of being too happy, but that is what I am accused of. So
> you have a happy First Minister. They should be very happy they
> have a happy First Minister and that I am not some miserable
> sod sitting up here in Stormont planning some way to bring
> disaster to the country.[23]

He was not just staying on, but was going to keep on chuckling.
And in December, Paisley told the *News Letter*:

> I was elected by the people of Northern Ireland to do a four year
> term and I am going to do a four year term. They did not say to
> me 'you go in there and then go home'. They said at the election
> you stay with us and there is no turning back. I am in good
> health and can do more than many of these younger fellas can
> do. I have a job to do and I am going to do it.[24]

All but one of these firm declarations about his future were made
after the September 2007 upset in the Free Presbyterian Church.
They contained an unambiguous message for the DUP. Paisley was
in for the long haul as First Minister.

This must have been incredibly frustrating for those hoping for
an imminent change at the top of the party. It seemed they still had
years of waiting ahead of them—and yet more embarrassed
squirming whenever their leader stumbled his way through
Assembly business.

Ian Paisley (*second from right*) at a 1966 protest march against alleged ecumenical tendencies in the mainstream Irish Presbyterian Church. (*Belfast Telegraph*)

Ian Paisley is escorted to a police car after throwing a snowball at the car carrying Taoiseach Jack Lynch for a Stormont meeting with Unionist Prime Minister Terence O'Neill in December 1967. (*Belfast Telegraph*)

Ian Paisley at a Derry counter-demonstration to the civil rights campaign. (*Belfast Telegraph*)

Ian Paisley leaving Crumlin Road prison in 1969, greeted by his wife, Eileen. (*Belfast Telegraph*)

Brian Faulkner, the unionist leader who headed the brief 1974 power-sharing administration at Stormont based on the Sunningdale Agreement with the nationalist SDLP. The 1998 Belfast Agreement was famously dubbed 'Sunningdale for slow learners'. (*Belfast Telegraph*)

Ian Paisley at a 1974 Larne protest against the Sunningdale Agreement. (*Belfast Telegraph*)

Ian Paisley and Peter Robinson arrested at a 1980 protest against a visit to Armagh by Taoiseach Charles Haughey. (*Belfast Telegraph*)

Less compromising times. Ian Paisley and DUP colleagues Peter Robinson (*left*) and Willie McCrea lead a Belfast City Hall protest against a visit to Northern Ireland by Dublin councillors. (*Belfast Telegraph*)

This 1984 DUP delegation included Jim Allister and Rev. Ivan Foster, who would later become leading critics of the party's 2007 power-sharing deal with Sinn Féin. (*From left*) William McCrea, Ivan Foster, Jim Allister, Ian Paisley and Peter Robinson. (*Belfast Telegraph*)

Ian Paisley poses with a sledgehamer to promote his 'Smash Sinn Féin' campaign in the 1985 local government elections. (*Pacemaker*)

Paisley features on a DUP poster campaign to 'Smash Sinn Féin and reject Republicanism'. (*Belfast Telegraph*)

Ulster Unionist leader David Trimble (*with yellow tie*) and a group of party colleagues get into a slanging match with top DUP politicians during the 2003 election campaign. The confrontation occurred outside UUP headquarters in east Belfast. (*Press Association Images Ltd*)

Done deal. The famous moment in March 2007 when Ian Paisley and Sinn Féin President Gerry Adams sit side by side to announce a power-sharing agreement. (*Press Association Images Ltd*)

Ian Paisley and his wife, Baroness Paisley, arrive at Stormont in May 2007 on the day of his appointment as First Minister. (*Alan Lewis*)

Let the chuckling commence. Pictured after the May 2007 launch of the new Stormont are (*from left*): new Deputy First Minister Martin McGuinness, Taoiseach Bertie Ahern, Prime Minister Tony Blair, Northern Ireland Secretary Peter Hain and new First Minister Ian Paisley. (*Press Association Images Ltd*)

Ian Paisley announces his ministerial team for the power-sharing executive that took office in May 2007. (*From left*): Nigel Dodds, Peter Robinson, Ian Paisley, Arlene Foster, Edwin Poots and Ian Paisley Jnr. (*Belfast Telegraph*)

A badge worn at the 2007 Belfast Gay Pride parade responds to Ian Paisley Jnr's comments about being 'repulsed' by homosexuality. (*Pacemaker*)

Junior Ministers Gerry Kelly and Ian Paisley Jnr launch a new superheroes comic to promote children's rights. (*Pacemaker*)

This photograph of the Paisleys with developer Seymour Sweeney (*centre*) made constant re-appearances in the media in late 2007, as the controversy over Paisley Jnr's links to the businessman deepened. (*Pacemaker*)

The Giant's Causeway, Northern Ireland's top tourist attraction and the subject of many of Ian Paisley Jnr's lobbying problems. (*National Trust*)

Former Eurovision song winner and conservative Catholic politician Dana—Rosemary Scallon—jokes with Ian Paisley and Baroness Paisley during her November 2007 book launch at Stormont. A tribute to Dana from Paisley at the event caused him trouble in his Free Presbyterian heartland. (*Press Association Images Ltd*)

us President George W. Bush with First Minister Ian Paisley and Deputy First Minister Martin McGuinness in the Oval Office in December 2007. (*Press Association Images Ltd*)

Junior Minister Ian Paisley Jnr joins with Sinn Féin Ministers Conor Murphy and Caitríona Ruane to help promote a 'Bike to Work' week. (*Belfast Telegraph*)

Junior Minister Ian Paisley Jnr at the launch of the January 2008 programme for his beloved North West 200 road racing event. Funding for the North West 200 was one of his 'shopping list' demands controversially raised with Prime Minister Tony Blair at the St Andrews talks. (*Press Association Images Ltd*)

Ian Paisley's daughter Rhonda, one of three Paisley children on his House of Commons payroll.

A new dynasty takes over. Peter and Iris Robinson with Ian and Baroness Paisley at the end of a May 2008 DUP event at the King's Hall, Belfast, to mark Paisley's retirement as DUP leader. (*Belfast Telegraph*)

Peter Robinson in happy mood with wife, Iris, after taking over from Ian Paisley as First Minister of Northern Ireland in June 2008. (*Press Association Images Ltd*)

Ian Paisley Jnr announces his resignation as Minister to the media. Observers noted that he was not flanked by any party colleagues as he made his departure statement. (*Press Association Images Ltd*)

Chapter 8
Land Deal Lobbying

'I believe that Ian Paisley Jnr should have withdrawn totally from involvement in this matter as soon as he became Minister.'

SDLP MLA DECLAN O'LOAN

Just as the worst of the Causeway lobbying storm seemed to be blowing over, another batch of unwanted headlines came along for Ian Paisley Jnr towards the end of 2007. They also centred on his repeated use of political access and influence in support of a potentially very lucrative business deal.

At the heart of the story once again was a property developer by the name of Seymour Sweeney. It emerged that Paisley Jnr had been persistently lobbying government ministers on the sale of publicly owned land in north Antrim. Sweeney was among the businessmen waiting in the wings to benefit from the proposed asset disposal.

To add to the mix, Paisley Jnr's lobbying on this issue even continued after he became a minister in the new Northern Ireland devolved government. It was discovered that he had gone to the lengths of protesting to a fellow minister that her department was seeking too much money for the land. Critics argued—not without reason—that he should have been seeking to maximise the sale proceeds, thereby boosting the funds available to his government for public services.

Different views have been expressed on the seriousness, or otherwise, of the land deal lobbying controversy. Paisley Jnr maintained that he had simply been pursuing the interests of constituents. The Sweeney connection obviously made it a bigger story. Clearly, there would have been less of a fuss had this particular businessman not been involved. But he was, and that meant there were 'cronyism' issues involved.

Imagine, for example, if a prominent New Labour minister in England was making strong representations to a Cabinet colleague in support of a land sale plan. How would the media react if a major beneficiary of this sell-off turned out to be linked to the lobbying minister, and a member of his constituency party? It's not hard to envisage that making front-page news in London. Paisley Jnr also made the situation worse for himself by the way he responded to criticism.

ACRES UP FOR GRABS

The background to this section of the Paisley Jnr downfall story stretched back almost four decades. In 1970, 96 acres of land at Ballee, close to Ballymena in north Antrim, were compulsorily purchased by the Stormont government of the day. The aim was to facilitate the development of a new town, but the plans never came to fruition. The landholding stayed in public ownership up to 2003 when the province's Department for Social Development (DSD) decided it was surplus to requirements. The plan was to sell off the 96 acres at auction, with the proceeds going to the public purse.

Former owners of the land objected to an auction, arguing that they should have first refusal on buying it back, in light of the compulsory purchase decades earlier. The DSD rejected their request, but found itself facing a judicial review challenge. In the background was a group of property developers, including Seymour Sweeney. They backed the legal challenge taken by the former owners, on the basis that the ex-landowners would sell the site on to them. Court documentation published from a hearing relating to the case shed some light on arrangements that had been put in place by early 2007.[1] It stated that the cost of buying the land from government would be met by the developers, who in turn would pay the ex-owners 10 per cent of this asking price to secure ownership.

Not for the first time, the efforts of Paisley Jnr were brought to light due to the Freedom of Information Act.[2] Released papers showed he had made several approaches to the DSD's then Direct Rule Minister David Hanson. It is clear—whatever Paisley Jnr himself thought—that Hanson's officials believed the Assemblyman was acting in some kind of quasi-negotiating role.

In December 2006, a paper was provided to the Minister by the MLA outlining the case for a government deal with the former Ballee land owners. In an email to a DSD civil servant, an official from Hanson's private office stated:

> As discussed, Ian Paisley Jnr has approached the Minister and has provided him with the attached document. He has stated that he is prepared to drop the judicial review if the suggestion he makes in this document is accepted. The Minister has asked for urgent advice on this matter to be with him by close of play tomorrow as he has undertaken to respond to Ian Paisley Jnr with a decision and would need to consider the evidence over the weekend.

Three days later, Hanson wrote to Paisley Jnr thanking him for the document. 'I have read the document with interest and note that it does not differ markedly from the skeleton argument already passed by the legal team for the former owners. I am also unclear as to what exactly the terms of the offer are,' the Minister said. 'If the former owners now wish to make an offer, for the purposes of clarity, it should perhaps be made between their legal team and ours.'

An offer of £9 million was duly made to the DSD the following month by two law firms. There was a problem with this figure, however. It was almost £28 million lower than the government's official valuation for the 96 Ballee acres, as set the previous year. There is no evidence that Paisley Jnr actually endorsed the £9 million figure. But he did make representations in connection with the offer, contacting the Minister within a few weeks of it being tabled. He wanted to know from Hanson why there had been no response from the Department.

The DSD Minister replied on 6 February 2007, explaining that the offer had been rejected. The Minister also stated: 'For information, the site is currently on the Departmental asset register at £36.7 million and will be subject to a fresh valuation by the Valuation and Lands Agency before any possible sale.' A valuation update made particular sense given that property and land prices were surging in Northern Ireland at this time.

Later in February, however, legal representatives for the ex-owners made a £36.7 million settlement offer, presumably in the hope that the government's revaluation plan would not be pursued.

Paisley Jnr continued using his influence behind the scenes. A DSD briefing paper to the Minister—dated 2 March 2007—noted that the MLA had 'again been in contact'. This memo was prepared in advance of a planned meeting between Hanson and Paisley Jnr three days later. It said: 'Mr Paisley has complained that the Department is moving very slowly in considering the former owners' offer to settle the case.' The memo set out the current position for the Minister and said a new valuation would be produced as soon as possible. Amid an exchange of emails between civil servants around this time, one official from the government's valuation agency commented: 'I am somewhat uncomfortable about what appears to be an attempt by the applicants to rush through a deal.'

In mid-March 2007, the ex-owners tabled a fresh offer of £50 million, leading to court proceedings in the judicial review being adjourned. By this stage, the government was moving towards a settlement, and £50 million had been cited as the new official valuation for the land.

In early April, the DSD sent letters to ex-owners advising them that the Minister 'has agreed to seek to negotiate a sale'. This document stated that the land 'will be sold at a price reflective of the current market value which will be agreed without undue delay'. That was a pretty strong indication that the £50 million figure was necessarily not the end of the matter. The negotiations appear to have been a very protracted affair, with a number of different ex-owners involved. According to DSD documentation, one of the former owners had still not entered into the process by late May 2007. That month also brought another complication—the official valuation for 96 acres at Ballee was raised to £75 million. An email from the government valuation agency stated: 'This assessment was based on recent sales and on the market evidence which had not been available at the date of the previous valuation.'

Paisley Jnr was in government by this stage, a junior minister in a devolved administration that was facing a significant slowdown in public spending. He complained strongly in June 2007 to new DSD Minister Margaret Ritchie, a member of the SDLP. In a letter to Ritchie, he stated:

> Given your publicly stated position on house prices it is extortionate to say the least that lands the DSD valued at £6.5m in 2003 are now being valued in excess of £50m. I feel my constituents have been taken for a ride by the valuation office, and that this will ultimately conclude in a detrimental impact on the ultimate housing project and house price values that will one day be realised on this site.

At one level, this was yet another example of the aggressive lobbying style used by Paisley on Sweeney-linked business projects. But there were particular problems with the contents of this letter, leaving aside the small matter of a government minister arguing against a bid to increase public income.

The fact was that the allegedly 'extortionate' new price tag was not coming from Ritchie's department at all. It had been set by the Valuation and Lands Agency, which came under the Department of Finance. So Paisley Jnr should have been venting his anger at Finance Minister Peter Robinson. Instead, he was acting the hard man with an SDLP minister over a valuation process outside her department's direct responsibility.

The logic of Paisley Jnr's bombastic argument is also worth noting. Was he really suggesting that the expert opinions of government valuation staff should be set aside? And did he actually believe that officials within an agency of Peter Robinson's department were deliberately out to take his constituents 'for a ride'? For what reason? If a government minister is going to level such an accusation about civil servants in the course of a lobbying push, he should at least produce some evidence to back it up. There was none whatsoever in his letter to Ritchie.

Robinson's successor as DUP Finance Minister, Nigel Dodds, has stoutly defended his department's handling of the Ballee valuation process. Answering an Assembly question in 2008, Dodds said: 'This work was carried out promptly and professionally by experienced senior staff in the Agency and I am confident of the quality of both the valuations and advice provided to DSD.'[3] Whether he intended it or not, that Assembly reply from Dodds represented a categorical rejection of Paisley Jnr's claims.

The angry missive to Ritchie about the 'extortionate' land valuation came around the time the DSD was seeking to finally settle the Ballee legal dispute. An offer to sell it to the ex-owners for £70 million was made and duly rejected.

On 13 June, a DSD official sent an urgent memo to his permanent secretary, expressing concern about the state of play in the judicial review. Reporting that the case had resumed in court, he stated: 'The judicial review has not gone well for the Department and the judge seems very hostile to our case.' The memo requested approval to settle, in line with legal advice.

A £50 million purchase price was agreed and announced to the court the next day. One of the conditions of the agreement was that it would be completed within six months. But when December 2007 arrived, it was still not concluded. By coincidence, that was the month that Paisley Jnr's lobbying on Ballee came to light.[4] A bundle of DSD documents was released under FOI, including the records of his representations to ministers over the past 12 months. Paisley Jnr did not respond to queries from the *Belfast Telegraph*, but gave a detailed interview to the BBC. It failed to head off a controversy.

His main argument was that he had been acting on behalf of his constituents in his capacity as an Assemblyman, rather than a minister. But a number of his comments to the BBC, if anything, added to the questions facing him. For a start, he seemed reluctant to speak publicly about Sweeney's role, saying: 'There's six businessmen involved in this case. At some point I have been in touch or spoken to the majority of those businessmen.'

When pressed on whether he had spoken to Sweeney, he said: 'Well if Mr Sweeney contacted me of course I did.' He added: 'I've spoken to six. There are six businessmen involved in this. I have spoken to the majority of those businessmen throughout this case.' It wasn't quite 'I know of him' but it was hardly a frank and open reply.

During the interview, Paisley Jnr tried to blame the DSD for the valuation increases. 'Let's be clear about this, when the department asked me could I get them the £37 million, I did,' he claimed. 'They then turned that down and said, "Could you get us £50 million?" I did. And they then turned that down. When they then started to take the mickey on this, "We want £75m, we want £100m", there is no way my constituents were going to be ridden over in that way and I supported their interests.' In reality, the Department did not ask him to get £37 million. That was the figure quoted in early 2007, prior to an updated valuation being obtained. And if anyone was really trying to 'take the mickey', it was an agency of Peter Robinson's department.

Paisley Jnr was then questioned on the terms of the agreement the developers currently had with the former Ballee land owners. This was a vital matter. After all, if Sweeney and co. were still going to pay the ex-owners 10 per cent of the sale price, would a £75 million valuation not have meant more money for them? 'I have no idea in terms of the business agreement that is in place between my constituents and their business partners,' Paisley Jnr said. 'You have mentioned percentages. So I'm not privy to any of that, don't want to be privy to any of that.'

But given such deliberate ignorance, how could he be sure he was acting in the best interests of the former owners? Paisley Jnr could have argued that an excessive price for the land would have scuppered the deal, thereby depriving his constituents of their windfall and the government of the sale proceeds. But he did not make that argument, either in the BBC interview or in his letter of complaint to Ritchie. The letter only referred to a higher price having a knock-on effect on the value of properties built on the site. That was hardly a clinching public interest defence.

Paisley found himself being challenged on his Ballee lobbying by a leading expert in public standards, Sir Alistair Graham. Sir Alistair is a former chairman of the Committee on Standards in Public Life, a London-based watchdog established by the Westminster government. Speaking on the Ballee land lobbying, he urged Paisley Jnr to spell out his Sweeney links.[5] 'We are dealing with a property deal in which the public purse may gain many, many millions of pounds,' Sir Alistair said.

> And of course it is important that we maximise the amount of money to the public purse if public assets are being put up for sale. And therefore I think there is a heavy duty on the Junior Minister to lay out his exact interests in this matter. For example, I understand a key player in all of this is a fellow member of the DUP, the same political party. Therefore that should be absolutely clear, what contacts there has been. Is there any obligation in any way to this businessman? Has he for example had any property deals with this businessman?

It was not the first time that the Junior Minister had been challenged to fully detail all his connections with Sweeney. Once again, the call went unheeded.

In the end, the Ballee lobbying story mattered—and not just because it kept the Sweeney links row going. It was symptomatic of an attitude to public life and government that reflected poorly on the Junior Minister. He had thrown his weight about and in some instances got his facts wrong. Also, he had left himself open to the accusation of not paying proper heed to the public interest.

SDLP north Antrim MLA Declan O'Loan made the most telling criticism, stating: 'I do not see how it can be proper for a Minister to argue against the Executive interest in a matter involving many millions of pounds. I believe that Ian Paisley Jnr should have withdrawn totally from involvement in this matter as soon as he became Minister.'[6]

It also transpired that protocol concerns had been expressed privately at a high level within the civil service. This unease over Minister Paisley Jnr's lobbying even led to an intervention by the head of the civil service. The details were made public by Brian Barrington, who had been Margaret Ritchie's special adviser at the time in question.[7] Barrington said Paisley Jnr's ministerial office had phoned him twice in one day, but he had declined to take calls from the Junior Minister on both occasions. Paisley Jnr contacted the special adviser the following day personally and asked him what was happening on the Ballee land deal. Barrington said this was the only time he had been contacted by the Junior Minister during his time as a special adviser. He informed DSD's permanent secretary Alan Shannon of the phone calls, after which Shannon reported them to civil service head Nigel Hamilton.

This was confirmed officially in brief government statements issued through Stormont press offices.[8] A DSD spokesman said:

The department can confirm, in relation to the interactions between Mr Barrington and Mr Paisley Jnr over the Ballee land sale, that Mr Paisley Jnr did ring Mr Barrington, that Mr Barrington did raise the matter with the DSD Permanent Secretary and that the DSD Permanent Secretary did refer the matter to the Head of the Civil Service.

A spokesman for Sir Nigel—he had just received a knighthood—said: 'The matter was referred to the Head of the Civil Service and was dealt with by him at the time.'

Little more has been disclosed about what exactly transpired. O'Loan sought to extract further details with an Assembly question to First Ministers Paisley Snr and McGuinness. In a brief reply, they stated: 'We have been advised that, following referral of this matter by the Permanent Secretary of the Department for Social Development, the Head of the Northern Ireland Civil Service dealt with this matter by way of a private discussion with the Junior

Minister.'[9] O'Loan later pressed for more details, and was told by First Ministers Robinson and McGuinness that the 'private discussion' between Sir Nigel and Paisley Jnr related to ministerial protocols. They also stated that the matter was 'dealt with satisfactorily at that time'.[10]

There are grounds for believing that the intervention had the desired effect. Ritchie's special adviser Barrington did not receive any further calls. Paisley Jnr, meanwhile, had no comment to make on what was said to him by the civil service head in the 'private discussion'. But he rejected criticism from the SDLP that he had used the machinery of government in pursuit of constituency representations. 'There are proper procedures put in place that allow for my diaries to be combined—my private constituency work would be combined with ministerial duties,' Paisley Jnr said. 'The only meetings that were arranged and calls that took place was a civil servant making that arrangement.'[11]

Ballee remained in the news right through to February 2008, thanks in no small measure to Paisley Jnr himself. Declan O'Loan had called for an investigation into the lobbying, to establish if it was in line with Code of Conduct provisions for both ministers and MLAs. The focal point of his complaint was the Ministerial Code, as the land sale price had a bearing on funds available to the Stormont Executive. He therefore wrote to the First Ministers' department seeking an examination of the facts. In addition, O'Loan submitted a letter to the Assembly's cross-party Standards and Privileges Committee, the authority for investigating alleged breaches of the MLA code. In line with normal procedures, the Standards Committee complaint was forwarded directly to Standards Commissioner Tom Frawley for assessment.

In late January, details of a letter sent by Frawley to the Committee were leaked to the News Letter. The source of the leak is, needless to say, unknown. But the paper's coverage could hardly have been more positive for Paisley Jnr. It reported that Frawley had cleared him of breaching the Ministerial Code and the Code of Conduct for Assembly members.

Paisley Jnr followed this up a few days later—on 1 February

2008—with a press release entitled: 'Ombudsman dismisses O'Loan's complaint'. His statement referred to O'Loan launching 'a personal attack on me claiming I had breached the Ministerial Code'. It continued:

> The Assembly Ombudsman has examined this complaint and on the 17th December wrote to the SDLP chairman of the Standards and Privileges Committee stating that the complaint by the SDLP MLA did not even constitute a proper complaint, and that I did not breach any rule under the terms of membership. He also ruled out any investigation into an allegation that the Ministerial Code has been breached.

It seemed Paisley Jnr was finally able to launch a determined fightback against his critics.

At least one other media outlet was contacted by him at a senior level and asked why it had not followed up on the *News Letter*'s revelations. There was a slight problem with this, however. The *News Letter* had got it wrong.

Frawley had not in any shape or form cleared Paisley Jnr of breaching the Ministerial Code. His remit, as Standards Commissioner, extended solely to the separate Code of Conduct for MLAS. It was also stretching it to say that Frawley had unequivocally cleared him on this front. Indeed, the Standards Committee—which included DUP MLAS—was concerned enough about this to take the unprecedented step of making the Commissioner's private conclusions public.[12] In his letter to the Committee, Frawley firstly noted that the 'substance' of O'Loan's complaint was in respect of 'alleged breaches of the Ministerial Code'. 'This is a matter wholly outside the remit of the Committee,' the Commissioner stated. He further noted that the complaint was based solely on media reports on the Ballee issue.

Under Assembly standards rules, complaints stemming from the media are not 'normally regarded' as a substantiated allegation. It was Frawley's opinion in these circumstances that O'Loan's letter did not actually constitute a complaint to the Standards

Committee. The Commissioner added that if the SDLP man provided 'supporting evidence' he would be 'happy' to advise further.

This was hardly a case of Paisley Jnr being vindicated, or having complaints against him 'roundly dismissed'. Firstly, Frawley had not touched the Ministerial Code issue, the main focus of O'Loan's complaint. Secondly, O'Loan's letter was not deemed to be a complaint to the Standards Committee, although 'supporting evidence' could be considered if provided.

The cross-party Standards Committee sought to clarify the situation with a public statement posted on the Assembly website—another unprecedented move.[13] It said: 'In short, there was no detailed investigation by the Committee therefore there was no vindication in respect of the allegations made in the complaint. Rather, the complaint was not accepted by the Committee in the first place.'

The Standards Committee also published a letter it had sent to the *News Letter*, complaining of 'damaging' inaccuracies. It said the paper's report that Paisley Jnr had been cleared of breaching the Ministerial Code was 'totally disingenuous'. 'Such an alleged breach could only be examined under the Ministerial Code which is a matter for the First and Deputy First Minister,' the Committee added.

But what of O'Loan's complaint to the First Ministers? It turned out that there was no Stormont mechanism for an independent examination of alleged breaches of the Ministerial Code. That meant citizens aggrieved over a possible non-compliance had just one option—the highly expensive business of a judicial review case in the High Court. O'Loan challenged Paisley Snr over this situation in the Assembly in early February 2008.[14] He asked the First Minister how there could be 'confidence in ministerial conduct if there is not a clear mechanism for the enforcement of the ministerial code'.

In reply, Paisley Snr echoed the boasts of his son:

The Member talks energetically to the media about complaints that he has lodged with my Department and others. Let me be clear: there is nothing to investigate, and he knows that. He could not even lodge a credible paper or proper complaint with the Assembly Ombudsman on the same matter. He was knocked down. The fact is that no such complaint of substance exists, and the Member has failed to make even half a case.

So that was how the government would deal with an allegation that a junior minister had been lobbying against the public interests on asset sale proceeds. No independent examination of the complaint would take place, or was even possible under the system. And the junior minister's father would simply decree to the Assembly that there was 'nothing to investigate' anyway.

But it was not entirely the end of the affair. Standards Commissioner Frawley had, after all, stated that further material from O'Loan would be considered. Within a few weeks, the SDLP MLA obliged, providing a much more detailed complaint. The substance of it was that Paisley Jnr should have declared certain links to Seymour Sweeney in the Assembly Register of Interests. That prompted an investigation that lasted more than a year.

Chapter 9
Out with the Old

*'Like Mandela in Africa, he has become a father figure
here, a pivotal influence on whether this country's
experiment in power-sharing can survive.'*
From a newspaper column naming Ian Paisley as Northern
Ireland Man of the Year for 2007

First Minister Paisley finished 2007 in grand style. His bizarre
Chuckle Brothers act with Martin McGuinness was still a big
draw, however much some of his old fans hated it. It seemed
the pair could not appear together in public without hearty
laughter and big smiles for the cameras ensuing.

In December 2007, the chortling First Ministers made a high-
profile joint trip to the United States with the aim of wooing US
investors. Baroness Paisley and Ian Junior went too. The tour took
in New York and Washington, and looked very much like a victory
lap for Northern Ireland's power-sharing triumph. With the
American economy on its way to near-collapse, it was possibly not
the best time to go looking for corporate sugar daddies.
Nevertheless, the visit did put the province's new image on
international display.

The First Ministers held discussions with President Bush,
Hillary Clinton and Teddy Kennedy, and received enthusiastic
praise for their peacemaking. There was also a meeting with
Ballymena-born Hollywood actor Liam Neeson. 'I never thought in
my lifetime that I would ever see Ian Paisley and Martin
McGuinness together laughing, sharing jokes and doing the
country proud, the people of Northern Ireland proud,' Neeson
said.[1] Paisley also held private talks during the trip with famous US

billionaire Donald Trump. Any reservations the ageing preacher had about a tycoon with major interests in casino gambling were not made public. Trump was encouraged to consider extending his business empire to Northern Ireland. He was also invited to attend the US Investment Conference in Belfast planned for May 2008. He did not make it.

In image-projection terms, the American trip was a big success for Paisley and McGuinness. A picture of the two men at the US's largest electronic stock market, the NASDAQ, was even beamed onto New York's Times Square. Paisley said: 'The opening of the NASDAQ stock market has been presided over by some of the world's most prestigious political and business leaders so it is an honour for us to be included in such an elite group.' McGuinness added: 'There can also be few better ways of having such a positive image, representing the political progress we are making, beamed into the heart of American life.'[2] Sinn Féin's revolutionary socialist rhetoric must have been left back home in Ireland.

The First Ministers had barely returned from the US when they were smiling for the photographers again, this time at the opening of Northern Ireland's long-awaited first IKEA furniture store. A report on the event in the *Times* neatly caught the atmosphere.

There have been many bizarre photos of Ian Paisley and Martin McGuinness since Northern Ireland's political 'odd couple' came together at the head of the Stormont power-sharing government. But of all these moments, few have been quite as surreal as the sight of Ulster's onetime arch-enemies grinning inanely together on a bright red Ikea sofa in front of the slogan, 'Home is the most important place in the world'.[3]

The House of Paisley had good reason to feel pleased with itself by the end of 2007, notwithstanding the church setback for Senior and the controversy surrounding Junior's lobbying activities. The church saga would soon be over, with a new Moderator due to be elected in January. And the criticisms of Junior could all be blamed on lazy journalists, or similar reprobates. What does it matter anyway, when you are being fêted by the President of the United States himself?

The success of the American trip helped end the year very positively for the Stormont devolution experiment. As thoughts turned to the 12 months just past, there was a general feeling of wonderment at how well power-sharing had bedded in. An editorial in the *Independent* commented on an 'extraordinary level of cooperation' between unionists and republicans in government. The London paper continued: 'Dr Paisley and Mr McGuinness have run the show in the most amicable and even jovial manner, nipping over to see George Bush together, occupying a sofa at the opening of Belfast's enormous new Ikea store, joking and joshing as though they had never been sworn enemies.'[4]

The Irish-American paper *Irish Voice* named Paisley its Man of the Year.[5] The same accolade was bestowed by the *Belfast Telegraph* columnist and editor-in-chief Ed Curran. Curran recalled the run-ins between Paisley and his newspaper in the 1960s, when it was supporting liberal unionist Prime Minister Terence O'Neill. His memories included watching the future First Minister stage a torchlight protest against the paper and branding its reporters 'scribbling serpents'. Curran's end-of-year article concluded that Paisley was 'now as vital to Northern Ireland as Nelson Mandela has been to South Africa'. He added:

> Like Mandela in Africa, he has become a father figure here, a pivotal influence on whether this country's experiment in power-sharing can survive. For that reason, and without question, Ian Richard Kyle Paisley is my Northern Ireland Man of the Year. And, in writing that in today's Telegraph, I wouldn't even begin to countenance what my old editor from the 1960s would make of my judgment.[6]

The Deputy First Minister declared himself full of optimism for 2008. McGuinness's New Year message spoke of the new Stormont government having laid solid foundations. 'I think the last seven months, since the restoration of devolution, is a snapshot of what the future is going to be like with people working together to build a better society.'[7]

But another Derry politician, the DUP's Gregory Campbell, was much less upbeat. In his seasonal message, Campbell once again registered his displeasure with all the Stormont bonhomie, the chuckling and the photographs. He said the benefits of the St Andrews Agreement were 'obvious' but also stated:

> In 2008, we have to dispel the impression that DUP is enjoying doing business with Sinn Féin. This is not merely some quibble of who stands beside whom in photographs but is a definitive message being given to present and future generations about how former terrorists must be treated by democrats.[8]

This was a blatant rebuke for the laughing leader from a senior DUP figure. Campbell was from the Peter Robinson generation within the party, and indeed was made a Stormont minister by Robinson following Paisley's departure in 2008. His pointed New Year message showed that away from the publicity shots and the plaudits, all was not well in DUP land. The truth was that—at home at any rate—Stormont's Chuckle Brothers were starting to lose their novelty value.

At one level, it seems ridiculous that so much trouble was caused by two senior ministers in a coalition government being at ease in each other's company. But a government led by the DUP and Sinn Féin was no ordinary coalition, and Paisley and McGuinness were no ordinary double act. It is also worth pointing out the Chuckle Brothers routine had started to annoy more than just DUP diehards. Even those who would describe themselves as in the middle ground of politics felt somewhat uncomfortable by the apparent cosiness of the former foes. Such people were pleased, obviously, that the Troubles were finally over and that a stable-looking devolved settlement was in place. But there was still something a bit galling for them in seeing two destructive forces—the Provos and the Paisleyites—ending up at the top of the pile. These two forces were now sharing the political spoils of peace between them, and their leaders seemed to be finding the whole thing hilarious.

Mick Fealty, founder of the influential blog 'Slugger O'Toole', drew a striking analogy in May 2007 in the early days of the new power-sharing government. His inspiration came while reading one of his children a book by famous author David McKee, creator of such legends as Mr Benn and Elmer the Patchwork Elephant. The book Fealty found himself reading was *Two Monsters*, a tale of two gruesome characters who lived on either side of a mountain.[9] They got into an angry argument about whether sunset was day leaving or night arriving. A vicious fight broke out, with the monsters throwing rocks from each side of the mountain until it was flattened. Then they each walked into the middle of the mess they had made to watch the departure of the day and the arrival of the night together. 'That was rather fun,' giggled the first monster. 'Yes, wasn't it,' chuckled the second. 'Pity about the mountain.' Fealty commented simply: 'Remind you of anyone?'[10]

SUNNINGDALE REVISITED

Seamus Mallon, former Deputy First Minister, famously dubbed the 1998 Good Friday Agreement 'Sunningdale for slow learners'. To the untrained eye at least, there was not a great deal of difference between the Sunningdale deal that produced the brief 1974 experiment in power-sharing and its successor in the early part of the twenty-first century. Both involved partnership government in the north, along with recognition of a southern dimension through the creation of cross-border structures.

These elements were also at the heart of the 1998 Good Friday Agreement and its offspring, the 2006 St Andrews Agreement. In many eyes, St Andrews was not just Sunningdale for slow learners, but Sunningdale for the bad boys in the class. So, even as the DUP–Sinn Féin pact was being viewed elsewhere as a peacemaking template, some people in Northern Ireland could not help thinking about the previous attempted accords that the two forces had helped stymie. For 'pity about the mountain' read 'pity about the last 40 years'.

On the subject of Sunningdale, it is worth quoting from Brian Faulkner, the Ulster Unionist leader who signed up to that deal. Speaking at the outset of the 1974 power-sharing administration that the DUP and the Provisional IRA would in their own ways help bring down, Faulkner said:

> Virtually everyone of judgement now agrees that it has been a great source of weakness and instability to Northern Ireland over half-a-century that its Roman Catholic community, representing one-third of the population, has not played a commensurate part in the life and affairs of the province. We can argue until the cows come home about whose fault that has been over all those years. We can go on attributing mutual blame up to and beyond the point where the rest of the world grows sick of us. All I know is that we have now found the means to work together. Are we now to say to that community, 'democracy is simply majority rule, and if that means you are to sit in opposition for half-a-century more, it's just too bad'? I ask the opponents of all that we in this Executive represent, 'What is your answer?'[11]

It turned out, 33 years later, that the solution from Sunningdale's chief opponents was not that different from Faulkner's.

DEVOLUTION BLUES

It is also interesting to note that few if any middle-ground voices were raised in support of Paisley when his position started to look shaky in 2008. While some hardline ex-supporters believed he had betrayed them, another strand of opinion could not quite forgive him for taking so long to sign up to power-sharing. The ageing leader hailed for bravely leading his people into a new Jerusalem was not sustained in power by a popular centrist uprising.

In truth, Northern Ireland did not feel much like a new Jerusalem under DUP–Sinn Féin rule. Durable devolution was back for the first time in a generation but the day-to-day experience of it was sometimes proving underwhelming. Some of this disillusionment was down to specific policy issues, including a damaging stand-off that had developed on educational reform.

Sinn Féin Education Minister Caitríona Ruane had pressed ahead with the scrapping of the 11-plus transfer test for post-primary schools. However, there was nothing close to a cross-party consensus on what should replace it, leaving the system heading towards unregulated confusion. The deep uncertainty this created for children, parents and teachers did nothing to enhance Stormont's reputation.

An appointment of a Commissioner to champion the interests of Troubles victims and their families was delayed, fuelling speculation that Paisley and McGuinness could not agree on who should fill the post. In the end, not one but four Victims Commissioners were named. That decision looked a lot like a costly compromise, and also became the subject of a legal challenge. Plans for a new multi-sports stadium at the site of the former Maze Prison also started to unravel, principally because of opposition within the DUP.

Aside from such specific policy issues, there was often little going on of real note within the Assembly. Debates and committee sessions were routinely of poor quality. A benign explanation for the often lacklustre performances was that the members were new to power and had to be given time to develop the necessary skills. On the other hand, a significant proportion of them had been in taxpayer-funded political jobs for years in the previous, non-functioning Assembly. Given the sums of public money they and their parties had received over this period, it was not entirely unreasonable to expect some expertise. There was precious little sign of it in the first year of the new Stormont.

At some point, people were going to expect a little more than an absence of war from the new devolved government. A couple of chuckling First Ministers was not going to be enough in the long run. But Paisley kept on laughing, despite the wishes of senior party colleagues. According to a senior DUP source, Paisley's Junior Minister son was used as the conduit to deliver a plea for an end to the chortling. It did not work.

This may have been just old-fashioned Paisley stubbornness at play once again. Another explanation is that the First Minister kept on smiling as an act of defiance against his critics within his own church. Free Presbyterianism was still beset by friction behind the scenes, despite his imminent replacement as Moderator. The 'truce' agreed after the September Presbytery had quietly come apart due to a number of internal controversies. To many in the outside world, they would not have seemed particularly important. But in the narrow confines of Free Presbyterianism they were very emotive.

Among the issues that troubled the faithful was a Stormont reception for a new book by Dana, the Derry singer turned Irish politician. The one-time Eurovision Song Contest winner would have been known to Paisley, as both were past members of the European Parliament. Paisley was a special guest at the Stormont launch of Dana's autobiography and praised her as 'a woman of great faith and steel who had stood up for what she believed in'. He also stated that he was 'glad to stand with her' and added: 'I hope that when everyone on this island reads this book I hope [sic] they ponder what it says.'[12]

These comments caused surprise, if not horror, in some Free Presbyterian quarters. Dana was one of Ireland's most prominent conservative Catholics and one of her best-loved songs was 'Totus Tuus' (Totally Yours), a 1979 tribute to Pope John Paul II. This was the same Pope who Paisley had regularly denounced as the Antichrist. When John Paul II visited the European Parliament in 1988, a heckling Paisley was ejected from the chamber.

There was further concern within the Free Presbyterian family when Paisley met with a former target of his church's ire, Rev. David Armstrong. As a mainstream Presbyterian minister in the town of Limavady, Armstrong had been angrily condemned by Paisleyites in the 1980s for establishing friendly links with his local Catholic counterpart Father Kevin Mullan. He was forced to leave the area with his family after his own church passed a vote of no confidence in him.

Armstrong met Paisley at the Dana book launch at Stormont. It was subsequently reported by one newspaper—and strongly denied by Paisley—that the Free Presbyterian Moderator had apologised to the former Limavady clergyman for the way he had been treated. Armstrong, for his part, has declined to comment on the contents of his private conversation with the First Minister. But he did say it left him 'much happier' and that he thought Paisley was a 'very changed man'.[13] He also told the author that Paisley and his wife both spoke amicably to him at the Stormont book launch event. 'I found Mrs Paisley very, very gracious. She had a good knowledge of what had happened to me. She was extremely warm and felt sorry for me,' the clergyman said.

Probably the most serious tremor within Paisley's church at the end of 2007 came as a result of a thanksgiving service for the Scouting movement. He participated in the event, giving an address to the scouts. That was hardly a great surprise given that the service was held in Ballymena, in the heart of his constituency. But also taking part was a local Catholic priest, Father Paul Symonds, who said prayers at the service. Again, this would hardly be earth-shattering in most people's eyes. But this was Paisley, who for many years had hounded other Protestant churches and indeed unionist politicians over any hint of a dalliance with ecumenism. Back in 1964, Paisley even denounced liberal unionist Prime Minister Terence O'Neill for being photographed beside a Catholic crucifix. 'Whether willingly or unwillingly, aware or unaware, Captain O'Neill has, by countenancing this Roman idol, given food to the Roman propagandists,' Paisley said.[14] In his firebrand heyday, Paisley might very well have led a noisy picket against a Protestant cleric who had participated in a Scouting service involving a Catholic priest.

The Armstrong, Dana and Fr Symonds cases were all highlighted in detail on the website of Rev. Ivan Foster. When BBC Northern Ireland's influential religious affairs programme 'Sunday Sequence' took an interest in the Scouting service early in the New Year, Paisley came out fighting. A savage broadside launched from the pulpit of his Martyrs Memorial Church on 20 January 2008 once again illustrated the divisions within Free Presbyterianism. It also showed that Paisley believed he was being 'persecuted' because of his work for God—and that those against him were doing Satan's work.

In truth, the bitter fall-out with his fellow believers stemmed from his power-sharing deal with Sinn Féin. Its root cause was politics, not religion. Paisley's angry retort from the pulpit was launched just after he had handed over the church Moderator's position to his deputy, Rev. Ron Johnstone.[15] It also came amid media speculation that senior DUP colleagues wanted him to set a date for standing down as party leader.

Paisley firstly announced to his congregation that the clerk of the church's Kirk Session had a statement to read out. This statement began with a declaration of support for Paisley's 'integrity' and 'faithfulness'. The fact that the Kirk Session even felt the need to say that after all his years at Martyrs Memorial was an indication of how deeply the feelings went.

The statement continued: 'Having worked with him closer than anyone save his own family, we cannot be silent when his character is abused, his Christianity called into question and the enemies of the gospel are used on certain websites to tarnish his life and witness.' The Kirk Session clerk also referred to 'vilification' and 'savage accusations', and said the report of an apology being made to Rev. David Armstrong was a 'colossal lie'. The congregation was told that the Devil had 'inspired these attacks' because 'more and more people' were being reached by the gospel. The statement also said: 'Apostates, evil speakers, breakers of the moral law, those living in breach of the commandments have all been recruited into the campaign to destroy our Minister.'

Paisley himself then rose to give his sermon. It provided a fascinating insight into his state of mind at that time. He spoke of how the Gospel of Matthew exhorted people to be 'exceeding glad' when they are being 'satanically persecuted' for Christ's sake. Dealing with some of the specific accusations against him, Paisley denied making any apology to Rev. David Armstrong. He also described the newspaper that carried the story as 'wicked', 'salacious' and 'immoral'. In relation to the Ballymena service for scouts, Paisley said he had not known a priest would be present. He told the congregation that he would have 'walked out', but for the fact that young scouts were due to take a vow of allegiance to the Queen.

The strongest words in the Martyrs Memorial sermon were directed at critics within Free Presbyterianism. Paisley said 'so-called friends' had caused him to be 'wounded'. 'And some of these people owe their souls to me,' he claimed. There was also an ominous warning of 'severe happenings', 'evil speakers' and 'false accusations' in the days ahead. 'How hard people become when they forsake the ways of God and turn into the byways prepared for them by the devil himself,' he said. 'Yes, we are in for a period of persecution. We have no friends in the press.'

Paisley had clearly convinced himself that he was the victim of a Hell-inspired campaign of vilification, designed to stop him doing God's work. 'It is my duty to be exceeding glad,' his sermon added. 'I have been accused of being a chuckler. Well I don't know what exceeding glad is, but I would think an exceeding glad man would be a man with a face that's smiling and joyful. And I intend to be that.'

The chuckling was clearly going to continue, despite what critics in the DUP or the church wanted. This was a man who had no intention of backing down. 'I'm surprised that people think Ian Paisley is weak,' he also warned. 'Well, they'll see, maybe.'

Yet less than six weeks later, the same man would announce that he was stepping down as First Minister and DUP leader. This sudden change followed a series of dramatic and unforeseen developments.

His politician son had more than a walk-on part in the drama.

Chapter 10

St Andrews Bombshell

'*The Prime Minister has considered your requests …*'
Document reveals controversial lobbying of Tony Blair by
Ian Paisley Jnr

The House of Paisley could have done without a fresh
lobbying controversy involving Paisley Jnr at the start of
2008. But that it is exactly what it got.

Once again the name of Seymour Sweeney loomed large in the
story. In terms of the internal dynamics of the DUP, this saga was
particularly serious. It involved Paisley Jnr's behaviour at the St
Andrews talks—the negotiations in October 2006 involving the
Northern Ireland parties and the British and Irish governments.
This intensive three-day session in Scotland produced the
agreement which laid the basis for the power-sharing deal of the
following year.

It emerged in January 2008 that Paisley Jnr had engaged in some
high-level lobbying during the St Andrews talks on behalf of
constituency projects.[1] A list of six priority projects—nicknamed
his 'shopping list' by the media—went all the way to Prime
Minister Tony Blair, who agreed to respond 'positively'. Some of the
requests, such as a road upgrade and a hotel investment, were
hardly contentious. But also on the list were two long-standing
Sweeney-related subjects—proposed visitor facilities at the Giant's
Causeway and the legal wrangle over the government-owned land
at Ballee, Ballymena.

When the details of the lobbying emerged, there was a furious
political row. Paisley Jnr had left the DUP open to accusations of
seeking side deals during all-important talks on the future of
Northern Ireland. He was by no means the first politician to try to

take advantage of a situation and push pet schemes. But in this particular context, it was highly embarrassing for his party.

St Andrews will always be a sensitive topic for the DUP. This was where the party publicly moved towards abandoning its outright opposition to sitting in power with Sinn Féin. If it was not the scene of the actual full U-turn, it was the spot where the indicators went on and the manoeuvre began. The bulk of the party has subsequently been able to convince itself that this was the right decision given the political realities it faced. But that did not mean it was ever going to look back on St Andrews with glowing pride or nostalgia. Nevertheless, the DUP will always assure its base that it maintained a tough line in the Scottish talks and secured the best outcome possible in the circumstances. That line was dented by the suggestion that one of its negotiators had not spent all his time there fighting for the cause. He had instead been seeking constituency sweeteners from Tony Blair.

To add to the pain, there was also the small matter of who had unearthed the St Andrews lobbying details. They came to light as a result of a freedom of information (FOI) request to the Northern Ireland Office by ex-DUP MEP Jim Allister. Allister had been the most high-profile departure from the party over its devolution deal with Sinn Féin. By January 2008, he was rallying anti-power-sharing unionists around his fledgling new grouping, Traditional Unionist Voice (TUV). To make matters worse, the DUP was only weeks away from facing its first electoral test since Paisley's elevation as First Minister. The Dromore council by-election in County Down was fixed for mid-February and the TUV was fielding a candidate.

Allister had tabled the FOI request on the basis of suspicions about St Andrews. He had been part of the DUP delegation at St Andrews and had picked up whispers about lobbying during the talks process. 'I knew something went on,' he says. 'I knew from putting the pieces of the jigsaw together that there was something there to get.'

The key document obtained by Allister was a letter sent to Paisley Jnr by NIO Minister David Hanson, written on the last day of the Scotland talks. It listed the six north Antrim 'shopping list' demands, including the Ballee land dispute and the Causeway. Also featured were a road upgrade between Ballymena and Ballycastle, planning approval for a hotel resort spa scheme, a pledge to consult Ian Paisley Snr on potential future uses for an army barracks site, and a funding commitment for the North West 200, an annual motorbike race on the north coast.

The document sent to Paisley Jnr by Hanson stated: 'The Prime Minister has considered your requests and has agreed that we should try to respond positively. I will ask my officials to scope the issues set out below and will report back to you once I have considered their findings.' It also said: 'This letter should be regarded as a statement of intent.'

Allister made the correspondence public on 15 January 2008 in a press release entitled 'St Andrews bombshell'. The MEP declared himself 'appalled', adding:

> With unionists back home hoping and believing that the DUP leadership was there negotiating hard for the best deal possible in defence of the union, I believe most will be outraged to discover that Ian Paisley Jnr was wasting valuable leverage on securing concessions from the PM no less, not on matters of importance to Unionists, but on issues of mere commercial or constituency import.[2]

Allister's freedom of information request had found its target. 'I was well pleased that I got as much as I did,' he admits. 'It exposed the abuse of the process and the waste of leverage. You only have so much leverage at these occasions.'

Questions can be asked about the readiness of the NIO to release the documentation. Anyone with experience of FOI knows that some government bodies are more open than others. There are also more than enough exemptions in the legislation for authorities to hide behind if they wish. The NIO could have attempted to withhold the Hanson letter on the basis of the catch-all exemption that release would prejudice the effective conduct of public affairs. A successful appeal to the Information Commissioner against nondisclosure could have been stranded in the complaints system for years—long past the time when the Paisley Jnr lobbying details were politically sensitive.

Instead, the NIO chose to issue the paperwork in full to Allister, presumably in the full knowledge that it would cause severe problems for the Junior Minister and his father. This is not to suggest a Machiavellian NIO plot to help shepherd both Paisleys out the door and usher in the Peter Robinson era. It's just to note that the NIO could have done more to aid the Junior Minister's cause.

Faced with Allister's revelations, Paisley Jnr went on an immediate counter-attack, but failed to provide a coherent defence of his actions. This was by now a familiar pattern, though at least he did not claim that he merely 'knew of' St Andrews. The Junior Minister made an apology of sorts for any embarrassment caused to the DUP, but paradoxically also maintained that he had done nothing wrong. 'If I have caused embarrassment to someone, if my party feel there was embarrassment, I have no problem apologising for that,' he said.[3]

The strident tone of a press release dismissing Allister's 'bombshell' as nothing more than a 'damp squib' was in contrast to the offer of an apology. 'My eagerness in resolving my constituency cases is not a political issue or a matter which causes me any embarrassment,' the statement said. 'The fact that Jim Allister chooses to make an issue of this at the time of a by-election in Dromore highlights the poverty of his activities.' In one interview, Paisley Jnr said the lobbying of ministers during the talks had taken place 'over a cup of tea'. He also denied asking for his requests to be raised with Blair.[4]

Unfortunately for him, his arguments failed to inspire party colleagues to rally to his cause. There were several reasons for this lack of support. Firstly, other DUP politicians who were at St Andrews had not been lobbying on constituency matters. If they had been given such an opportunity, they might well have come up with much more worthy projects than two Seymour Sweeney money-making enterprises. Even if they had bumped into Tony Blair in the dining room queue and bent his ear about a school closure or a rundown hospital wing, what response would they have received? They are unlikely to have been issued with a 'statement of intent' promising to respond 'positively'. That was because their surname was not Paisley.

Blair had not become involved with Junior's north Antrim shopping list because of its intrinsic merits. His government was going all out for a power-sharing deal as one of the principal positive legacies of his time in power. Keeping Paisley Snr onboard was crucial to this goal. As a result, Paisley Jnr's influence in the corridors of power had grown enormously.

Both Downing Street and the NIO had good reason to be cagey about him. He had played a key role behind the scenes in the collapse of a previous bid to restore devolution. Hopes of a deal in 2004 after talks at Leeds Castle in Kent fell apart when Paisley Snr demanded 'sackcloth and ashes' humiliation for the IRA on decommissioning. It had been his son who had ensured a BBC camera team was present to record the all-important 'sackcloth and ashes' speech to party members in Ballymena.[5] Recalling Paisley Jnr's overall contribution to the deal-making process, a source from the NIO says: 'We were wary of him and we took him seriously. We were very keen not to annoy him.'

With his ageing father becoming increasingly reliant on him, Paisley Jnr had found himself right at the centre of the negotiating process that would restore devolution. He chose to take advantage of that privileged situation while at St Andrews to promote a fairly uninspiring set of personal priorities. It was simply ridiculous to claim his lobbying—and the Hanson letter it produced—had no connection with the St Andrews talks.

There is only one explanation for the keenness of Blair and co. to respond favourably—they saw it as part of the price to be paid for a power-sharing deal. Paisley Jnr inadvertently provided evidence for this obvious conclusion when trying to refute Allister's claims. Explaining his motivation for raising the constituency matters, he stated: 'I said, you know, I've an opportunity here to talk to these ministers about issues which quite frankly every single one of these issues on my list were issues I'd raised for years as an

MLA and had got nowhere with them.'[6] That begs the question why he received such an enthusiastic response on this occasion, with even the Prime Minister weighing in. The answer is obvious. The British government was determined to keep the Paisleys biddable. If that involved a few constituency sweeteners for Junior, so be it.

Party colleagues were clearly less than impressed when the St Andrews lobbying details were made public. Allister and his newborn TUV had been handed a valuable propaganda coup close to a by-election. The new revelations also ensured a fresh wave of negative publicity about pro-Sweeney lobbying. All told, the relentless media coverage of Junior was doing the DUP no favours. The party issued a statement denying that any of the six shopping list demands had any connection to its St Andrews negotiating team. 'They were not raised by or with the party, nor were they included on any shopping list considered and approved by the party officers,' it asserted.[7]

Journalists did not have to try too hard to get off-the-record quotes from angry DUP 'sources'. A BBC report referred to an unnamed 'very senior source' in the party expressing 'anger' at what had emerged.[8] The *Belfast Telegraph* quoted a DUP insider saying: 'Obviously there are a number of very senior people in the party who are not happy about what has happened and will have questions to raise. He was obviously on a solo run.'[9] Another source told the same paper: 'This will leave a bad taste in the mouths of people who were at St Andrews and who had no idea that this was going on.' The *News Letter*, the newspaper closest to the DUP, reported:

Ian Paisley Jnr cut a lonely figure yesterday, standing in the Great Hall at Stormont. There was no supporting cast of DUP colleagues standing by his side as he tackled yet another round of questions from the media on his behind-the-scenes political dealings. Instead, senior figures in the party were putting distance between themselves and the North Antrim MLA … None would be publicly drawn into commenting on his situation. No words of support. And off-the-record, at the top level of the DUP, they were 'spitting feathers', 'fit-to-be-tied' and 'deeply angry'.[10]

Perhaps because he sensed the hostile mood, Paisley Jnr publicly admitted for the first time he could have handled questions about his Sweeney links better. 'I think there have been mistakes in it. Of course, I'd accept that,' he said.[11] He also claimed to the same interviewer: 'This is not a hot topic, as some people would like us to believe.' Not even his DUP colleagues could have believed that anymore.

By this stage, there was also wider unease within the party about Paisley Jnr's powerful role at Stormont. He was a near-permanent fixture by his father's side and a number of MLAs had started regarding him as being effectively in charge. One DUP Assembly source voices a view that was shared by others in the party: 'Ian Junior was the unofficial First Minister. His father was not able to be on top of everything that was going on. There was a feeling that the young boy held all the cards, had access to everything that was happening.'

Allister successfully scored more points against the DUP on the St Andrews lobbying issue later in 2008, thanks to further FOI disclosures. It transpired that senior government officials had been tasked with providing a substantive response to the six-point shopping list tabled by Paisley Jnr. A circular issued to the high-ranking civil servants on 9 November 2006 said Minister Hanson wanted the reply to be 'as positive as possible'. It also stated that Hanson wished to write to Paisley Jnr 'well in advance of 24 November'. That was not a random point in the calendar: 24 November 2006 had been pencilled in under the St Andrews Agreement as the start date for the restoration of devolution. The timetable subsequently slipped to May 2007. But clearly, in Hanson's mind at least, Paisley's shopping list and a power-sharing deal had not been unconnected.

Allister's persistence on the FOI front later yielded another interesting internal document. This involved a civil service memo dated 16 October 2006—just after the St Andrews talks. It raised further questions for the DUP, as it mentioned its leader's name in connection with the six north Antrim demands. The high-level memo stated:

> At last week's talks, Rev Ian Paisley and Ian Paisley Jnr took the opportunity to raise with the Prime Minister a number of issues on which they were seeking a positive outcome. Ministers here have been asked to pursue these and we have in turn been asked to make a report to David Hanson and SOFs [Secretary of State] by the end of the week.

Having obtained this document, Allister argued that it implicated Paisley Snr in his son's lobbying and demolished the 'solo run' claims made by the party. He challenged both the DUP and its leader to 'come clean'. Neither issued any response.

There are grounds for questioning just how much Paisley Jnr actually gained from his St Andrews lobbying—apart from serious embarrassment when the details were eventually made public. An NIO source says its efforts to keep him contented largely involved 'flattery' and lots of high-level access. As a previous chapter of this book has documented, Hanson did eventually agree in principle to sell the Ballee land in Ballymena back to its former owners—with Sweeney and co. poised to purchase it from them. But there is little sign of any great breakthrough having been made on the other St Andrews shopping list items.

On the Causeway project, there was the complication that government planning officials were strongly recommending a refusal decision for Sweeney. An approval would have been hard to defend, especially given the Direct Rule administration's central role in seeking a public sector visitor centre. If it had announced any verdict, the chances are that it would have been a refusal for Sweeney. It instead did nothing and left the decision to the tender mercies of devolution.

A funding announcement for the North West 200 event came within days of Direct Rule ending in May 2007. Presumably, preparatory work on this allocation had been ongoing in government for some time. Purely in the interests of accuracy, it should be pointed out that the North West 200 is not actually in Paisley Jnr's constituency. It takes place in the neighbouring constituency of east Londonderry. As a tourist attraction that draws biking fans from near and far, it obviously has some knock-on benefits for north Antrim. Paisley Jnr is a motorbike enthusiast himself. On 9 May 2007—the day after devolution had been restored—he attended a dinner for the North West 200 in Portrush. He was transported there in a ministerial car, although his department has stated that it was not officially represented at the event.[12] When the £150,000 allocation was announced a few days later, North West 200 organisers paid a warm tribute to Paisley Jnr for his role in helping secure the funding.

Praise was not the predominant response to his St Andrews lobbying efforts. Overall, the Allister-inspired controversy affected his standing within the DUP. Some colleagues were appalled at his use—or abuse—of a delicate negotiating session. Others may well have taken a less principled view and been simply annoyed that he got caught out. Again, there was a cumulative impact. The Giant's Causeway row had marred the early months of devolution and caused problems for Arlene Foster, a much-admired Minister. The repeated disclosures about Paisley Jnr's pro-Sweeney lobbying were hardly enhancing the DUP's image. And the Ballee land deal case had raised yet more questions—and brought yet more unwanted publicity. With the St Andrews 'bombshell', he had put his party on the defensive ahead of a by-election.

A well-placed senior DUP source confirms that there was high-level annoyance at Paisley Jnr in the wake of Allister's discovery of the six-point shopping list. 'None of us was aware of that,' the source says. 'The collective leadership of the DUP—the party officer team—were not aware of these issues until they came into the public domain.' The source also comments:

At one level, people can admire someone who can work hard for their constituency but there is a limit to that. I think what concerned people was that whilst it may not have been done directly the inference was certainly that Ian Junior was asking for issues relating to his constituency and that if they were delivered implied that that would make it easier for them in terms of making key political decisions. That is not the way the DUP works. There would have been no one else in the DUP who would have sought to use the access afforded by those negotiations.

Given the barely concealed anger about him within the party in January 2008, it was not that surprising that a rumour about Paisley Jnr resigning as a minister circulated briefly. It still seemed an unlikely development to most commentators. His dad was still the boss and at 81 would surely struggle to cope with the demands of the job without his son beside him. One DUP MLA told the author around this time: 'The problem is if Junior goes, Senior goes too.' Likewise, the *News Letter*'s political editor, Stephen Dempster, referred to Paisley Jnr being regarded as a 'protected species'. Dempster added: 'Those who think they smell blood will have to be spilling it on the carpet to dislodge the DUP Junior Minister.'[13]

The resignation rumour faded quickly and was soon laughed off by Paisley Jnr himself. He spoke of receiving great support from constituents for his lobbying efforts. 'I intend to stay around for a very long time,' he added. 'I notice my father has extremely good genes—and I'm not talking about Levis—and I hope that they are inherited.'[14]

That interview was broadcast on 3 February 2008. Fifteen days later, Paisley Jnr was standing in front of Stormont Castle announcing his resignation.

Chapter 11

Other People's Money

'The rich man in his castle, the poor man at his gate,
God made them, high or lowly, and ordered their estate.'
From the hymn 'All Things Bright and Beautiful' by CECIL
FRANCES ALEXANDER

January 2008 really should have marked a turning point in Ian Paisley Jnr's fortunes. The revelations about his side deal efforts at St Andrews had not been pretty, but he had come through them. The month then ended with what looked like a pivotal moment in the long-running controversy about his lobbying for Seymour Sweeney.

Environment Minister Arlene Foster announced that she was refusing planning permission for Sweeney's Causeway visitor centre application. Her September 2007 position of being 'of a mind' to approve was abandoned, although the key facts of the case had not changed in the intervening period. Foster revealed her decision to the Assembly, with Junior Minister Paisley Jnr positioned right beside her in the chamber. If he was feeling embarrassed or uncomfortable about sitting there, he did not let it show. He obviously would have wanted the decision to go the other way. On the plus side, it did appear to signal the end of the story.

DUP member Sweeney was not getting approval from a DUP minister and the prospect of the developer taking centre stage at Northern Ireland's top natural attraction had receded.

In terms of ending all the negative media focus, this was actually good news for Paisley Jnr. To those in the press who had been covering the story, it looked like it was over. Leads had been chased, Freedom of Information requests made, sources milked for information. It seemed that all that could be unearthed about Paisley Jnr's Sweeney links was now in the public domain. Some of it had been serious and pretty damaging, but it had not cost him his job. He had boasted about there being no 'smoking gun', and it appeared he had been proved correct. So just how did he end up resigning in the middle of February?

The answer can be found in a furore about politicians' expenses that spread over to Stormont from Westminster, and an unexpected outcome in the Dromore council by-election. 'Perfect storm' has been deemed to be one of the most overused phrases of recent years.[1] But it does capture the way a random series of events knocked the highly confident Junior Minister off his perch. The Dromore by-election will be the subject of Chapter 12. But first it's time to delve into the unedifying subject of Assembly expenses.

Paisley Jnr was by no means the only MLA to face questions about his use of taxpayer-funded allowances. Nobody else came close to losing their jobs, though. His problems stemmed from two separate factors. It was firstly learned that he had been receiving payments from his father's House of Commons expenses for work as a parliamentary assistant. This remunerated role had continued when he became a junior minister at Stormont, meaning he had three jobs—MLA, government minister and MP's assistant.

The Westminster-funded salary was later confirmed as being between £9,000 and £11,000 a year during his time as a minister.[2] The part-time job included dealing with his father's parliamentary constituency case workload for north Antrim. As critics pointed out, Paisley Jnr was himself a full-time north Antrim representative in the Assembly. Therefore, the caseload that was coming through the DUP's doors in the constituency was bringing with it two separate remuneration streams for him.

The second expenses-related controversy involved a showpiece Ballymena advice centre the two Paisleys had opened in the summer of 2007. It turned out to be costing taxpayers three times more than any other MLA constituency office. There was also the small matter of a link between the property and Seymour Sweeney. On top of this, the company that owned it—and was getting the mortgage paid off by public funds—involved Paisley Jnr's father-in-law. If this weapon was not smoking, there were at least traces of gunshot residue around it.

All this expenses-related information tumbled out—along with details of how other MLAS were using taxpayers' cash—in a heady period in February 2008. The immediate cause of this flurry was a scandal at the Commons surrounding a Conservative MP called Derek Conway. He had been paying his son Freddie for parliamentary-related research work. The trouble was that young Freddie was also a full-time student studying for a degree well away from Westminster. That led to a major media focus on allowances claimed by politicians. The Assembly was particularly unprepared for such analysis, and particularly vulnerable to public outrage. That was down to a lack of leadership and foresight at Stormont over a number of years. Therefore, all the flak it received was entirely its own fault.

The political class generally hates media coverage of its pay and expenses. It is true that journalists can be tempted into simplistic generalisations on the subject. But that does not negate the overwhelming case for media scrutiny of the subject. When it comes to taxpayers' money, politicians should be setting an example. They should understand the importance of not just being above reproach, but being seen to be above reproach. There should also be a simple rule for anyone using public money, whether for a personal hotel bill, an office rental claim or a multi-million-pound consultancy contract. If you would not feel comfortable about the details being made public, you should think very carefully about proceeding. There may be cases when the expenditure is still justified. But some cognisance should still be given to how it would be defended to the people who are actually picking up the bill—the taxpayers.

Politicians need to do more than grudgingly accept that the media will take an interest in their pay and expenses. They should acknowledge that this attention is actually in the wider public interest. The same goes for the boost for transparency brought about by the Freedom of Information Act. Details of how government bodies allocate their funds should be disclosed as a matter of principle. They are spending other people's money, after all. On top of this, it needs to be understood that transparency is a vital safeguard against misuse. A questionable claim is much less likely if the details are going to be made public.

The political class at Westminster has not been covering itself in glory in recent years on pay and allowances issues. Serious shortcomings in its approach to pay and expenses have been exposed. Yet, compared to Stormont, the House of Commons has almost been a model of good practice. The Assembly managed to sleepwalk into problems, rather than take action to prevent them developing. While sensible private and public sector organisations around the world got to grips with concepts like 'governance' and 'reputational risk', Stormont slumbered complacently.

This problem dated back well beyond the 2007 power-sharing deal, and was evident in the fitful attempts at devolution that followed the 1998 Belfast Agreement. In early 2002, a mini-conflict occurred behind closed doors that would set the pattern for years to come. Annoyance had been expressed among MLAs about the attitude of the Assembly Finance Office. It seemed that staff members had been quite strict about expenses claims made by the politicians. Instead of applauding this vigilance with taxpayers' money, the Stormont powers-that-be decided to initiate a high-level review. No less a person than a senior official of the House of Commons was signed up for the process.

The confidential report from this exercise made quite disturbing reading.[3] The Assembly expenses system had been largely based on practice at Westminster. So a chief remit of the review was to establish if the rules were being applied too strictly to MLAs in comparison with MPs.

The answer was no. But the Assembly Finance Office was nevertheless warned to be nicer to the delicate politicians. The review report stated:

Although one of the reasons for commissioning this review was the perception that the rules were applied in an overly rigid fashion, no substantive evidence of this was discovered. However, the way in which the Finance Office goes about service delivery lacks customer sensitivity and this may have given rise to the belief that MLAs were being refused support for legitimate claims.

This laughable idea of greater customer care for the MLAs was reflected elsewhere in the report. It noted that there was no 'meet and greet' facility for the Stormont politicians when they made a personal visit to the Finance Office. Perhaps it should have gone further and recommended a personal shopper for MLAs to guide them through the range of expenses available. An official in the Assembly Finance Office found himself moved to a post elsewhere around this time. No doubt that had absolutely nothing to do with a desire to pacify annoyed MLAs.

The review by the senior House of Commons official did manage to make some telling points. It said:

> To mitigate the almost wholly negative messages concerning the Finance Office staff dealing with Members' allowances, it would be helpful if some more positive messages could be relayed to them. The Finance Office's application of the rules has in no small measure contributed to a lack of media opportunity to pillory Assembly members in the same way that MSPs have been pilloried in Scotland.

In other words, the staff who were being subject to 'almost wholly negative' attitudes were actually protecting MLAs as well as the public purse. The internal report also stated:

> The Assembly needs to consider the impact that the introduction of freedom of information legislation might have on the ability of the media to demand information about how Members spend their allowances and what use they make of travel facilities. There is a danger that an unprepared Assembly will have to give out piecemeal information.

Six years later, the Assembly was still adopting a piecemeal approach to Freedom of Information disclosures. By that stage, its integrity had been damaged by almost five years of inaction.

Devolution was suspended between October 2002 and May 2007. During that time, Assembly members continued to get paid, albeit at a reduced rate of £31,817 a year. Almost all Northern Ireland's MPs also sat in the Assembly. These 'double jobbers' receive the full Commons rate and have their Stormont salaries reduced by two thirds. They are also entitled to full expenses from both legislatures. Sinn Féin's MPs do not receive a Westminster salary, as they do not take their seats in the House. However, the rules were changed in 2001 to allow them to claim MP expenses.

Stormont expenses continued to be paid in full to all MLAs through the suspension years. That included the important Office Costs Allowance (OCA) of up to £48,000 a year which enabled them to staff and run constituency advice centres. The overall salary and expenses bill for Assembly members ran at around £9 million annually during suspension. That played very badly with the public, and quite rightly so. MLA stands for Member of a Legislative Assembly, but during suspension they neither assembled nor legislated. In their defence, they pointed to their busy constituency caseloads. But they were not elected to be glorified social workers, and £9 million a year could have been much better spent on enhancing non-political community advice centre networks.

Other costs were also incurred during suspension that did nothing to build voter confidence in the political system. Over £500,000 a year was pumped into the pension fund for MLAs during this period.[4] Touchingly, the pension scheme trustees—a cross-party grouping—were the only Assembly body to keep meeting right through the suspension years. It also transpired that catering facilities for MLAs continued to be subsidised to the tune of £845 a day.[5] That included the exclusive Members' Dining Room with very fine food at extremely reasonable prices. The Assembly also found itself obliged to keep paying a broadcasting company to cover non-existent proceedings from its non-sitting chamber. This worked out at around £100,000 a year up to 2005, when it was able to put a new, less expensive contract in place.[6]

Incredibly, no one seemed to notice when MLAs ended up with

higher mileage rates than MPs—even though the Assembly was not sitting. The car journey expenses paid out by Westminster and Stormont had at one stage been the same, with rates of up to 56.1p a mile. But in 2005, the House of Commons rate was reduced to bring it into line with standard Inland Revenue-recommended levels of up to 40p per mile. The Stormont rate remained the same, until this was discovered by the author in May 2006 and reduced by Secretary of State Peter Hain that summer.[7] Once again, the MLAs had managed to stumble carelessly into hassle. Their 56.1p rate was the highest paid to elected representatives anywhere in the UK and they were not even doing their jobs at the time.

The mileage discrepancy might not have mattered massively by itself. However, the fact that they had failed to spot it, let alone address it, was a symptom of a much deeper problem. The truth was they were not sufficiently clued in to recognise the importance of a defensible remuneration framework. The Assembly elected in 2003 got through a four-year term without a minute of devolution to occupy its time.

Those MLAs who stood down or lost their seats in the March 2007 election were each paid a 'resettlement allowance' of £15,908— a sort of redundancy payment for politicians. Among the recipients was SDLP member Marietta Farrell, who had only joined the Assembly a couple of months earlier, as a replacement for a colleague who resigned. 'I was under the impression that it was going to be just a tiny fraction of what I ended up getting,' she said. 'Nobody was more surprised than me when I got the cheque.'[8]

Stormont also failed during the suspension years to keep pace with important changes introduced at Westminster on rental allowances. The fact that this happened by default—due to the Assembly not actually meeting—is not much of an excuse. The Direct Rule regime in the Northern Ireland Office (NIO) was in charge and could have ensured that the necessary changes were applied in the province. So too could MLAs, if they had been on top of the issue. A joint letter to the Secretary of State from the parties would probably have sorted out the anomalies. They remained in sleepwalking mode instead.

In 2004, the *Belfast Telegraph* reported on a loophole that had developed between London and Stormont on constituency office allowances. The Commons had introduced a new rule, preventing MPs from renting at taxpayers' expense premises owned by family members. This new regulation was not extended to Stormont.[9]

The Westminster change had followed standards investigations into a number of cases. One of these involved a veteran Ulster Unionist politician, so the Assembly parties really should have been paying attention. UUP East Antrim MP Roy Beggs had been the subject of a 2001 inquiry over payments claimed for a Larne constituency office owned by his daughters.[10] The then Commons Standards Commissioner, Elizabeth Filkin, conducted a typically forensic investigation that resulted in Beggs repaying the Commons £2,454 for overclaimed rental sums. Filkin's report concluded: 'He increased his family's income at public expense.'

The MPs who made up the parliamentary Standards and Privileges Committee were somewhat gentler with Beggs. But they did call on the Commons to address the 'question of financial transactions between Members and others which are not "at arm's length"'. That recommendation helped to bring about the ban on MPs channelling office rental expenses to members of their families. In another important move, the Commons also made it compulsory for members who were leasing premises from their political parties to obtain independent rental valuations. That reform was also not introduced at the Assembly.

These oversights—or errors of judgment—later brought trouble down on MLAs' heads. The least that can be said about the expenses loopholes is that they did not build public trust. Confidence was not that high anyway in the wake of the long period of suspension. Anger over MLAs still being paid during these years became an increasingly important factor in political debate.

Peter Hain, as Secretary of State, milked the situation effectively as part of the push to get the DUP and Sinn Féin into government together. There were repeated threats from him of salaries and expenses being halted if NIO deadlines for restoring devolution were not met. This may have been resented by the homegrown politicians, but it proved an effective lever.

In March 2007—around three weeks before the DUP–Sinn Féin deal was finally sealed—an opinion poll found strong support for the Hain line.[11] Seventy-five per cent of those surveyed agreed that all pay and allowances should be halted by the end of that month if there was no devolution agreement. Hain trumpeted the poll finding as a 'clear message to local politicians from the people of Northern Ireland'. The fact that quite a few members had a wife or other family members on their Stormont payrolls helped increase the pressure.

A senior source from Hain's team is in no doubt about the importance of the threat to stop paying Assembly members. 'That in the end had as much impact as almost anything else we did. It was the most popular thing on the street as well.'

It was all just tactics. The British government had been content to keep throwing money at the suspended institutions for years. When the devolution pact was agreed, Hain marked the happy event by giving the MLAs even more. He raised the Office Costs Allowance (OCA) from £48,000 to a whopping £70,000. By April 2008, it had climbed again to £72,660.

Some sceptics have dubbed the OCA the 'nepotism allowance' because of the many members who used it to employ relatives. There had been suspicions for years about the extent of this practice at Stormont, but no obvious way of quantifying it. Such staffing and personnel matters are exempt from freedom of information legislation. So it seemed the details would always stay hidden from view, barring the unlikely event of MLAs or their parties making voluntary disclosures.

Then the Derek Conway scandal broke in late January 2008 and changed everything. It caused major turbulence in British politics, and the icy blast that hit Westminster made it across the Irish Sea to Stormont. Within a few weeks, it had formed part of the 'perfect storm' that slapped Ian Paisley Jnr in the face.

IT'S A FAMILY AFFAIR
It quickly became clear that openness was the best response to the

hostile public reaction to the Conway revelations. Westminster politicians began giving details of relatives on their payroll and the jobs they did. The Stormont parties followed suit, one at a time. It produced a pretty long list.

Disclosures from the four governing parties revealed a total of 50 relatives of MLAS and MPs working in support jobs.[12] The DUP alone accounted for 27 of this officially declared employee tally, with the UUP having 11, the SDLP 10 and Sinn Féin two. It was stressed by the DUP that its 27-strong list was from an overall party staff team of 136. That illustrated the extent to which politics had started to resemble a mini-industry or, more accurately, a taxpayer-funded job creation scheme.

The DUP had been the last Northern Ireland party to make its details public and the delay ensured it received more attention than the other parties. Announcing the figures, its chief whip, Lord Morrow, said: 'Whilst there has been much discussion about MLAS who employ relatives, it must be noted that the focus should be on whether the employee is effectively doing the work for which they are paid.'[13]

That was not an unreasonable point. It also underlined the need for transparency. An important control against potential abuse of the system was to have mandatory declarations by elected representatives of any family members on their payrolls. With the basic facts in the public domain, a politician would be unlikely to abuse the system.

The House of Commons brought in a fairly swift reform, requiring MPs to declare employment details of relatives in the parliamentary register of interests. The Assembly did not show quite the same urgency. At an early stage, its Standards and Privileges Committee deferred its deliberations to see what course of action would be taken by Westminster. It then agreed a similar reform to the Commons, based on register of interest declarations. This was in the context of a wider and long-running review of the Code of Conduct for MLAS. By the beginning of June 2009, the new rule had still not been adopted and only a small number of MLAS were making voluntary entries in the register on employment details. This was hardly a proactive response to the situation.

In fairness, there are arguments to be made in support of some family members being on MLA staff teams. A lack of job security at Stormont must have deterred potential recruits to backroom posts. The future of the Assembly had seemed decidedly dodgy during the suspension years, with the British government threatening to close the place down. Against that background, few people would be willing to give up employment elsewhere and bank on Stormont always being able to pay the mortgage. It is therefore not necessarily that reprehensible that many MLAs turned to their nearest and dearest to help make up the numbers.

Expecting politicians to hire all staff by open competition also seems somewhat naïve. They need like-minded people around them. Politics is also very much a minority interest in Northern Ireland and there are not necessarily droves of people queuing up to dedicate their lives to it. It is not primarily concerned with the affairs of state that occupy great minds in other jurisdictions, but is instead chiefly about communal friction with 'the other side'. And local councils—the breeding ground for politics—are normally unappealing places in the province, with limited powers and constant bickering between party blocs.

The best way to attract new people is to develop a new form of politics. But the prospect of that happening in the foreseeable future look fairly remote. It should be stressed, though, that the 'nepotism' factor plays really badly with the public, for quite understandable reasons. Few commentators have gone so far as to argue that politicians should be totally barred from hiring family members. But that was the hardline position backed by 67 per cent of people in a poll in Northern Ireland in 2008. Only 18 per cent actually agreed that the practice should be permitted.[14] That was another indication of the credibility gap between the people and their representatives on the Stormont hill.

But MLAs seemed largely unwilling or unable to address the problem. There was no open debate about ways to widen recruitment procedures, attract more people and cut down on the numbers of wives and children taking home taxpayers' money.

They even managed to drag their feet on adopting the basic reform of requiring register of interest declarations on related employees.

The most eye-catching revelations of this period came courtesy of the DUP's two dynasties—the Paisleys and the Robinsons.[15] It was confirmed that no fewer than six Robinsons were in paid political posts. Peter Robinson (Minister, MLA and MP) was employing a son and a daughter in full-time roles. Wife Iris (MLA, Assembly committee chair and councillor) had their other son working for her full-time, plus a daughter-in-law on a part-time basis. This was the same Peter Robinson who liked to warn about Northern Ireland's dependency culture and how its overlarge public sector had to be trimmed down. Maybe a radical shift towards the private sector might even reach his household some day.

The Paisleys mustered five members in political posts, including the big man himself (First Minister, MLA and MP) and his Baroness wife with her seat in the House of Lords. Two of their three daughters were also in the family firm: Rhonda, a former DUP councillor, was her daddy's diary secretary and parliamentary assistant, while her sister Cherith was his office manager. And then there was Ian Jnr.

The facts about his extra pay from his father were not readily made public. At the height of the Derek Conway story, a previously unnoticed entry in the Junior Minister's register of interests jumped out. It said in the section for remunerated employment: 'Assistant to Dr Ian Paisley MP MLA, Leader, Democratic Unionist Party.' Both he and his party failed to respond to *Belfast Telegraph* enquiries, specifically on whether payments from his father had continued when he was made a junior minister.

Sir Alistair Graham, former chair of the Committee for Standards in Public Life, then publicly urged him to disclose details of his additional remuneration. 'I would call on him to explain to the people at large how much public funding he's actually been accessing, so that taxpayers can determine whether they are getting value for money,' Sir Alistair told the *Telegraph*.[16]

Paisley Jnr then confirmed to the BBC that he was still on his father's Westminster payroll as a parliamentary assistant. He declined to give details at that stage over the salary involved. It was only when a complaint was made to the Parliamentary Standards Commissioner that he stated that the arrangement involved £9,000–£11,000 a year from the Commons.[17] That was on top of around £60,000 for his ministerial and MLA jobs at the Assembly.

At best, continuing with the Westminster job looked like a case of bad judgment. He and his father were each receiving £70,000 a year in Assembly expenses to staff and run north Antrim constituency offices. Over £100,000 was also available to Paisley Snr from the Commons for staffing and other office costs. It is hard to imagine how anyone could have thought it wise to channel some £10,000 of this to Junior on top of his other well-paid roles. His workload as an MLA might not have been overly onerous prior to devolution returning. But being a Stormont minister is a very time-consuming business.

Three of the then ministers—Paisley Snr, Peter Robinson and Nigel Dodds—were also sitting MPs at the time. But being an MP is not a contracted employee post. The amount of time and effort they devote to the job is ultimately between them and their constituents. Paisley Jnr does put in many extra hours when it comes to politics, not least on the constituency representation front. But that commitment presumably stems from his belief in the DUP cause. It should not necessarily need an extra £10,000 or so a year, on top of what most people would regard as a more than ample wage packet.

The complaint against him to Westminster—from a member of the public—was eventually thrown out a few months later by parliamentary standards commissioner John Lyon, after a preliminary enquiry. Lyon initially rejected the idea of even a preliminary enquiry, but agreed to it after a second letter from the complainant. Judging from his eventual letter of response, his approach to the job is somewhat different to former commissioner Elizabeth Filkin, the woman who took UUP MP Roy Beggs to task.

Filkin infuriated MPs with her investigations, and was effectively pushed out of the post. It would seem unlikely that Lyon will suffer the same fate. In his response to the complainant on the Paisley Jnr pay question, Lyon said he had consulted Dr Paisley and the Commons authorities and concluded that 'sufficient work' was carried out to justify the money.[18] He also stated:

> Dr Paisley has told me that the constituency work undertaken by Mr Ian Paisley Jnr and remunerated out of his parliamentary allowances is exclusively in respect of his parliamentary duties. Only Mr Paisley Jnr carries out constituency casework on Dr Paisley's behalf: he directs all the work and inquiries and reports progress to Dr Paisley. I understand from Dr Paisley that Mr Paisley Jnr's tasks include dealing with press inquiries, writing speeches, handling constituency inquiries, including constituency casework, directing secretarial staff and meeting constituents on Dr Paisley's behalf. Given the nature of Mr Paisley's work and his level of experience, the salary with which he is provided from Dr Paisley's parliamentary allowances would reasonably meet the cost of some 9 or 10 hours work a week. I believe it is reasonable to conclude that Mr Paisley is undertaking at least this amount of work as Dr Paisley's parliamentary assistant.

And that was that. Lyon's letter did not detail the investigations he had conducted into the breakdown of Paisley Snr's constituency caseload between devolved Assembly matters and subjects still under Westminster's remit.

It was also interesting to note that the tasks involved in Paisley Jnr's remunerated parliamentary post included 'dealing with press inquiries'. That would be aside from those dealt with by the full-time press officers in the DUP and the First Ministers' department. According to Lyon's findings, Paisley Jnr was working 9 to 10 hours a week in his Commons-related job. That is the equivalent of around a day per week—alongside the demands of his minister's job and his own MLA constituency work. That would surely drain the energies and focus of any mere mortal, if not Paisley Jnr.

Lyon's blessing for the third pay packet was a boost for the

Paisleys. But there was a twist to the story later in the year, in the shape of an official Assembly pay and expenses report. This study by the Whitehall-based Senior Salaries Review Body (SSRB) predictably recommended a wages boost for MLAs. But a research paper for the report made some interesting comments on Assembly job remits.

This document was compiled for the SSRB by the Hay Group, a management consultancy company.[19] It openly questioned the feasibility of politicians holding jobs at both the Assembly and Westminster—and the fact that they were entitled to two sets of constituency office expenses. Reflecting on its conversations with a sample of Assembly members, the Hay Group stated: 'None of our interviews suggested there are two amounts of constituency work generated for MLAs who also serve as MPs in the same constituency.' It also said it found 'no compelling argument' why those who were double jobbing as MPs and MLAs should receive anything more than their Westminster salary and allowances.

GOING RENTAL

The fact that Assembly members were still permitted to claim rental expenses for offices owned by family members also came to the fore in February 2008. A small number of MLAs, from different parties, were discovered to be engaged in the practice. They included Billy Armstrong, Ulster Unionist MLA for Mid Ulster.

It turned out he had been renting a prefabricated constituency office from his wife up to the end of 2007.[20] It was located on their farm, not far from their family home. That was handy enough as his wife and one of his daughters also worked for him, both on a part-time basis. Armstrong's party explained that he had ceased claiming the rent at the end of 2007 as all the costs associated with it had been covered by that stage. That meant his family had gained new prefab office premises on the farm at public expense. One senior Ulster Unionist, when asked in private conversation for his thoughts on the matter, replied: 'Billy is Billy.' It was not exactly the finest case for the defence ever mustered.

The embarrassment grew when the Department of the

Environment decided that Armstrong had to apply for retrospective planning permission for the prefab.[21] Armstrong was at that time a member of the Stormont Environment Committee, which scrutinised the performance of the Planning Service.

Other MLAs were also revealed as keeping rental money in the family in early 2008.[22] Alliance's Kieran McCarthy was claiming £5,400 per year for a unit owned by his wife in the County Down town of Kircubbin. UUP Health Minister Michael McGimpsey was renting an office in Sandy Row, south Belfast, for £5,500 a year from a property company linked to his brother. DUP Minister Edwin Poots confirmed that he had previously claimed rental money for a Lisburn office bought by his wife in 1998. He said he had never been 'entirely comfortable' with the situation and the property had been sold on in 2002. The purchaser was a company called Iveagh Properties, who rented it to him for a further two years. Iveagh was part of a chain of property investment syndicates including people from Orange Order circles. Poots himself was among a large number of shareholders in Iveagh. Another senior DUP figure, Gregory Campbell, was renting a Coleraine office from his wife for £12,600 a year. She also held a full-time job on his staff.

A number of other Assembly members, meanwhile, located their constituency offices in premises owned by their parties. This practice was particularly prevalent among Sinn Féin members. At differing times during the financial year 2007/08, three of their west Belfast representatives—Paul Maskey, Fra McCann and Sue Ramsay—were based in Sinn Féin's Connolly House on the Andersonstown Road.[23]

Due to the Assembly's failure to keep in line with Westminster rules, there was no requirement on MLAs to provide independent rental valuations on party-owned offices. This is not to say that any of the figures claimed were out of step with market rates—just that good practice should require outside independent verification as a safeguard for everyone involved.

Other members were revealed in an Assembly freedom of information disclosure to be renting from little-known cultural organisations.[24] The landlord of Deputy First Minister Martin

McGuinness was listed as Tyrone Cultural Society. His Sinn Féin colleague Michelle O'Neill was renting from an organisation called South Derry Cultural and Heritage Society. According to official Assembly information, O'Neill's rental expenses came to £18,000 a year for an office in a small County Derry village called Gulladuff. That figure made it the second most expensive MLA advice centre.

But it was dwarfed by the sum claimed for another office. Its tenants were Ian Paisley and Ian Paisley Jnr and it would be the subject of the year's longest-running expenses controversy.

JUNIOR'S 9–11

The Paisleys moved into their spacious new constituency office at 9–11 Church Street, Ballymena, in the summer of 2007. They had just taken up their posts as government ministers and doubtless wanted a new address becoming to their elevated status in society. Their new Church Street base stretched over some 3,000 square feet with individual offices, a large meeting room and parking facilities. It had previously been a discount shop.

Reflecting their delight at the location, the Paisleys held an official opening in November that year. A full-page feature was run in a weekly Ballymena paper on the new centre with Junior declaring it 'the best appointed constituency office of any party in north Antrim, if not further afield'.[25] This was the house of the House of Paisley. Small and functional it was not.

The facts behind the acquisition tumbled out almost accidentally. They began on a nondescript day in January with the author casually filing a freedom of information request about rental expenses claimed by each MLA. There was no great expectation that the details would be issued, or that they would show anything dramatic. There was definitely no advance knowledge that the figures for the Paisleys would be out of the ordinary.

In early February, ahead of releasing the information, the Assembly circulated draft rental expenses totals to MLAS for checking purposes. The list showed the Paisleys were claiming some £62,000 between them from the public purse for their

Church Street premises. That made it some three times more expensive than the next highest sum. Eyebrows were raised in senior DUP circles at the figures—probably in frustration as well as surprise. Here was another unwanted batch of expenses-related headlines on the way.

Worse was to come. It emerged that the landlord of 9–11 Church Street was a company called Sarcon 250. Developer Seymour Sweeney had played a key behind-the-scenes role in this firm.[26] He had been Sarcon 250's sole director and shareholder after the company was formed in the first half of 2007. And, crucially, the Bank of Ireland mortgage that funded the purchase of the Church Street building had been obtained when the businessman was Sarcon 250's boss.

The Sweeney–Sarcon link was by far the most significant revelation to emerge in all the months of controversy surrounding Paisley Jnr. Up to this point, all the favours and lobbying had been in one direction. Sweeney had made it clear that he had never donated a single penny to the Paisleys or their party. Supporters of Junior could argue that he had simply pressed the case of a prominent entrepreneur in his constituency, while receiving and expecting nothing from him. But now it was clear that Sweeney had performed a service for the DUP father-and-son team.

He had agreed to be the only director of a company that had the sole purpose of buying a new constituency office. Furthermore, his name and financial standing had presumably assisted the task of securing the mortgage. This was not an insignificant deal—papers lodged in the government's land registry showed that the purchase price had been £500,000. There was also a key issue of timing. Just as Sarcon 250 was in the process of being formed with Seymour Sweeney at the helm, Paisley Jnr was aggressively lobbying a fellow Stormont minister on the proposed Ballee land sale that was linked to Sweeney. The mortgage and purchase arrangements for 9–11 Church Street were concluded on 31 July 2007. Around six weeks later, Paisley Jnr was on his feet in the Assembly attacking critics of Sweeney's plans for a Giant's Causeway visitor centre. Hours before that Stormont debate, he uttered the famous words 'I know of him' when asked about the businessman. Sweeney had at that very moment been the head of the company that owned his new constituency office.

The draft rental figures hit the public domain through a *News Letter* report on 15 February. By later that day, the all-important details of the Sweeney–Sarcon link were known to both the *Belfast Telegraph* and the *News Letter*.

Paisley Jnr was in trouble and he seemed to know it. Having stonewalled *Belfast Telegraph* queries for weeks, he was suddenly on the phone to the paper seeking to explain himself. A brief statement was issued to the two newspapers chasing the story. 'I can confirm that a company called Sarcon 250 owns the DUP office at 9–11 Church Street and has done since the summer of 2007,' he said.

> During the run-up to the purchase, for a period of weeks, Mr Sweeney as a member of the DUP gave advice on the purchase of the office and became a director of the company to ensure that the purchase could be completed. He subsequently resigned before any rent was due under the lease, in favour of a new director, as it was never intended that he would have any further role or be in receipt of any benefit.

That meant Sweeney had provided his assistance free of charge. This was not just giving advice 'on the purchase of the office', but taking on the legal responsibilities of being a Sarcon 250 director, and putting his name and good financial standing on the mortgage deal.

Another problem for the Paisleys was that Sweeney was still listed at the Government's Companies Registry as Sarcon 250's sole director. That raised more questions, and Paisley Jnr was back trying to explain himself to journalists over the course of the weekend.

He said Sweeney had actually relinquished the post during 2007. His replacement had been the Junior Minister's father-in-law, James Currie. Sweeney's Sarcon resignation date was later disclosed, through a backdated Companies Registry filing, to have been during October 2007. This would have been at the height of

the Causeway cronyism row. The link to the father-in-law was
hardly going to make the story go away.

Paisley Jnr said: 'There is no profit for Sarcon from the rental
payments. It goes directly to the bank to furnish the mortgage.'
That still meant taxpayers were footing the entire bill for a large-
sized commercial property that would remain in private
ownership. It was quite a bill too. Paisley Jnr challenged the draft
£62,000 rental figure that had been circulated by the Assembly,
claiming the true total was 'at most' £56,000 per year. That was
hardly a massive reassurance. Moreover, when the Assembly
released the official figures a few days later, they gave 9–11 Church
Street's annual cost to the public purse as £57,200 a year.

Hinting at the increasing strain on him by this stage, Paisley Jnr
said: 'I have been under a lot of pressure and received undue
attention for issues that also affect other MLAs. I take it on the chin
and move on.' He said the rental rate was set in line with the market
rate after professional advice was considered. Questions were
nevertheless asked about the fact that a building bought for
£500,000 was earning £57,200 a year—a yield that has been
described as 'exceptional' by one expert.[27]

Paisley Jnr further claimed that the Church Street arrangement
had been 'validated' by the Assembly. But there was no validation
process or independent valuation arrangement. It would also be
unrealistic to expect officials to challenge rental claims made by the
First Minister and his Junior Minister son. A staff member tempted
to raise a question internally might have been aware of the rumpus
caused back in 2002, when people within the Finance Office dared
to seek further details on expenses.

Paisley Jnr confirmed he had been the 'the mover and shaker'
behind the purchase of the property, adding:

I have absolutely done this correctly. I did not want to buy the
property myself and rent to myself and put my father in an
awkward position of renting from me. My understanding is that
I could have bought it or put it in my wife's name and she could
have charged me. I did not do that.

So that's all right then.

He later announced that his father-in-law was being replaced as Sarcon 250's director. That change took effect later in the year.

It was by no means uncommon to hear the phrase 'no rules have been broken' in connection with Paisley Jnr's troubles in 2007 and 2008. It is true to say that there was nothing to stop MLAS renting from family members, no official limits on the size of their constituency offices, and no system for checking the market basis for their rental claims. Even so, the phrase 'no rules have been broken' is a cop-out. For a start, it should be remembered that the limited rules—as enshrined in the Assembly Code of Conduct—are set by members themselves.

MLAS—on the Standards and Privileges Committee—also have the final say on whether one of their number has breached the rulebook. It's hardly a robust and independent framework for keeping propriety at the heart of public life. That goal requires politicians to understand the importance of being beyond reproach. It's not really that big an ask.

MLAS and MPs often delight in grilling civil servants about their stewardship of public funds. Nervous government officials can find themselves bombarded at lengthy committee sessions on overspends, underspends, wastage and poor management within their departments or quangos. That is as it should be. But suppose a civil servant was found to have been allocated public funds to rent office premises in a particular town. Would it be acceptable for him to arrange for a relative to buy a property and then rent it from him at taxpayers' expense? And would it also be no big deal if there were no checks on whether the rent was in line with market values, or if the office was larger than actually required? How would MLAS treat an official who admitted to such a situation at an Assembly committee hearing? Would they be in any way satisfied with the argument that there were no rules against it? The answer is obvious, so it begs another one. Should politicians demand higher standards from civil servants than they apply to themselves?

The Assembly had allowed a mess over expenses to slowly develop over a number of years. The First Minister's son was the one sitting in the middle of it in February 2008. His chances of surviving in government had meanwhile been dealt a blow by people power. Hours before the Ballymena office details started coming into the public domain, voters in a place called Dromore had inflicted a shock election snub on the DUP.

Chapter 12
Surprise in Dromore

'The hare was once boasting of his speed before the other animals. "I have never yet been beaten," said he, "when I put forth my full speed. I challenge any one here to race with me.'
'The Hare and the Tortoise'[1]

By the end of 2007, former Ulster and Ireland rugby player Tyrone Howe had had enough. He announced that he was quitting Banbridge Council, where he had represented the Dromore area for the UUP for some two and a half years.

In a more normal political environment, Howe would have been quickly fast tracked by party bosses for a high-profile role. Observers had long been lamenting the small number of young people involved in public life in Northern Ireland. And here was one who also happened to be a well-known sports star. Having performed extremely well at the polls in 2005—topping the poll in Dromore while the UUP was being generally thumped elsewhere—Howe nevertheless found himself marooned in the Banbridge council chamber.

Work commitments were cited for his resignation decision, but he had also become disillusioned with local government politics. Like many other councils across Northern Ireland, Banbridge had its share of pettiness, bickering and general negativity. Putting up with that week after week was not what he had in mind when he stood for election. In departing the scene, however, Howe did manage to make a major difference. The Dromore by-election to find his replacement, in February 2008, played a pivotal role in toppling the House of Paisley.

The DUP expected to win the seat but failed, with the Ulster Unionists instead claiming a surprise victory. Jim Allister's new anti-Agreement grouping, Traditional Unionist Voice (TUV), showed it was capable of eating into the DUP's core vote. Most significantly of all, the DUP was handed concrete evidence that the father-and-son Paisley team had become an electoral liability.

The party would have been nothing without Paisley Snr. But now his chuckling antics were hurting it. This was never just about the constant laughter with the Deputy First Minister. It was about how it grated with supporters who had been told for decades that compromise was wrong, power-sharing was wrong, Sinn Féin had to be smashed—and that anyone who suggested otherwise was acting contrary to God's wishes. Not everyone felt able to ignore or forget their past and giggle along with Paisley.

Dromore had never before been viewed as a political cauldron, or a key unionist battleground. The February by-election poll produced a 39 per cent turnout. This was actually quite high for a council by-election, but it still meant that six out of 10 potential voters stayed at home. But those who did cast their votes had a huge impact on Northern Ireland politics.

The campaign started inauspiciously—and predictably—with an inter-party bust-up. The DUP agreed to an Ulster Unionist co-option to fill Howe's seat—on the grounds that it would be taken by veteran ex-UUP councillor William Martin. These terms were rejected by the Ulster Unionists, who instead selected local woman Carol Black as their candidate.[2] She was a constituency office worker for the party's Lagan Valley MLA Basil McCrea. Black proved not to the DUP's liking and a co-option was opposed. The by-election date was duly set for 13 February, with the count to take place the following day. The failure to agree on a co-option clearly did not trouble the DUP.

A by-election was attractive to the party for a number of reasons. It had been on the march electorally since 2001, not just replacing the UUP as the main unionist party but hammering it with increasing ease. This would be the first time it would face voters as a pro-power-sharing party, given that its Assembly 2007 manifesto had left its options open on a deal. Dromore was as good a place as any for the electoral test, as it was not regarded as a particularly hardline unionist area. Towns in other parts of Northern Ireland like Portadown, Larne and possibly even Ballymena would have been viewed as posing a greater risk, due to the likelihood that they contained stronger pockets of hardline sentiment. Dromore had been solid Ulster Unionist territory for many years, until the party's vote fell apart as Protestant attitudes to the Belfast Agreement hardened.

The area's most prominent politician, Jeffrey Donaldson, epitomised the changes that had taken place. He defected to Paisley's party from the UUP in opposition to David Trimble's leadership in 2004, and took most of his voters with him. The local government elections of the following year showed that Dromore was now firmly in the DUP camp. While Tyrone Howe topped the poll, the next three across the line in the proportional representation battle were all DUP candidates. The fifth and final seat went to the SDLP.

At first glance, the February 2008 by-election was simply a UUP hold, with Carol Black retaining the seat vacated by Howe. But in reality it was a DUP defeat, as it held three of the five seats in the district and the UUP had just one. The DUP had won those three Dromore seats in 2005 by securing 49.8 per cent of the first preference votes.[3] By contrast, the Ulster Unionists received 31.3 per cent. The actual votes cast were 3,000 for the DUP and 1,884 for the UUP. That was quite a lead for Paisley's party to take into the by-election.

There were also grounds for thinking that the 2005 figures flattered the UUP. Howe was viewed as on the liberal wing of the party, and it is likely that his vote was boosted by the absence of a candidate from the middle of the road Alliance Party in the field. Alliance's candidate in the 2008 by-election, David Griffin, was well known in the area as a former school vice-principal. It was not unreasonable to anticipate some of his votes coming from UUP territory.

The Ulster Unionist bid to retain its single Dromore seat did not exactly make a glorious start. Internal frictions surrounding the selection of candidate Carol Black spilled out into the public domain. Defeated would-be candidate Stephen Warke, who worked for another UUP MLA, denounced the selection process as a 'shambles'.[4] He protested at the way the local party meeting had been called and conducted, and said he was taking legal advice. Warke also used the words 'incompetence' and 'mismanagement' and alleged the selection process had been 'seriously contaminated'.

Then during the election campaign, former Dromore UUP representative William Martin endorsed the DUP candidate.[5] Martin was the ex-councillor the DUP had wanted to see co-opted into the vacant seat. His subsequent switch of allegiance suggested the UUP had been right to look elsewhere.

The Stephen Warke and William Martin developments hardly helped the UUP rebuild its reputation, after the years of fragmentation. Nor can they have boosted self-esteem or morale in a party that looked to many as if it was in its death throes. At the 1997 Westminster election, the UUP had 10 MPs elected. By the end of the count in the 2005 General Election, it was down to just one.

In the context of that dramatic slide, the DUP could be forgiven for feeling super-confident ahead of the Dromore by-election. The poll also offered it the enticing opportunity to put one of the UUP's few rising stars, Basil McCrea, in his place. McCrea was by no means universally admired, even in his own party, but he had developed a high media profile. Carol Black's candidacy was closely linked to him, as her employer and prominent backer. However, the real prize for the DUP in Dromore was the scalp of Jim Allister.

Allister had formed his anti-Agreement Traditional Unionist Voice organisation in December 2007, just a few weeks before the Dromore by-election was called. The poll offered him an opening, but also represented a major risk. The DUP must have been almost drooling at the thought of inflicting a humiliating defeat on the fledgling TUV. It mustered all its resources—and considerable electioneering expertise—to achieve such a victory. Running for the DUP was Paul Stewart, a constituency office employee of Jeffrey Donaldson.

The fact that two of the leading Dromore candidates—Stewart and the UUP's Black—were on Stormont payrolls illustrated the extent to which the parties were benefiting from public funds. Allister's candidate Keith Harbinson had a job outside politics as a solicitor in the town.

From the very outset, the DUP played up its confidence about teaching the TUV a lesson. First Minister Paisley had set the tone in December, greeting the formation of Allister's grouping with the words:

> I have little comment to make about that. It will be of no use. He will use it to get his face in the political limelight but it will be forgotten, if it's not forgotten already. They will disappear. If there was an election tomorrow, they would disappear out of sight.[6]

The leader of the DUP grouping on Banbridge Council David Herron was equally upbeat after the by-election was confirmed. 'If that means a TUV candidate coming forward, so much the better,' he said. 'We'll see them off no problem. The electorate doesn't want to go backwards. DUP has never been stronger.'[7]

Similar confidence was expressed during the campaign. DUP MLA Alastair Ross said:

> This will be the first time since May that voters will be able to go to the polls and give their verdict on the hard work and progress that has been achieved as a result of strong DUP leadership. I do not believe that any fringe unionist candidate will pose any sort of electoral difficulty as ultimately people want to see politicians who look for solutions to problems, rather than eternally portraying a pessimistic view on everything.[8]

And DUP candidate Stewart said: 'I am surprised at the amount of support we have been getting.'[9]

It is normal in politics for parties and candidates to talk up their prospects. However, all the indications are that the DUP was very positive about the Dromore result, and simply did not see the defeat coming. Winning had become an ingrained habit for the party year after year, and its optimism must have been further boosted by the early squabbling within the UUP on its candidate selection. The DUP could also point to the 2007 Assembly poll and the failure of anti-Agreement unionist candidates to win a single seat. There was a crucial difference then, however, as the deal with Sinn Féin had still to be struck. While the DUP was confident, it would be unfair to portray it as complacent. It took the by-election seriously, canvassing every area and bringing the party's big names to the town during the course of the campaign.

The TUV also did not give the impression that it was anticipating a major breakthrough. Candidate Keith Harbinson told the *Sunday Tribune*: 'We'll perform strongly but, whatever the result, we'll build on it. I'm a Leeds United fan. I've not forsaken them no matter how far they've dropped. I've conviction and loyalty.'[10] Given that Leeds United were languishing in English football's third tier, having suffered one of the worst slumps in the history of the game, this was not the most positive of analogies.

The *Tribune* report concluded: 'DUP insiders predict the party should win around 50% of the vote with Stewart elected on the first count. The TUV hopes to thwart this but stresses it's "starting from scratch".' In the event, Stewart came nowhere near 50 per cent or to being elected on the first count. He did top the poll with 1,069 first preference votes.[11] But that represented a 28 per cent share—well down on the DUP's 49.8 per cent in 2005. In second place came the UUP's Black with 912 votes and 24 per cent of the vote. Harbinson finished third with 739 votes—a 19.5 per cent share.

It took five stages of the 14 February count to produce a final result. Black drew level along the way—largely thanks to transfers from the eliminated Alliance candidate. The crucial moment came when Harbinson was excluded and his second preferences shared out. Black received 50 more transfers from the TUV than Stewart, sealing victory for her by a margin of just 66.

The DUP had suffered its first reversal at the polls for many years. Its opponents enjoyed the moment. A TUV supporter sought to wind up the DUP at the count by playing a tape of Paisley's famous 'Never, Never, Never' speech at a Belfast rally against the 1985 Anglo-Irish Agreement. UUP deputy leader Danny Kennedy succeeding in coining the phrase of the day. With just the right amount of hyperbole, he described the result as a 'St Valentine's Day massacre for the DUP'.[12]

The DUP naturally tried to minimise the outcome, with reference to the fact that the seat had previously been in UUP hands. But that ignored its strong overall lead in Dromore in 2005, which had made it the clear favourite. Its slice of the vote had dropped by some 20 per cent since then, to the clear benefit of Jim Allister's TUV. And its share of the unionist vote was down from 61 per cent to 39 per cent. A similar swing across Northern Ireland at the next Assembly elections would be the stuff of nightmares for the DUP. Just 3,776 people cast valid votes in the Dromore by-election, 2,720 of them for unionist candidates. They managed to confound the commentators and seriously unsettle Northern Ireland's largest governing party.

Various factors influenced the outcome. The TUV was definitely boosted by its choice of candidate. Keith Harbinson was a prominent member of the Orange Order in the area and also worked in the legal practice of one of the province's most senior Orangemen, Drew Nelson. The Orange Order was active in the area during the by-election campaign, protesting in defence of the display of unionist emblems at Banbridge Council's headquarters.

The TUV is viewed by its critics as mainly comprising a collection of ageing ex-Paisleyites and other jaded veterans of unionism. At 24, Harbinson did not fit that description. The DUP's Dromore candidate, Paul Stewart, was also in his twenties and deeply involved in the local Orange Order. However, some in his party wondered if he was the right choice, on account of his family's involvement in a pub–restaurant business. It has been suggested that this connection may not have played well among the conservative church-going Protestant voters who normally flocked to the DUP's side. 'It would not have mattered in a Belfast constituency,' is how one party source puts it.

There is also a view that Dromore has quite a few retired security force personnel among its population. It is possible that some ex-police officers are now among the most disgruntled sections of the Protestant community. The reform process that changed the RUC into the PSNI stuck in many of their throats. And even the most liberal former officer who served through the Troubles might suffer the occasional twitch of anger at the sight of Sinn Féin ministers in suits with government cars. So the ex-cop vote may be chalked up as another potential factor in the Dromore result.

There are other areas for speculation too. It could be that the lingering controversy over the brutal border murder of Paul Quinn the previous October had soured attitudes among parts of the unionist electorate. Allegations had been made—and denied—that the south Armagh IRA was responsible for Quinn being beaten to death in County Monaghan.

On a more general point, by-elections are traditionally tricky for all governing parties as they give voters an opportunity to humble them. The DUP did not just speculate on the reasons for its Dromore setback. In keeping with its reputation as a tightly organised party that left little to chance, it conducted a detailed post-mortem. This review identified the prime causes for the defeat.

Two of them were called Paisley.

WHAT JUST HAPPENED?
A senior DUP source who spoke to the author insisted that the Dromore campaign was well run. In a frank assessment, he also confirmed that the party expected to win the seat. The district had 'switched significantly' to the DUP over recent years and was 'certainly one of our strongest areas' in the 2007 Assembly elections, he said.

> I would say that we were quietly confident we would hold the seat, but not taking anything for granted. Paul Stewart was a good candidate, a local man, well connected. The campaign was

run very efficiently. We canvassed the urban area three times and we did the rural area as well. We had good teams out on the ground. On the doorsteps, we were received in a polite way. It was very rare that people raised political issues on the doorsteps with us.

The DUP source described the TUV entry into the field as 'the unknown factor', adding: 'We just did not know how that would go.' The feedback from the campaign trail was not alarming. 'There was no sense from the doorsteps that there was any major rebellion, any major turning away from the party. The result therefore came as a disappointment.' In the DUP's eyes, it had been hit by a by-election protest vote. 'We set about analysing what people were protesting about,' the senior source disclosed.

We did some local surveying and we talked to people. We made it our business to go and talk to people that we knew had voted for the TUV. There were a number of issues that became apparent. The primary issue was the Chuckle Brothers issue. People said we understood the decision to go into government with Sinn Féin and we supported that, but we didn't expect people to enjoy it.

The DUP had, after all, promised a 'battle a day' with Sinn Féin at Stormont. 'The reality was that we were having battles with Sinn Féin, but the perception, which in Ulster politics is often nine tenths of reality, was that it was more jolly and enjoyable than people had expected.'

The by-election review also indicated that the DUP had suffered in rural districts, with 'traditional Presbyterian unionists' backing the TUV. The Dromore area had the distinction of two Free Presbyterian congregations, he added. 'I would say probably a majority of the Free Presbyterian vote in Dromore went as a protest to the TUV,' the DUP insider argued. That was quite a stunning conclusion. It meant Paisley's political party had suffered because Paisley's church had turned against it. The DUP source continued:

Another issue that undoubtedly had a negative impact was the Ian Paisley Jnr stuff. Church going Protestants who would be traditional DUP voters always regarded the DUP as a party that would have integrity. They were very concerned about a series of events that occurred where there were allegations made against Ian Paisley Jnr which caused people concerns. That also impacted negatively with the traditional church-going rural Protestant voter base of the DUP. The perception was that there were issues here.

There were indeed. Some of the most serious Paisley Jnr controversies broke right in the teeth of the by-election campaign. These included the revelations about his side deal lobbying of the British government at the St Andrews talks. Then came the disclosure that he was on his father's Westminster payroll as a parliamentary assistant, while also an Assembly member and minister at Stormont. The DUP's Dromore post-mortem highlighted a third cause, aside from the Chuckle Brothers and Paisley Jnr. 'There would also have been an element of the TUV vote who were people who would just never agree with the DUP being in government with Sinn Féin,' the party source said.

There probably was not that much the DUP could do—in the short term at least—to win over such diehard opponents of power-sharing. But senior figures did have the capacity to deal with the Paisley problems, however painful that was going to be.

The senior DUP source also readily admitted that his party was 'spooked' by the Dromore result. 'There is no doubt about that. It had been progressing in successive elections, its vote had been going up. This was the first reversal for the party in the period since it came to dominance in 2003. I think it was a wake-up call. There was a message there from voters.'

To add to the DUP's woes, the result had also given an unexpected confidence boost to its unionist rivals. In the words of Jim Allister, Dromore gave the TUV 'a bounce across the country'. 'The phones in my office the next day were red with people from right across the province saying: "We thought there was something wrong with us that we thought like that, that we were the only people who thought like that. We're just amazed and surprised that so many think like that.'"

Allister also admits to being 'pleasantly surprised' at the outcome of the by-election. 'I didn't know what to expect. I put a lot of time into Dromore and I knew as we were doing the doors that we certainly weren't going to be shamed.' Allister had correctly assessed that the Chuckle Brothers image of Paisley and McGuinness was playing badly. One of the key messages of the TUV campaign was to encourage unionists to 'wipe the smile' off the faces of the First Ministers. 'The whole Chuckle business I suppose epitomised the attitude of a lot of people,' he says.

> At that time too, the shenanigans of Junior weren't doing us any harm at all. I remember on the Saturday before the election being in the same part of Dromore canvassing as the DUP were. Junior was just a couple of streets ahead of us, knocking on doors. At a number of doors I went to, people commented adversely on who'd just been to the door. I knew that his shenanigans weren't impressing, as they shouldn't have.

One of the most intriguing aspects of the by-election result was the fact that the Ulster Unionists received more second preference votes from the TUV candidate than the DUP. The UUP had backed going into government with Sinn Féin years earlier. So the way Keith Harbinson's preferences were distributed suggests that his vote did not just come from hardline power-sharing opponents.

It is generally agreed that the alphabetical order of candidates' names on the ballot paper can have a significant bearing on PR election transfers. The names of Harbinson and the DUP's Paul Stewart were beside each other at the bottom of the ballot sheet, while Carol Black's was at the top. Many TUV supporters therefore put Harbinson one and went to the top of the paper to give the UUP woman their second preference. That helped decide the outcome of the by-election.

Jim Allister has an explanation for the transfers between the two opposing unionist camps.

> That was voters saying to themselves: how can we best poke the
> DUP in the eye? I've no doubt of that, from people I canvassed
> stating to me, yes we're delighted to vote for you and we are
> going to vote for the Ulster Unionists because the people we
> want to punish here are the DUP, who we've always voted for.
> That in fact was happening the other way as well. They never
> had to be counted, but from simply watching the ballots it was
> quite clear to me from the Ulster Unionist first preferences, that
> we were taking a great deal of their second preferences. That was
> Ulster Unionists—not in policy agreement, but because they
> too voted to poke the DUP in the eye.

UUP MLA Basil McCrea also saw the by-election campaign at first
hand, as he canvassed alongside candidate Carol Black, his
constituency office employee. 'It was an unexpected victory. I don't
think we'd won anything for about 10 years, against the head,' he
says. 'Nobody saw it coming, even within the UUP.'

McCrea agrees that the Chuckle Brothers and Paisley Junior
were factors. But he also saw something more significant at work.
'People didn't like being misled. There was just a feeling that the
DUP said one thing and then did the complete opposite.' The
decision to go into government with Sinn Féin had left strong DUP
supporters 'absolutely livid', the UUP Assemblyman adds. 'In my
opinion, the DUP brand is wrecked.'

McCrea also believes there was arrogance at play in the DUP
campaign. 'They brought in big guns—they had every MLA coming
in. It was all a bit bemusing for people.' He also states: 'I think they
thought they could do two things—I think they thought they could
take me out and they also wanted to nip the TUV in the bud. They
also didn't think they could lose, because the numbers were quite
dramatically in their favour.'

McCrea was clearly not overly confident at the outset of the
campaign about his party's prospects. 'You were certainly aware at
the time that there was a pool of unhappy people. How big was that

pool was the thing that we really wanted to find out.' Recalling his mood a week before polling day, he states: 'I kept saying to Carol, it couldn't be that we're picking up so many negatives about the DUP that there isn't going to be some positive swing for us. I suppose at the end of the day it was a triumph of hope over adversity.'[13]

The DUP's chief strategists swiftly recognised the significance of the Dromore result. But its ageing leader defiantly dismissed the result as a 'flash in the pan' and proclaimed: 'We did extremely well.'[14]

Parties across the world will always seek to put the best possible gloss on electoral setbacks. But Paisley Snr's 'extremely well' comment was so far over the top as to invite ridicule. It also gave the appearance of an old man who was unwilling or unable to come to terms with political reality.

Chapter 13
All Fall Down

'Some people bring joy wherever they go. Some people bring joy when they go.'
Green Party statement welcoming Ian Paisley Jnr's departure

Monday 18 February 2008—the date Ian Paisley Jnr resigned as a junior minister. Barely nine months after he and daddy had taken their places in Northern Ireland's new devolved government, here he was standing alone in front of the media announcing his departure. The Junior Minister everyone once regarded as flameproof was gone.

It had been quite a week for both him and his party. First had come that disturbing defeat in the Dromore by-election. Only 66 votes separated the DUP candidate from the UUP winner in the end. If a few more people had made it to the polling station, or used their second preferences in a different way, the result could have been altered. But they had lost, and the feedback was quickly placing much of the blame on the Chuckle Brothers act and the constant Junior problems.

The votes at Dromore had barely been counted when yet another controversy came along, involving the Paisley advice centre in Ballymena. As Chapter 11 detailed, these premises were costing taxpayers some three times as much as the next most expensive MLA office. The connection between the premises and Seymour Sweeney made the story much more serious. The developer had been the first director of the company that owned the building, and the mortgage for its purchase had been secured in his name. The press—in the shape of the *News Letter* and *Belfast Telegraph*—were crawling over the details of the arrangements by the weekend following Dromore.

Meanwhile, senior figures in the DUP were asking questions too. The fact that the *News Letter* was running hard with the story was a sign of how things were turning against Paisley Jnr. The paper did not exactly go out of its way to annoy the DUP normally. Its strong coverage of the Ballymena office saga was an indication that Junior's standing in the party was not what it had been.

Another piece of bad luck came along at exactly the wrong moment for Junior. By unhappy coincidence, the weekend after the Dromore defeat saw much of the DUP parliamentary party heading off to Portugal for a strategic think-in. Paisley Snr could not make it, which meant that the views of deputy Peter Robinson and his closest allies would take centre stage in the discussions. That was hardly good news for Junior. The DUP gathering in Lisbon addressed the Dromore by-election defeat and the never-ending problems attached to the leader's son. There was no mood to rally behind the Junior Minister.

Back home, it was a weekend for speculation and gossip—two of the main ingredients in political and journalistic life. The consensus that Paisley Jnr was a protected species while his father was in office was weakening. Some DUP sources had previously muttered off the record in connection with his lobbying at the St Andrews talks. But now the whispers were getting louder and more personal. 'People in the party are just sick to the back teeth of all of this,' was how one DUP figure put it.[1] A backroom party source told the author he did not think Paisley Jnr would last the week as a minister. Forces in the DUP were by now effectively briefing against the leader's son.

By the morning of Monday 18 February, his position was even bleaker. Another of the party's politicians gave what turned out to be a very accurate off-the-record comment: 'There is no doubt that a head of steam is building up. I would say Ian Junior's position is precarious.'[2] A further source captured a growing mood among MLAS, saying: 'There is a feeling that if it had been anyone else they would have been out long ago.'[3]

That Monday morning, the author had a brief conversation with another DUP politician, who was reluctant to speak even off

the record. It was suggested to him that the whole situation about
Ian Jnr would be resolved within the next 48 hours. 'I think it will
be much sooner than that,' came the reply.

He was right. By lunchtime, the word was out that Paisley Jnr
was resigning. He appeared at the steps of Stormont Castle, his
departmental headquarters, to confirm the news. Not a single party
colleague or backroom aide stood beside him. There was no
obvious hint of emotion as he read out his statement:

> I have been honoured and privileged to support my father, the
> First Minister, during this period of historic change for our
> country. To be a minister in the government of Northern
> Ireland for the past 10 months has been an absolute honour. I
> entered elected political life in 1996 and have been driven by a
> desire to be a faithful servant to my constituents in North
> Antrim. I am also pleased to have played some small part in
> helping to secure the current political stability of the political
> institutions that our country and people enjoy now so freely. I
> take personal pride in ensuring that the Democratic Unionist
> Party in negotiations secured from Sinn Féin not only the
> signing up to support for the police but insisted that they made
> a pledge of support to the police in the assembly. However, the
> past 10 months have not been without controversy. Personal
> criticism, unfounded allegation, innuendo and attacks on me
> personally, followed by ombudsman's reports that have cleared
> me. This relentless period of criticism by those who have
> decided on this path has been unceasing. The criticism has been
> a distraction and has got in the way of the activities of this
> government and importantly, has got in the way of the activities
> of my political party. There is no doubt that the message and
> good work that I have done as a junior minister in this
> administration has been overshadowed by this personal
> controversy. I accept that there are those who wish for me to be
> a convenient distraction of the DUP's political message. I will
> not serve that purpose. What is more, I refuse to be a convenient
> excuse to attack the position of the leader of my party. I will not

serve that purpose or indeed the purpose of those who would seek to undermine him, indeed one of Ulster's finest sons. I have considered these factors and with a certain degree of sadness, I have informed the First Minister of my intention to resign my ministerial office. My resignation will take effect after my replacement has been found but I expect that within days not weeks. I cannot express strongly enough that I am not going because of some hidden or some revealed wrongdoing on my part. I have no intention of stopping my political activity or relinquishing my position as a member of the legislative assembly for North Antrim. Unlike my critics, I believe in putting my constituents first. Working for their interests is something I believe I can do with more success from the backbenches than from the current position that I hold as minister. I have relished the opportunity to be part of the government but I have grown increasingly frustrated by this campaign of personal bitterness, of jealousy and indeed of perception against me.[4]

The statement was nine-tenths bravado. Some of it was frankly nonsensical, not least the concluding sentence about a campaign of 'jealousy' and 'perception' being waged against him. No doubt Paisley Jnr did actually believe that his critics were just jealous of him. That's an indication of how he regarded himself. The overall impression was that he had been driven from office by a malicious campaign that was entirely without foundation.

But what kind of minister, government or political party would allow such a thing to happen? Who would forsake all the influence and trappings of power, just because some nasty people in the media were being unkind? Ministers with defensible positions tend to fight back rather than run away. So do their parties.

Paisley Jnr resigned because he had become an embarrassment to the DUP. His judgment had been shown up as poor, and his excessive and at times inappropriate lobbying for a controversial property developer—and party member—had been uncovered. Furthermore, he had involved himself with this same businessman while fashioning a constituency office deal funded entirely by taxpayers.

The most telling part of his resignation statement was his refusal to 'be a convenient excuse to attack the position of the leader of my party' or to serve 'the purpose of those who would seek to undermine him'. It may well be that he thought his departure would bolster his dad's position. In the event, the opposite occurred. Without his son by his side, the elderly Paisley Snr was seriously exposed and his future immediately became the subject of intense scrutiny. Junior's resignation announcement implied that the attacks on him were really aimed at his father— that the 'campaign' was really all about damaging the esteemed First Minister.   There have been similar whispers in political and media circles since, suggesting a co-ordinated plot was hatched to bring down Paisley Snr by targeting the son. Some people have even reached the conclusion that figures in the DUP might have been behind it all. This is nonsense. There was in fact no centralised Machiavellian operation. A relatively small number of reporters simply followed the story wherever it took us. There was no rocket science involved.

The information that damaged Paisley Jnr came out bit by bit mainly through freedom of information disclosures, cross-checking public records, following up on tip-offs and gossip. It was good old-fashioned journalism in action and it was entirely justified, not least by the fact of Paisley Jnr's departure from government. DUP sources had a minimal role in assisting the investigations, aside from a few off-the-record critical comments on certain revelations.

It's true to say that the party's big guns did not come out blazing in Paisley Jnr's support. But that might just have been because some of his actions were hard to justify. It is also true to say that the resignation did not appear to have left Peter Robinson and co. heartbroken. The deputy leader issued a fairly brief statement, referring to media coverage of Paisley Jnr being 'a distraction from the important business of the Executive'. Robinson added: 'Today I believe Ian Paisley Jnr has taken the right decision for the right reason. In drawing this particular chapter to a close, I think it is important to record that in the last 10 months Ian Paisley Jnr has made a significant contribution to both the office of the first and deputy first minister and to the work of the wider Executive in often difficult personal circumstances.'[5]

Another of the senior party figures, Gregory Campbell, repeated the 'distraction' line, adding:

> We had the Minister for Finance announcing a three year freeze on regional rates, something which impacts on everyone, but in the same week there were more revelations about Ian Paisley Junior and when the two ran in tandem it was the good news about the rates which was dropped. News outlets prefer to run with salacious and juicy stories rather than good news. Hopefully this move will end that distraction and we can get back to business at Stormont.[6]

Neither Robinson nor Campbell expressed any view on whether the press coverage of their party colleague had been unfair.

The political reaction to the resignation outside the DUP was generally unfavourable to Paisley Jnr. The UUP's deputy leader, Danny Kennedy, talked of 'public trust and confidence' having been 'sapped'.[7] Sinn Féin's Daithí McKay said: 'This is certainly not the end of it for Ian Paisley Jnr. There are still a number of questions that he needs to answer in relation to the Giant's Causeway and other developments.'[8] Alliance leader David Ford commented: 'Ian Paisley Jnr's behaviour has severely damaged the credibility of the Executive. However, the questions being asked relate to his behaviour as an MLA. This would suggest he must resign as MLA too.'

Declan O'Loan of the SDLP made a correct prediction on the wider implications for Stormont. 'The spotlight now switches on to Ian Paisley Senior,' he said. 'I think the public will be saying one Paisley has gone, when is the other going to go?'

But the comments were not all negative. Secretary of State Shaun Woodward was at his most sycophantic, declaring:

On the public front it is obviously a matter for the DUP and obviously a matter for the Executive and Assembly. But on a private front I think one also has to acknowledge that, for the Paisley family, it is a very difficult time. These matters are always very, very hard and for them, a family who has given a huge amount to Northern Ireland, my thoughts are also with them.

Meanwhile, a poignant little statement was issued by Seymour Sweeney. He said: 'It is a very sad day for democracy and one can only hope that given his considerable political dedication and expertise he will be encouraged to continue his valuable work as an MLA.'[9] The Green Party, not surprisingly, took a different view with its south Belfast spokesman Dr Peter Doran claiming Paisley Jnr should never have been appointed in the first place. Doran added: 'Some people bring joy wherever they go. Some people bring joy when they go.'[10]

One of the most telling reactions came from DUP MP and MLA Sammy Wilson, who would later that year be made a minister by Peter Robinson. In a frank interview with the BBC 'Spotlight' programme, Wilson said the 'adverse publicity' Paisley Jnr had 'attracted to himself' was 'one of the factors' in the Dromore by-election.[11] He also voiced his opinion on the lobbying at St Andrews by his leader's son. 'If you ask me would I have done it, the answer is no I wouldn't. And I've got to be honest about that,' he said. He further told 'Spotlight':

As far as I was concerned, at St Andrews we were there negotiating about the bigger political issues, and issues which affected the whole of Northern Ireland. It wasn't an opportunity to collar a Minister and say look, you know, can you get this sorted out for me, can you get that sorted out for me. That is not how I saw those arrangements.

Wilson confirmed that Paisley Jnr's position had been discussed by the MPs on their Portugal trip—and that the Ballymena office revelations were also on their minds. 'Obviously it was in the news at the time about Ian's rental arrangements and, of course, we would have discussed it,' he said. Asked about the reaction of the MPs to the office controversy, Wilson said:

> There was dismay that the good things that our Ministers were doing were lost in the kind of publicity, and the only publicity the DUP were getting was the publicity centred around Ian. Anything which distracts from the main work of a political party, you've got to find ways of dealing with that and the only way, of course, of dealing with that was for Ian to make a decision to go. But he reached that decision himself independently. Had he not reached that decision independently, then I suppose the question is would we have encouraged him to make that? And I think that, yes, in any party that would have been the case but we didn't have to do that because he did the right thing by the party by putting his own resignation in.

In other words, if he hadn't jumped, he would have been pushed. Paisley Jnr would have been well aware of that too, so the extent to which his decision was really his alone is open to question.

The Wilson interview on 'Spotlight' did not contain a single adverse remark on the media's role. That is worth recording, not least because back in the autumn of 2007 Wilson had been fiercely critical in private about press reports on Paisley Jnr's lobbying. The interview also contained an interesting comment on the future of Paisley Snr. Wilson said: 'Dr Paisley has quite openly spoken about, you know, the need of transition and that, you know, he's not going to be around for ever and everything else. He has publicly, you know, made those kind of statements.' This was the same Dr Paisley who in December 2007—just two months earlier—was still insisting that he would be serving his full term.

The First Minister made no public statement on the day of his son's resignation announcement. But many observers saw deep symbolism in the sight of him sitting by himself on the Assembly's benches that day, looking isolated and old. The image was picked up in an *Irish Times* report on Junior's departure, which stated:

'The effective forced resignation of his son is a huge personal blow to Dr Paisley, who for a considerable period of the Assembly sitting yesterday sat alone on the DUP front benches.'[12]

From that day, the talk was all about when the First Minister would be going. Peter Robinson's day was coming.

OUT OF THE SHADOWS

It seems somehow unlikely that Peter Robinson is a big fan of actress and singer Martine McCutcheon. But her hit 'Perfect Moment' would supply an ideal soundtrack for his life in early 2008. He had been Paisley's deputy leader for around 30 years. Now, his time to take the helm was approaching.

For a start, there was general agreement that Junior's fall had brought Senior's departure closer. There were strong doubts over how the 81-year-old First Minister would cope with the demands of his busy government job without his son constantly beside him. Also, the fact that the party leader had been unable to prevent his own son from exiting office was another indication of his ebbing strength. This was just a few weeks after Paisley Snr had officially vacated his role as Free Presbyterian Moderator and it all added to a sense of a dying dynasty. The succession issue was also likely to be less complicated for Robinson with Junior's influence drastically diminished. Speculation had rumbled for years over whether Paisley Snr would seek to eventually hand the leadership to his son. That would have been a very difficult task, even if Junior's lobbying activities had not landed him in trouble. It would have required Paisley Snr to stay in power well beyond 2008, thus giving his son the opportunity to build up his position.

On top of this, Junior lacked his father's charm and had irritated people in the party over the years during his rise to prominence. A realistic challenge to Robinson for the DUP leadership was probably always beyond him. However, he could still have caused problems internally—for instance by seeking to negotiate a top role for himself in return for declaring his support for Robinson's candidacy. The Paisley name would always carry clout and Junior could have set himself up as kingmaker. That was not going to happen in 2008, given the discomfiture he had been causing the party, his resignation from ministerial office and the resultant damage to his standing. Robinson could therefore plan for the future without worrying about keeping Paisley Jnr happy.

The DUP deputy leader had also been fortunate in other ways. His senior party colleagues knew full well that they found themselves in government with Sinn Féin as a result of Robinson's gameplan. As one high-level party source put it: 'The agreement that was reached was negotiated by Peter Robinson. Peter Robinson is the master strategist within the DUP and the master tactician.'

Yet Robinson had suffered much less damage than his party leader from the power-sharing U-turn. Paisley had been the one who emerged diminished—partly because of his unbending 'Never, Never, Never' rhetoric and posturing over the years. His Chuckle Brothers act with Martin McGuinness was also an important factor in the end, with the Dromore by-election clearly demonstrating that the hilarity was not playing well with unionist voters. Even hardline elements in the party were becoming increasingly convinced that a change of leadership was required. They might once have regarded Robinson with a level of suspicion. By February 2008, he was nevertheless preferable to an out-of-touch old man who refused to change his style and was harming the party's prospects.

Events—many of them well beyond his control—had been very kind to Peter Robinson in the first 10 months of devolution. This was indeed his perfect moment.

PAISLEY MUST GO

The desire for a change at the top was clearly evident within the DUP parliamentary party by this stage. But they faced an obvious problem on how to bring it about. Paisley Snr could not be counted upon to go quietly. There had been some talk in private from him about passing the burdens of leadership on to a younger generation. Yet in public, he kept on insisting that he would be serving his full timespan as First Minister.

A 'palace coup'—similar to the Conservative Party revolt that toppled Margaret Thatcher—was not an attractive option. It would at the very least have been messy and potentially very damaging to the party. Grass-roots members would never love Robinson the way they loved Paisley, and could cause trouble if the man they had followed for decades was harshly dumped. He would instead have to be eased out the door. The trick, as one DUP source has hinted to the author, was to make Paisley feel like it was his idea.

The task facing the leadership-in-waiting can be compared to a family trying to persuade a grandfather that he was getting too old to drive. It's not always easy to convince senior citizens that they are past it. Another analogy can be drawn from the world of football, and the tough decision Nottingham Forest took in 1993 in replacing the legendary Brian Clough as manager. Clough was able to resign with dignity, but would surely have been sacked if he had refused to go. It should be stressed that Clough's powers had been diminished by alcoholism, which is where any comparison with Paisley obviously ends.

The moves to ensure a friction-free succession in the DUP did not run entirely smoothly. One tactic used was to give briefings to selected national newspapers at key moments. That helped ensure ongoing conjecture about Paisley's future. It was akin to currency speculators starting a run on the pound.

A significant article appeared in the *Irish Times* in mid-January 2008—just before Paisley officially stood down as Moderator.[13] The article was written by the paper's London editor, Frank Millar. Millar is an acknowledged expert on unionism, and held a senior backroom post in the Ulster Unionist Party in the 1980s before switching to journalism. During that time, he and Peter Robinson were members of a joint unionist task force that pressed unsuccessfully for a new direction for their parties, involving a move towards power-sharing devolution.

Millar's January 2008 article stated that Paisley would be retiring from Westminster politics when the next British general election was called. 'The news will fuel feverish ongoing discussions among senior DUP MPs and Assembly Members about the possible timetable for the eventual election of Dr Paisley's successor as party leader,' it stated. Millar suggested that Nigel Dodds could be a contender alongside Robinson, in the event of Paisley finally declaring his intention to stand down. The article said:

> A majority of the DUP's MPs are now privately indicating their belief that this should be sooner rather than later, with some advocating a handover as early as this summer in order to allow a new leader to establish himself ahead of the general election in which the party hopes to increase further its Westminster representation.

It also suggested that one possible permutation involved Paisley relinquishing the DUP leadership, but staying on as First Minister until 2011. Millar quoted one unnamed MP pointedly questioning Paisley's 'capacity to continue doing the job' in light of his advanced years. 'The MP confirmed there was "no plot" to force the pace on the leadership issue, insisting "that isn't the nature" of the now widespread discussion about the timing of the succession,' the article concluded.

The *Irish Times* piece drew a frosty response from Paisley. Standing outside the Dungannon meeting where he handed over the top position in his church, he said: 'No Dublin newspaper will drive me out of a job.'[14] But there was no statement from the DUP parliamentary party refuting Millar's claims.

Three days after the *Irish Times* article, Paisley hit out at his church critics from the pulpit, claiming he was being 'satanically persecuted'.[15] That sermon even cited a scriptural basis for his chuckling routine—the injunction from the book of Matthew to be 'exceeding glad' while under attack.

Maybe he still had some battling left in him. However, the fall of Paisley Jnr the following month placed his father's prospects right at the top of the political agenda. Two days after his son's resignation, the First Minister found himself facing a press conference at Edinburgh Castle during a trip to meet his Scottish counterpart, Alex Salmond. Paisley reacted angrily to questions about his future, telling one reporter: 'I have a fairly hard rhinoceros skin—and I think I will not be skinned by you or the likes of you.' He also said: 'It's a wonder they didn't tell you I was dying of all sorts of diseases and that soon I would be carried out in a box—that's usually added to make it more spicy.'[16]

The speculation kept on coming. To add insult to injury, Irish bookmaker Paddy Power even tried to cash in on the situation, opening a book on when Paisley would step down. He had preached against gambling for years, and here was a Dublin bookie making his departure from office before the end of 2008 the odds-on favourite option. 'It's expected that Ian Paisley will resign, it's just a question of whether he'll do it sooner or later,' a spokeswoman for Paddy Power said.[17]

It was also a question that would not go away. Party sources kept playing their part in this regard, muttering quotes in the ears of journalists. On the day after the Edinburgh visit, the *Guardian*'s chief political correspondent, Nicholas Watt, quoted a 'well-placed DUP figure' as saying:

> There is no doubt the resignation of Ian Jr is a big blow to his father. If you'd asked anyone six months ago about his position you would say that he would have served a full four-year term as First Minister. But that has changed. He will now go sooner rather than later.[18]

The *Guardian* article also referred to a 'gentle campaign' at the 'highest levels' of the DUP to ease Paisley out. And it quoted a senior British government source saying: 'It is now expected that Ian Paisley will be gone by May.'

On the very same day that this article appeared, Frank Millar ran another well-sourced piece.[19] It stated that Paisley was 'being pressed by senior colleagues to set and name a date for his retirement later this year'. Millar said key party figures had approached the leader 'within the past few weeks' and before his son's resignation. His report also stated: 'Senior MPs and Assembly members keen to see an early handover are also stressing their desire to protect Dr Paisley's "legacy" and to allow him to go "at the moment of his choice". That is exactly how it turned out in the end.

The *Sunday Tribune*'s Suzanne Breen was also well informed on the situation, again thanks to DUP sources.[20] She reported that there was not a single senior DUP figure saying Paisley should stay on longer than a few months.

> The insistence that it's time to go unites all wings of the party: from the slick Robinson modernisers to the country-and-western Free Presbyterian fundamentalists. A seamless transition to a new leadership under Peter Robinson, with Nigel Dodds as his deputy, has already been discussed. It seems there will be no other challengers.

That prediction also proved 100 per cent correct. It was beginning to look like senior DUP personnel were using the press to send smoke signals to their leader. Whether or not he was getting the message was very much open to question at this point.

Loyal wife Baroness Paisley was not ready for him to go. Speaking to the *Belfast Telegraph*, the woman Paisley called 'Mammy' said:

> I want him to stay on, especially since he has been in this new government leading the country. He is doing a jolly good job. If he was not I would be the first one to say to him 'give it up'. His health is excellent, his mind is sharp and his body is strong. I would like him to continue until he has done what he set out to and that is achieve peace and prosperity and normality.[21]

A DUP source was having none of this, telling the paper:

> It is a very close and loving relationship and they have always shared everything. His wife is his most trusted and closest confidant, even more than Paisley Jnr. She would like him to stay but he is more accepting of the fact that that is not achievable. Given all the circumstances it is coming to the latter stages. There is a growing acceptance that it is going to happen, despite Mrs Paisley's wishes.

Baroness Paisley was fighting for her husband in private, as well as in public. This was the woman who the previous year had used the pages of her church magazine to savage critics of 'God's anointed leader'. She did not hold back within the DUP either. During an internal party meeting, the Baroness launched a stinging attack on MP and MLA Sammy Wilson. Wilson himself was not present to hear the onslaught. It is suspected as having been prompted by his BBC 'Spotlight' interview, when he voiced some criticism of Paisley Jnr and spoke briefly about Senior stepping down. Wilson was also a former boyfriend of one of the Paisley daughters, Rhonda.

The attack on him by Mammy did not play well within the party. It also highlighted that a smooth leadership succession might not be easy. Baroness Paisley's motives in wanting her elderly husband to stay in power can only be guessed it. But it is a safe assumption that the thought of Peter Robinson taking over did not fill her with unbounded joy. There is not an excess of warmth between the Paisley and Robinson households. The Baroness is never believed to have been over-burdened with affection for her husband's deputy, and was definitely never going to become Honorary President of the Iris Robinson Appreciation Society. The Ian Paisley–Peter Robinson relationship had been through some tricky patches over the years. In 1987, Robinson actually resigned as DUP deputy leader. No public explanation was ever given. Robinson returned to the post a couple of months later, and carried on as if nothing had happened.

Robinson's influence within the party grew steadily over the years following 1987. The DUP became much more professionally organised, with power and influence increasingly centralised around Robinson and his lieutenants. The east Belfast MP has been likened to Lenin and called a control freak by his critics. But his supporters can point to his success in steadily building the party into the dominant force in unionism.

Living with an unpredictable and headstrong leader like Paisley cannot always have been easy for a forensic organiser and planner like Robinson. There must have been times when the deputy anxiously held his breath while his leader went off on a rant at a press conference or meeting. Robinson could never be exactly sure what Paisley would say next, nor could he publicly disown his comments once they were made.

It is also clear that there were tensions in the long run-up to the 2007 devolution deal with Sinn Féin. Ex-DUP politician Jim Allister remembers Robinson being 'very uncomfortable' about one-to-one meetings between Paisley and Tony Blair. Allister says:

> Peter would have told me stories of Paisley having these meetings, the Northern Ireland Office or Downing Street officials not believing what they were hearing, ringing Robinson and saying we want to get this clear, Hain tells us that the DUP's position is x and Robinson saying let me tell you the DUP's position is nothing like x. That frustrated Peter immensely.

Allister cannot be regarded as a neutral witness, given his acrimonious split from the DUP over power-sharing. But his account is echoed by the recollections of a Downing Street source about the 2006 St Andrews negotiations that led the way to a deal. This source says there was a clear gap between Paisley and other DUP figures at the Scotland talks.

Stances taken by the party leader in exchanges with the British government did not find favour with DUP colleagues. 'They were saying Paisley's position is finished, he's really shot himself in the foot by taking this line, we don't support him,' the Downing Street source adds. While accepting that this apparent disagreement might have been a negotiating ploy, the source adds: 'It looked real.'

Internal DUP unease over Paisley's unpredictability can hardly have lessened much after devolution arrived. The 'senior moment' gaffes in the Assembly—when he read out the wrong answers to questions from the floor—must have been hard to watch. Party meetings at Stormont were also said to be less than focused at times. And then there was Paisley's refusal to tone down the jocularity with McGuinness when the First Ministers appeared together in public. All this fuelled a growing desire for change within the party's Assembly team. Paisley, though, was facing pressure on the home front to stay in power. It looked like a way would be needed to help shepherd him towards the door.

Around this time, documentation calling for action on the leadership issue was circulated for DUP Assembly members to sign. The available evidence, such as it is, points to this being a planned operation. One party source has described it as a way of gauging opinion within the Assembly team on the leadership. The documentation more closely resembled a letter than a petition. MLAS have privately said they signed it individually with no sight of the other names that may also have backed the call.

The full facts of the internal manoeuvre may be permanently lost to the history books, as a result of the DUP's strict confidentiality regime. Just like the mafia, *omertà*—the code of silence—applies here. As one member put it when talking somewhat nervously off the record: 'We're not allowed to comment on the letter. We're not allowed. There will be no comment on the letter.'

It seems the secret documentation never actually got as far as Paisley himself. But it is believed he was alerted about unrest in the ranks by Stormont Minister Edwin Poots, a long-time ally of the Paisleys. It seems too neat to suggest that it was actually part of the plan to have someone like Poots warn the party leader about the situation. But the fact that the 'message job'—to borrow another phrase from the mafia—was delivered did the operation no harm at all.

The fevered atmosphere within the party at the time the Baroness spoke out was intensified by Paisley Jnr. On 29 February, two days after 'Mammy' had gone public with her views on the leadership, new backbencher Junior was back in the news.

Seymour Sweeney confirmed he would be challenging the refusal on his Giant's Causeway centre scheme through the planning appeals process. Paisley Jnr responded with a press release backing the developer's move. It claimed the 'merits' of the proposal had been 'somewhat distorted by political comment and controversy over the applicant'. Supporting the appeal meant supporting Sweeney against DUP Minister Arlene Foster's decision.

That was not welcome news in the party. Hopes that Paisley Jnr would keep his head down for a few months following his ministerial resignation had been dashed. Worse was to follow.

Later on 29 February, it was announced that Paisley Jnr was to be one of the DUP's representatives on the Northern Ireland Policing Board. A vacancy had arisen because MP and MLA Jeffrey Donaldson had replaced Paisley Jnr as a junior minister.

Being on the Policing Board is one of the most high-profile political roles in Northern Ireland outside of government. The decision on Donaldson's replacement had been entirely down to Paisley Snr as party leader. His choice of his son caused anger within DUP ranks, understandably in view of all the adverse publicity Junior had been attracting to the party. It was also viewed by some observers as a de facto declaration of war against those agitating for a new leader.

First the Baroness had spoken out, then a plum frontline job was handed to the boy. It seemed that the Paisley clan might be sending out its own 'message job'. Yet just four days later, the old man was calling it quits. With the benefit of hindsight, the Policing Board appointment now looks more like a parting gift to the son.

Despite all the whispers, the abruptness of Paisley's retirement announcement took many by surprise. It was made through an interview with UTV's political editor, Ken Reid, broadcast on the teatime news slot on 4 March 2008. Paisley confirmed he would be standing down both as First Minister and DUP leader, shortly after a US Investment Conference planned for Belfast in May. This much-hyped Stormont government initiative was aimed at attracting new American money into the province.

Paisley's somewhat rambling UTV interview provided little insight into his reasons for quitting. His most recent public assertion that he would serve the full term had come in December, less than three months earlier. 'I'd like to have done that but I don't think that that is what I should do, and I became convinced that my decision was a right one, and I'm more convinced of that than ever I've been,' he told Reid. He also stated: 'I came to this decision a few weeks ago, when I was thinking very much about the conference and what was going to come after the conference. And I thought that that is a marker, a very big marker, and it would be a most appropriate time for me to bow out.'

The US Investment Conference did not look much like a 'very big marker' to anyone else, particularly with regard to the grave problems afflicting the American economy. It provided a convenient, if ultimately unconvincing, excuse for the sudden about-turn by Paisley.

His suggestion in the UTV interview that his mind had been made up 'a few weeks ago' was surprising. It would mean his decision to go had already been reached when his wife was telling the *Belfast Telegraph* that he should stay on.

The subject of his son was raised in the UTV interview. 'I think he has been wrongfully accused,' Paisley said. 'I think people who couldn't get after me got after him, thinking they could hurt me.' That conspiracy theory was aired in even stronger terms in a later interview that evening with BBC Northern Ireland's political editor, Mark Devenport. Paisley spoke of having 'attained what I wanted to attain' and passing the leadership on to the next generation. He denied being pressurised into retiring, claiming it was 'not easy' to push him around. 'I don't think I can be pressured, I'm too old in the hide for that,' he said.

His son's problems had not been a factor in his decision, Devenport was told. 'I never even considered it. I felt that my son was very badly treated but I knew, of course, and I'm not a fool, I have ears that are open and I have many people who inform me of what's going on,' Paisley continued. 'And of course I have people that thought they could get at me—they would get at him and in some way they would damage me by the damage that they sought to take out on him. But that didn't move me whatsoever.'

So there you have it—it was all about him. The Junior controversies were not really about public interest issues like accountability, lobbying, cronyism and use of taxpayer-funded expenses. They were all part of a fiendish plot against his dad.

Paisley's decision was met with warm tributes from the likes of Gordon Brown, Tony Blair and Bertie Ahern. Prime Minister

Brown said: 'Ian Paisley has made a huge contribution to political life in Northern Ireland and the United Kingdom.' Paula Dobriansky, George Bush's Special Envoy to Northern Ireland, stated: 'On behalf of the United States, I would like to congratulate Dr Ian Paisley on his service to the people of Northern Ireland, and his historic role in bringing about a peaceful political settlement that will ensure a better future for Northern Ireland.'[22]

Ian Paisley Jnr did not hold back on his emotions, describing his father as both standing 'in the pantheon of Ulster's greats' and being the 'finest son of Ulster'. He added: 'My tribute to him cannot be measured in the tape of words but in the silence of an ever-thankful heart, a bottomless cavern of gratitude, love, devotion and regard will forever echo his praises.'[23]

Paisley Snr brushed off questions about who should replace him as party leader. 'This is not the church of Rome,' he said. 'This is not apostolic succession and I have no right to say who'll succeed me.'[24] But it was immediately fairly obvious to everyone else that Robinson would take over, with Nigel Dodds as his deputy. The two positions were subsequently filled without an electoral contest taking place.

In the immediate wake of Paisley's 4 March announcement, Robinson and others set about trying to scotch allegations that a coup had been enacted. Ulster Unionist leader Sir Reg Empey, for instance, stated: 'This departure has been more brutal than that which was given to Margaret Thatcher in 1990. It was orchestrated, meticulously prepared and executed. It was a political coup.'[25]

Rumours were rife that almost all DUP MLAs had signed a petition calling for their leader to set a departure date. It was suggested that a special party officers' meeting would have been called in the event of a refusal. Paisley was said to have pre-empted the move by reaching his own decision to go before any documentation was handed to him. But Robinson said bluntly: 'Such a document does not exist.'

He confirmed he had spoken to Paisley about his departure plans, stating: 'The timetable I indicated to Ian when he told me he was considering this course was a timetable much longer than the one he has chosen. Ian Paisley has taken his decision and anybody who suggests it's anything other than that, I think doesn't know Ian Paisley.' Edwin Poots, meanwhile, stated: 'I never saw any letter; never signed any letter and I am absolutely sure there was never a letter handed to Dr Paisley at any stage.'

As Poots is understood to have told the Paisley camp about the conspiratorial whispers, the discontent in the party was actually conveyed without a letter having to be handed over. As for Robinson's declaration that such a document 'does not exist', this was actually a non-denial denial. The words he used do not rule out the possibility that paperwork had been shredded or otherwise destroyed by that stage. Also, the evidence indicates that there was never such a thing as a single document, as Assembly members had signed separate pieces of paperwork. That's unless the MLAs who did speak privately to the author of this book were making the whole thing up, for no discernible reason.

The word 'coup' does not really capture what happened in the party. It was more subtle than that. The essence of the approach had been captured by Frank Millar of the *Irish Times* in one of his well-judged speculation pieces quoted above. He wrote in February 2008: 'Senior MPs and Assembly members keen to see an early handover are also stressing their desire to protect Dr Paisley's "legacy" and to allow him to go "at the moment of his choice".'

He did in the end choose the exact moment, but they got their way as well. Put another way, he jumped before he had to be pushed. This meant, as one DUP source puts it, that he was able to go out 'with his head held high'. This same source, reflecting on the mood in the party, adds: 'There was never any Doc must stay campaign.' A public bust-up was avoided and no traces of blood could be seen on the carpet. It was all dependent on Paisley playing his part, not just in going but in saying the right things and not displaying any hints of resentment.

Like the old pro he was, he carried off the role extremely well. He said the lines, took the curtain call, and left the stage. The jibes about people attacking his son just to get at him provided the only hint of any lingering anger. There seems little doubt that there would have been a coup attempt had Paisley decided to stay and remain true to his word on a full term in office.

Whether he could have seen off the rebellion is highly debateable. His decades of experience would have told him that his chances of survival were limited, and that an open conflict would in any event be bad for the party. It was similar to the position he faced in September 2007 in his church. The choice on both occasions was between staying, fighting and very possibly losing— or just walking away.

The hard man of Ulster politics walked away both times. The official DUP history will record that his March 2008 decision to go was his alone. That is by no means the full story.

Chapter 14

Legacy Matters

'Who won the bloody war anyway?'
BASIL FAWLTY in the 'Fawlty Towers' episode 'The Germans'

'We're all part of the same hypocrisy'
MICHAEL CORLEONE, speaking to a politician in *The Godfather* II

Friday, 30 May 2008 was the date of the big DUP send-off for Ian Paisley.

The weeks since his resignation announcement of early March had been fairly uneventful. The US Investment Conference had been and gone, amid much hope and hype. No one stood against Peter Robinson for the party leadership, and Nigel Dodds was similarly unopposed for the vacated deputy role.

With the Robinson era beckoning, the party faithful flocked to the King's Hall in Belfast on 30 May for its official farewell to the old chief. It was here in 1998 that supporters of the Belfast Agreement had triumphantly chanted 'Cheerio, Cheerio' at Paisley after the 71 per cent referendum vote for the deal. They underestimated him and his party. But now it really was goodbye. Robinson would officially take over as party leader and First Minister over the course of the following week.

The Friday night farewell bash for Paisley at the King's Hall was a showpiece event. Besuited young DUP turks busied themselves around the conference hall, making sure everything was in place. The party faithful attended in force, as they were expected to do. Perhaps some of the grey-haired contingent there were still secretly troubled by the way it had all turned out. They had fiercely opposed power-sharing down through the years at their leader's urging. Also present that night were DUP personnel who had been eagerly pushing for Paisley's departure for months. But such thoughts were buried away, and affection for the departing boss was the emotion on display.

The big gathering would be followed by a more exclusive £100-a-plate dinner attended by such c-list dignitaries as the Speaker of the House of Commons Michael Martin and Northern Ireland Secretary Shaun Woodward. But the main event was the public farewell, which included a warm-up speech by Robinson and a slick video presentation on Paisley's career, entitled 'A Man for All Seasons'.

The man himself then entered the auditorium, cheered and clapped as he made his way to the platform. He looked a bit like a veteran heavyweight boxing champion putting in one last crowd-pleasing performance before finally hanging up his gloves. The sharpness and flourishes of the past were largely gone. His farewell speech stuck mainly to the script, reading out the prepared text with few of the rhetorical ad libs of the glory years. The content was padded out with religious quotes. Jut like an ageing boxer, he still had some of the old moves and routines. But they lacked the snap and the impact they once had.

The following Thursday in the Assembly, he was saying cheerio as First Minister.[1] His successor Robinson had some well-chosen warm words of tribute. 'He has laid the foundation for this new era, and it is now up to the rest of us to build on it,' he said. 'Ian, many of us are glad that you did say no and that you did say never. There are questions to which no and never are the right answers.'

In his speech, DUP chief whip Lord Morrow said: 'Prior to the arrival of Dr Paisley, unionism was led by "big house" unionists and landowners. Dr Paisley changed all that and provided a voice for the working class.' There was praise too from Sinn Féin President Gerry Adams. He told MLAs that he had not spoken directly with Paisley until 26 March 2007—the day the power-sharing deal was agreed. 'Throughout all of our engagements, I have found him cordial and respectful, and I am convinced that the good humour, grace and enthusiasm that he displayed in public were good for public confidence and for all the people of this island,' Adams added.

It fell to others to provide a less positive context. Alliance leader David Ford said history would judge 'whether Ian Paisley is remembered for 40 years of saying no or for one year of saying maybe'. Declan O'Loan of the SDLP stated:

> Future historians will wrestle with the enigma with which they have been presented by the actions of Ian Paisley over the past 14 months of his political career when contrasted with those of the previous 40 years. In these past 14 months, he has done the right things—indeed the only things that could create a society at peace. Those things involved the elements of partnership government and North/South co-operation for which this party has always stood. We cannot ignore the fact that Ian Paisley stood resolutely against those things for all those long years.

The Paisley enigma goes well beyond the issue of saying yes after decades of saying never. This was a man who could often be charming, humble, compassionate and humorous. Yet there were also many instances of venomous outbursts, incendiary language, egotism and all-round ungraciousness.

Northern Ireland's evangelical Protestant community—which provided some of Paisley's core support for many years—is also full of contrasts and contradictions. There is a degree of sincerity and warmth among many of them that often goes unrecognised. Against this, they can be judgmental, aggressive and well capable of starting a blazing row on an obscure point of morality or theology. They also have a reputation for abstemiousness, while quite a few of them could eat their bodyweight in steaks and buns given half a chance.

No one is ever going to come up with the definitive explanation of the central Paisley mystery, as described by Declan O'Loan in the Assembly. Just why exactly did he end up striking a deal with his sworn enemies in view of all he had said and done over the years? Historians—not to mention psychologists—could debate this question for ever. Theories are inevitably coloured by people's views of the agreement that he backed. That is clear from the various assessments that will be quoted in this chapter. Some recurring themes emerge from the different opinions, including the impact of the ill-health that almost claimed his life in 2004.

Paisley's brush with death occurred in the run-up to the unsuccessful Leeds Castle party talks on restoring devolution. Tight secrecy was maintained within his family and party over the cause of the problems. Rumours of cancer and a leaking heart valve were firmly dismissed. But Paisley later admitted to his congregation that he had walked 'along death's shadows'.[2] And his clergyman son Kyle spoke of his father using the phrase 'at death's door' about himself.[3]

A senior source in the DUP believes being close to death did influence Paisley's outlook. 'I think his illness convinced him that if he was to secure political legacy, then he needed to get on with the negotiations and to do a deal—not a deal at any price it should be said but in the right circumstances, he was prepared to make agreement.' This source also says:

Why did he do the deal? Number one, because he believed firmly that it was the right deal. Secondly, he had had a long and successful political career and he wanted to confound the old adage that all political careers ended in failure. He wanted to lead the unionist people into a future where the violence would be a thing of the past.

This DUP figure also believes that Paisley wanted to be remembered as a 'man of peace'—and recalls him using this very phrase outside 10 Downing Street in 2004. There are strong grounds for believing that Paisley and his wife became increasingly mindful of his legacy, and that the health factor helped to bring it into focus. Clearly, the suspicion that he would prevent Robinson and other underlings agreeing a political accommodation started to fade from 2004 onwards.

Peter Hain found himself pleasantly surprised by Paisley's

attitude on meeting him after becoming Secretary of State in May 2005. A Northern Ireland Office (NIO) source says: 'From the very beginning, Peter was quite shocked. Paisley was not what he expected and had already undergone some kind of conversion.'

According to a Downing Street source, Blair was convinced by 2004 that Paisley was up for an agreement. This view took hold following talks at Lancaster House in the first half of that year— even before Paisley's health crisis. 'Up until Lancaster House, Tony had been convinced that Paisley didn't want to do a deal,' the government source says. The Downing Street insider nevertheless believes that legacy and the serious health scare were important factors. 'He literally wanted to end up as Dr Yes rather than Dr No,' he claims.

Critics level charges of egotism, pride and desire for power into the mix. Paisley's conversion to partnership government only came after he and his party had muscled their way to the top in unionism. That meant he would be the head man in a new power-sharing administration. A keen amateur historian, Paisley was clearly very taken with the idea of being Northern Ireland's 'Prime Minister'—of sitting where previous famous leaders of unionism like Craigavon had sat. In his last Assembly speech as First Minister, Paisley said: 'Sixty years ago, I first came to this House to watch a debate. Little did I think that I would sit one day in the seat of the Prime Minister.'[4]

Jim Allister, who left the DUP over the 2007 Sinn Féin deal, believes the lure of the First Minister's post became irresistible. Asked to explain why his former leader said yes, Allister states bluntly: 'It has to be the desire for power and the ego. I wouldn't dismiss the psychological and political impact of Ian Paisley being, in his terms, kicked around for 40 years by the establishment and then seeing an opportunity to be the establishment and being unable to resist it.'

Allister also believes Tony Blair played on Paisley's ego in one-to-one meetings prior to the celebrated deal. There has been much speculation on the subject matter of those private Blair–Paisley discussions. Drawings by Paisley's daughter Rhonda for Blair's son

Leo were apparently handed over.

There were also conversations on theological matters, with reading matter provided for the Prime Minister. Just how much spiritual guidance Blair actually took from the head of the Free Presbyterian Church is debateable. It did not prevent him making his long-predicted conversion to Catholicism after leaving office. Allister says: 'They knew which buttons to press with Paisley. I remember him coming back to a party officers' meeting and him saying: "Blair's a very troubled man spiritually, he asked me for a bible." It wasn't me—I wish it had been—but somebody said: "Dr Paisley, do you think the Prime Minister wouldn't have a bible?"'

Blair had not always treated Paisley with the utmost respect. In his book on the peace process, Blair's chief of staff Jonathan Powell recalled Paisley being 'almost hysterical' with anger on the phone with the Prime Minister following the 1998 Belfast Agreement. Powell wrote: 'I spoke to Tony afterwards, worried that he would be in shock, but he said he could not really take the call seriously as he was with the children watching *The Simpsons* on TV at the time.'[5]

The Downing Street sweet-talking operation kicked in later, after unionist disillusionment had all but finished off David Trimble and the UUP. Powell recalled Paisley being 'clearly flattered' by the attention he received from Blair in 2004.[6] Former SDLP Deputy First Minister Seamus Mallon says: 'It is remarkable how even the most robust of unionists start to get wobbly at the knees when a British Prime Minister fawns on them. You'd think that by now they would know that it's not in their interests.'[7]

Mallon identifies key milestones in the journey made by Paisley and his party. These included the decision to accept two ministerial posts in the ill-fated power-sharing administration set up under the Belfast Agreement. The DUP thus became part of the government it was vowing to destroy. Its two ministers refused to take part in wider Executive business, due to Sinn Féin's presence. 'Having taken those two ministerial posts, without accepting collective responsibility or attending an Executive meeting—it simply pointed to party advantage with no beliefs whatsoever,' Mallon argues. 'I think the lack of conviction, the lack of firm belief in what they stood for became evident then. Men of principle, if they felt the way they said they felt about it, would have acted as an opposition, rather than take the positions of privilege and influence.'

The former Deputy First Minister also sees deep significance in Paisley securing seats in the House of Lords for his wife and other party colleagues. The man who fought hard against 'big house unionism' was making the 'ultimate leap into the establishment' by accepting places in the Lords, he says. 'That gave a fair indication that the Paisley of protest, the Paisley of anti-big-house unionism, the man of the people Paisley was part of his public presentation for a number of years to get power. It was very easily jettisoned when he got the sniff of power.'

But the former SDLP MP believes that in the end there was also something deeper at work than just the allure of high office. 'I did have conversations with him on a number of occasions,' Mallon adds.

> One of them was when he came back to Westminster after being very ill and I accompanied him from the plane. He was a very frail man. I got the feeling then of a man who was looking over the brink into eternity. I had the feeling there was more to it than just the lust for power or wanting to leave his mark on history. I think there was another dimension to it and I think that dimension was spiritual. I like to think that the motivation was to leave a better place than he had previously fostered. I like to think that he had this spiritual motivation; that he wanted to make amends as it were for the damage that he had done over many years—and it was substantial damage.

For his part, former First Minister David Trimble admits to being surprised that Paisley did finally sign up to an agreement. 'I knew that the Robinson camp wanted to do a deal. I also knew that the Robinson camp felt they couldn't sell a deal unless Paisley's thumb print was on it. I knew that Paisley was necessary for them,' he says.

Trimble's scepticism about Paisley was based on the experience of the 1975 Constitutional Convention, one of many failed devolution talks sessions over the years. A voluntary coalition between unionist parties and the SDLP was firmly on the agenda at the Convention, but was eventually opposed by the DUP. 'In 1975, a deal was done with the SDLP. Paisley endorsed the deal,' Trimble says. 'A few days later, Paisley turned turtle and what we understood was that he received a delegation from the Free Presbyterian Church, who told him that if he did this, the church would split.' Trimble therefore took the view that if Paisley had to choose between the church and politics, he would always side with the church. That's why he did not expect the 2006 St Andrews talks to turn out the way they did. 'I said to myself—when the crunch really comes, will he do it? I was surprised, I have to confess.'

Trimble believes the Robinson gameplan on devolution was devised years before St Andrews, and involved destroying pro-Agreement unionism and then slipping into its shoes. 'I think the Robinson camp had decided on this strategy probably sometime around 2000.'

It can certainly be argued that the settlement Paisley endorsed was a reasonable one for unionism, as the DUP constantly maintains. Writer and former Provisional IRA prisoner Anthony McIntyre has reached that conclusion. McIntyre says: 'It was a good deal for unionism. I dare say Paisley would turn down a good deal for unionism, if it wasn't good for him personally. He got the balance of what was good for him personally and good for unionism politically. That's what he got out of it.'

McIntyre contrasts the fortunes of Paisley with those of Sinn Féin President Gerry Adams.

Adams signed up to everything he tried to overthrow. The key dividing line here is the consent principle, which is the partition principle. If Paisley was to have accepted terms similar to Adams, what he would have accepted was a British declaration to withdraw, a Dublin declaration to overtake the north, and a united Ireland at some stage in the future. That would have been a major disaster for unionism, yet when republicans go for something of the same scale in reverse, it's considered a compromise.

The consent principle—that it is for the residents of Northern Ireland to decide which state to belong to—was enshrined in the 1998 Belfast Agreement, which Paisley so vociferously opposed. This point is acknowledged by McIntyre, who believes Paisley was 'standing on the shoulders of David Trimble' when he sealed his deal. 'There is no doubt that Paisley compromised,' he adds. 'He made major about-turns and major retreats. He's a very disingenuous and ambitious man. In terms of his personality, he made major somersaults. In terms of what unionism secured, he did not make the somersaults Adams did. Adams made somersaults personally and politically.'

Writer Danny Morrison, a former senior Sinn Féin figure, rubbishes suggestions that Paisley emerged victorious over republicanism. He says:

> A variety of fools subscribe to that school—some, former members of the republican movement, because they themselves need to invert their own sense of demoralisation and lack of programme by blaming someone like Gerry Adams; and others out of long personal animus to the ongoing success of republicans and the resilience of republicanism in handling all contingencies, including the challenges of the peace process and the demand for a pragmatic approach. Certainly, the unionist community do not believe it has triumphed and it has experienced massive problems coming to terms with the reality and assertion of political strength by the republican movement.

Morrison continues:

> Paisley's publicly stated agenda was to smash 'Sinn Féin/IRA' and instead he finally went into government with them, perhaps to be remembered as a peacemaker and help undo his tarnished image as a bigot and demagogue. The guerrillas fought and the

guerrillas are now in government would hardly be described by any revolutionary organisation around the world as a definition of failure! After he went into government with former IRA leader Martin McGuinness we heard no more of Paisley's classic rhetoric.

Morrison also states:

> Does anyone believe that three and a half thousand people would still have lost their lives if the Belfast Agreement had been signed on Good Friday 1969? In that respect, we all lost and we all failed and we all should feel guilty and that means the British government also owning up to the magnitude of state terrorism. For republicans the Belfast Agreement is a work in progress which they believe is an essential component in the transition to a united Ireland.

When bowing out of office, Paisley did not take the opportunity to finally provide a full and credible explanation for his actions. He was asked in one interview just before he stood down as First Minister if his brush with death in 2004 had influenced his decision. He replied: 'No, except that it brought home to me that if I was going to do something I need to do it quickly.'[8] In the same interview, he also said that such an experience 'concentrates your desire to achieve something that you feel you need to achieve'.

Paisley has spoken of his desire to write his own version of the talks process that eventually led to him heading a power-sharing government. Anyone expecting a candid no-holds-barred self-assessment is likely to be disappointed. In an interview for RTÉ's 'Late Late Show' in January 2009, Paisley said he had 'no regrets' about his life in politics.[9]

The question of exactly why he said yes after decades of saying no will probably never be fully resolved. There were occasional signs over the years of him being tempted in the direction of a potential devolution deal. The 1975 voluntary coalition initiative recalled by Trimble above is the most obvious example of this. A year later, an NIO official wrote in a confidential briefing memo: 'It is not inconceivable that Paisley would seek a political accommodation with the SDLP if he felt his position to be unassailable.'[10]

Another potential deal was in the air in the early period of Margaret Thatcher's Conservative government, when Sir Humphrey Atkins was Secretary of State. It seemed for a brief while then that Paisley—fresh from his poll-topping success in the 1979 European election—was pondering the notion of being Northern Ireland's Prime Minister.[11] Of course, the diehard DUP followers continued to be fed the old-fashioned 'No surrender' diet down through the decades, whatever hints of possible flexibility from their leader were being detected by the British government.

Paisley biographer Ed Moloney has scrutinised the mystery of Paisley's about-turn, and has wondered if maybe the wrong question is in fact being asked. He has suggested that the more appropriate question may be whether Paisley ever fully believed the message he propagated to his supporters.[12] Many ex-followers are still loyal to the political principles he preached, and a large number of them will probably end their days in bitterness and confusion. They obviously do not buy the idea that their one-time revered leader triumphed over republicanism.

Former close allies of Paisley are among those estranged from him these days. They include Rev. Ivan Foster, the now retired Free Presbyterian Minister, who threw snowballs with him at a visiting Irish Taioseach in the 1960s. Desmond Boal, the leading Belfast lawyer who co-founded the DUP with Paisley, is also in the ranks of the disaffected. So incensed was Boal at the Sinn Féin power-sharing deal that he returned Paisley-penned books that had been gifted to him by his old friend over the years.

Clifford Smyth, a onetime DUP politician and Free Presbyterian member, is also deeply critical. Smyth, the author of a book on Paisley published in the 1980s, looks at the Paisley legacy from an evangelical Christian perspective. He comments:

Throughout both his church career and in political life Ian

Paisley demanded standards from others which, when the challenge came, he wasn't willing to adhere to himself. To those who failed to match the standards that Paisley had set, whether doctrinal verities, women wearing trousers in church, or line-dancing,[13] the discipline of moralising Paisleyism was applied with vehemence and denunciation. Simple souls were uprooted and thrown out of churches, subjected to cat-calls by the Paisleyites and generally harassed. In politics, it was cage fighting for years, until unionism was a splintered wreck, leaving Paisley and the DUP astride the wood-chippings. It's hard to escape the conclusion that Ian Paisley's egoism and pragmatism undermined his own 'principled stand', exposing him to the charge that he was a hypocrite.

Smyth adds:

His party, the DUP, puts on a Sabbath face one day a week, but the rest of the time enters into the rough and tumble of worldly political activity with unholy zeal. The consequences of this fractured witness are devastating—many of the unshockable media are reinforced in their cynicism about life without meaning and convinced that Christian fundamentalism is bogus. Worsted in early encounters with rumbustious Paisleyism, the Irish Presbyterian Church has become withdrawn, pietistic, and middle-class; Paisley's own denomination is heart-broken and privately extremely disillusioned; while a deeply divided unionist electorate finds itself in an undemocratic, unBritish and sectarian constitutional arrangement in which violence has been rewarded, and the manipulation of public sentiment is the norm.

Paisley may well have convinced himself that he led his people to a famous victory over republicanism. Some of his erstwhile supporters fervently believe that it was actually a defeat. From another perspective, the central achievement for unionism—

acceptance of the consent principle—was actually notched up under David Trimble's watch. It is also straining credibility to claim that Sinn Féin has been entirely routed, given that it is now at the heart of devolved government. To rephrase Danny Morrison, the guerrillas fought and ended up part of the new establishment—and their old enemies have had to live with it. Maybe, instead of winners and losers, Northern Ireland has been left with something like a score draw. Thankfully, there seems to be little enthusiasm among the players or the fans for extra time or a replay.

There is no great feeling in the Protestant community of a great triumph having been achieved. The more common feelings are a growing disinterest in politics, or simply relief that the violence is over. The Protestant working class—supposedly rescued from the clutches of big-house unionism by Paisleyism—do not appear to be revelling in the spoils of peace. Even before the global economic downturn kicked in, there were signs of serious disaffection and neglect in Protestant urban districts. This is very evident in the crucial area of educational achievement.

The influential House of Commons Public Accounts Committee conducted an investigation in 2006 into numeracy and literacy levels in the province. This was not some trendy lefty review, incidentally—the Committee was chaired by Conservative MP Edward Leigh, a diehard old-school Thatcherite. Its report highlighted 'significant differences' in the performance of Protestant and Catholic children from working class Belfast communities at GCSE English and Maths.[14] It compared the situation to Glasgow, where there was 'a reasonable degree of consistency' between Catholic and non-denominational schools. This was 'certainly not the case' for the sector teaching Belfast's working class Protestants, the report stated. 'Here, schools with 40% or more pupils entitled to free school meals do disturbingly less well than their Catholic counterparts, as well as much less well than their counterparts in Glasgow.' The MPs concluded that the disparity was 'one of the major challenges' facing Northern Ireland. Yet the report barely registered on the local political scene, and was not pursued with any vigour by the DUP. It instead stuck firmly to its policy of vigorously defending the grammar school system.

Veteran journalist Eamonn Mallie has also tried to highlight what is effectively a crisis in education in some Protestant areas. He amassed figures showing that only a small percentage of children from working class Protestant districts are securing places in grammar schools. 'I am absolutely bewildered by the position taken by unionists in the Assembly who represent these areas, who are blindly affording these kids no opportunity,' Mallie commented. 'There is no way forward for these children in these areas.'[15]

It was claimed at the Assembly on Paisley's last day as First Minister that he had provided a voice for the working class. That has not been particularly evident in the education field.

Any appraisal of Paisley's legacy should include his religious ministry. After all, this must have been the abiding priority of his long life. According to his creed, spiritual battles always take precedence over passing political matters. In this arena, Paisley's record is not one of soaring success. For all its influence on politics through the DUP, the Free Presbyterian Church never came close to being a major denomination.

Back in the early 1970s, in the first years of the Troubles, Paisley's church declared that only an evangelical revival could save Northern Ireland from the 'engulfing tides of evil' it was facing. That meant the threat from the 'Roman Catholic state' across the border and the 'strong fifth column of sympathisers and compromisers within'. It added: 'The only effective answer to encroaching Romanism is a revived and revitalised Protestantism, believing the Bible, proclaiming the Bible and practising the Bible.'[16] By 2007, however, Paisley was claiming that the province had in fact been delivered through his own God-guided political leadership.

Seven months into his brief term as First Minister, in December 2007, a revealing survey was published by Christian organisations. The first ever opinion poll on biblical knowledge in the province had been commissioned by the Evangelical Alliance (Northern Ireland) and other groups. The findings shed light on the extent of a decline in religion in the province.[17]

Only 42 per cent of respondents knew there were four gospels in the Bible (Catholics—52 per cent, Protestants—36 per cent) while 54 per cent could name the Holy Trinity (Catholics—65 per cent, Protestants—45 per cent). In addition, a mere 31 per cent could say the first commandment (Catholics—39 per cent, Protestants—26 per cent) and 60 per cent were able to name the first book of the Bible (Catholics—54 per cent, Protestants—68 per cent). Just 31 per cent could identify Martin Luther as the man who started the Reformation.(Catholics—30 per cent, Protestants—32 per cent).

The Northern Ireland figures were even more startling for the 16–24 age bracket. For example, only 21 per cent of poll respondents in this age group knew there were four gospels and just 17 per cent could say the First Commandment.

Stephen Cave of Evangelical Alliance (Northern Ireland) commented: 'The results of this poll throw serious doubt on the claim that we are a "Christian country". Overall the figures are not good but the drop in knowledge, almost halved within a generation, indicates that the Christian faith is becoming less meaningful to those under 25 years of age.'

Announcing the poll results, the Christian groupings also cited research on church attendance in both parts of Ireland. A 2006 poll found that 67 per cent of people in the Republic attended church at least monthly while a more recent survey gave the figure for north of the border as 45 per cent.

Northern Ireland is obviously not alone in experiencing an increasing trend towards secularisation. And it would be somewhat harsh, to say the least, to put all the blame on Paisley for the ongoing decline in religious observance among Protestants. Set against that, it is hard to think of a more prominent clergyman in the province over the past half century.

His critics—including some within the evangelical community—can argue that he has not always presented a positive image of Christianity, or acted as a beacon of faith, hope and charity. Paisley has spent a lot of time in the limelight during his life, as the subject of countless hours of media attention. In politics, he eventually rose to the very top to become Northern Ireland's

First Minister. But in religious terms, the balance sheet from his high-profile career has been nowhere near as healthy. He proved in the end to be much more successful at winning DUP votes than persuading people to follow his spiritual message.

He is one of Northern Ireland's most famous sons and its best-known gospel preacher over many years. Yet his ministry was drawing to a close with over half the population ignorant of basic biblical details and staying away from church.

Chapter 15
Life After Paisley

'The creatures outside looked from pig to man, and from man to pig, and from pig to man again: but already it was impossible to say which was which.'
GEORGE ORWELL, *Animal Farm*, 1945

Just as Peter Robinson was preparing to take over from Ian Paisley as First Minister, the proud boasts about the stability of Northern Ireland's new political settlement were beginning to sound less convincing. Sinn Féin started to whisper that it might veto Robinson's nomination in the Assembly, thereby triggering a crisis that could lead to a fresh election. In the event, the veiled threat was not acted upon. But that did not mean Sinn Féin was happy. It instead put a block on meetings of the power-sharing Executive. The stand-off led to a backlog of decisions on issues that cut across more than one department.

Sinn Féin's main grievance was a lack of progress towards the devolution of policing and justice powers. This was a major piece of unfinished business from the 2006 St Andrews Agreement. The DUP was in no hurry to act, arguing that confidence in the unionist community was not sufficiently strong for the move. Sinn Féin was also frustrated on other fronts. Plans for the redevelopment of the former Maze Prison site, involving a conflict resolution centre as well as a new sports stadium, were being dumped. Another item on the Sinn Féin wish list, an Irish Language Act, was also being stymied by the DUP, and hopes of an agreed way forward on reforming the post-primary education system were fading fast as well.

Under the power-sharing system, mutual agreement was needed to progress major projects. Sinn Féin was discovering to its chagrin that changes it wanted to see could be vetoed by the DUP. The DUP's repeated proclamations to its supporters that it was running Stormont also hardly helped the mood in the republican base. So the stalemate kicked in and week after week passed without the Executive sitting down together.

The bizarre situation—a government continuing to rule without actually meeting—lasted for some five months. It was similar to a game of 'chicken' on the roads, where boy racers drive towards each other until one finally swerves away. At one point it seemed that the Assembly could be heading for an actual smash-up. But a secretive deal between the DUP and Sinn Féin led to Executive meetings finally being resumed in November. No target date for the devolution of policing and justice powers was announced, but some kind of agreed approach had been worked out.

At one level, the two parties could say that they both gained from the mini-crisis. Sinn Féin could claim to its voters that it was still more than capable of fighting its corner. And the DUP's new leader was boosted by being able to demonstrate that he could hold the line against republicans. The Chuckle Brothers era, which had ended up something of an embarrassment, was brought to an end.

As part of the November deal-making, pleas were made to the British government on public expenditure arrangements. This helped to secure a further one-year postponement of household water charges, to April 2010. The move was announced immediately after the first post-stalemate Executive meeting. Perhaps working up a threat to the whole Stormont system was the best way to prise some more money from the Treasury's depleted coffers. But the idea of a win-win from the stand-off only really worked from a political class perspective, which is an increasingly remote standpoint. In the real world, yet more damage was done to the reputation of the fledgling devolved institutions.

The Executive's repeated failure to meet in the second half of 2008 came on top of the five-year suspension of devolution between 2002 and 2007. It also coincided with a period when the global and local economies were deteriorating badly. Of course, there was relatively little Stormont ministers could have done to counteract the looming recession. But voters were entitled to expect some concerted action to help cushion the region from crisis.

The whole experience once again highlighted doubts about the structure of politics in post-conflict Northern Ireland. Predictions of a full-scale Assembly collapse nevertheless started to look a little foolish once the stand-off ended. Robinson and McGuinness struck a businesslike tone, while every effort was made by ministers to outline the many measures being taken to boost the economy. The DUP and Sinn Féin continued to have some set-piece spats—in particular from the backbenches—on traditional unionist-nationalist issues of disagreement. But at a senior level they also got on by and large with the job of governing together.

A separate source of friction did remain at the Executive—between the DUP and Sinn Féin on the one hand and the smaller government parties, the SDLP and the UUP, on the other. As a result, it became fashionable in SDLP circles by early 2009 to castigate the two-party 'politburo' in charge of the government.

There were still opportunities for the DUP and Sinn Féin to face both ways. The DUP repeatedly insisted that the 2009 European election—with three Northern Ireland seats again up for grabs—would be all about stopping Sinn Féin topping the poll. Its candidate, Diane Dodds, wife of the party's deputy leader, Nigel, was the only unionist capable of achieving this vital task, it stressed. The fact that the same Sinn Féin was also its main power-sharing government partner did not seem to cause any embarrassment at all. This DUP electioneering tactic boosted Sinn Féin as well. It could urge nationalist voters to help it achieve the apparently all-important poll-topping prize.

A stability of sorts was nevertheless in place. Paisley was gone and his son was a mere backbencher, for the time being at least. However, the other House of Paisley—the political construction he helped establish at Stormont—is still standing. It can at times be a nasty, blinkered and ill-tempered house, which is maybe a fitting enough monument to the man. But how well was the system actually serving the public?

MALFUNCTIONING MACHINE

It is easy to criticise MLAs and their parties for the performance of the Assembly. That is not to say there is no talent at Stormont, either in the ministerial ranks or on the backbenches. There are some very good and clever people in Northern Ireland politics. Unfortunately, the good ones are not always that clever and the clever ones are not necessarily good.

The Assembly has for the most part been uninspiring since May 2007. There is no collective responsibility in the Executive. Debates and other exchanges in the chamber are all too often lifeless. Votes are passed with no bearing on the decisions of individual ministers or the Executive. The cross-party committees have hardly terrified Departments with their scrutinising zeal. Overall, the place has what could politely be called a capacity deficit. But it is too trite to blame this all on individual politicians.

What passes for politics in Northern Ireland is very much part of the problem. The blunt truth is that elected representatives can easily get by with little or no knowledge of bread-and-butter policy issues. Their job has boiled down to being seen to lobby for their constituencies, while standing up to the 'other side' on time-honoured subjects like parade routes, flags and emblems and the carve-up of public resources. Politics in the province does not divide on economic or social affairs. It is fundamentally about who shouts loudest, and scraps hardest, for the Protestant and Catholic communities. In that environment, it is not that surprising that the DUP and Sinn Féin have risen to the top.

Elections are likewise not fought on who has the best programme for the economy, or the most generous spending commitments for the NHS. Over the long period of Direct Rule, a central role of Northern Ireland politicians was to keep on demanding more cash from the British government. Not that much has changed. Many of the big decisions are still taken in London, including those on taxation and overall expenditure levels.

Since 1997, such decisions have been the responsibility of a New Labour government without a single Northern Ireland vote to its name. The party of Tony Blair and Gordon Brown has never stood for election in the province. That raises an interesting—but rarely asked—question on whether Northern Ireland is really a democracy. It is the London government that sets the fiscal framework for Stormont's devolved administration. Whitehall also controls the main levers of economic policy—plus a lot more besides. Yet the New Labour central government has never sought a mandate from this section of the UK state, nor had to worry about the electoral consequences of its decisions.

Northern Ireland politics has remained distant from most of the big policy decisions and debates. Stuck within these limits, it has not moved away from its traditional sectarian patterns. This does not mean that its elected representatives are all hate-filled bigots. Some of them can even be quite nice. However, the political set-up they operate in is communal in nature, and based on Protestants versus Catholics.

A belated fully-fledged entry by Gordon Brown's party into the fray is unlikely any time soon, and would hardly make any difference at this stage. New Labour is not even capable of energising its base in Great Britain these days.

It is not just Labour that has contributed to the entrenchment of politics. In the heady months following the 2007 power-sharing deal, there was talk of Fianna Fáil extending into the north, or merging with the SDLP. Its enthusiasm for such a move quickly faded. The Irish Labour Party has also set its face against contesting elections north of the border.

The British Conservative Party has recently taken a different and somewhat strange approach. It has pursued a link-up with the Ulster Unionist Party that looks to be little more than an alliance— or dalliance—of convenience. Having been almost obliterated by the DUP, the UUP is presumably glad to have any friends left.

Meanwhile, Tory leader David Cameron wants to build up his standing in the UK regions to dispel the notion that his party's appeal is limited to England. At the time of writing, a full merger between the UUP and Conservatives was not on the agenda. Instead, an electoral pact was emerging under the less than snappy title of 'Ulster Unionist and Conservative—New Force'.

The link-up has greatly annoyed the DUP, so it has already worked for the UUP to some extent. Nevertheless, predictions that it could help transform the face of politics seem wide of the mark. Rightly or wrongly in Northern Ireland, unionist has meant, and will continue to mean, Protestant. The UUP had until relatively recently a formal connection with the Orange Order. It also ran the old majority rule Stormont government up to 1972, which was not exactly adored by the Catholic community.

The UUP has been coming under pressure from the DUP to agree an electoral pact on two Westminster seats—South Belfast and Fermanagh–South Tyrone—that could be won back from nationalists. That would make sense in traditional Protestant unionist terms, but is impossible to square with the idea of a new non-sectarian Tory–UUP political force.

The truth is that anyone hoping for a change in Northern Ireland politics is unlikely to receive much practical help from outside. It has been a long-standing goal of the British Establishment to keep the place at arm's length as much as possible. The Dublin government now has pretty much the same attitude. Thus, the place is being left to stew in its own juices.

It is not uncommon among the chattering classes of Belfast to hear the phrase 'We get the politicians we deserve.' But in truth the blame does not altogether rest on the home front. The political framework has very much favoured the status quo, with the current Stormont arrangements underlining this in-built bias very effectively.

STITCHED UP A TREAT

All members of the Assembly have to designate themselves as unionist, nationalist or other. This branding exercise has a purpose. In certain votes, where a cross-community majority is required, the votes of MLAs designated as 'other' do not carry the same weight.

Of the 108 current Assembly members, 97 of them belong to Stormont's four governing parties. That's almost 90 per cent. Of these, 63 are in either the DUP or Sinn Féin, the so-called 'politburo' parties. Both these parties are tightly managed from the centre. There is little danger of any of their MLAS going seriously off-message—or getting away with it. The DUP leadership has unsigned resignation letters from its members, which it could implement at any given moment to silence a dissident. The four governing parties also hold all the chairmanship posts of the Assembly's scrutinising committees. That reduces the chances of any committee seriously rocking the boat.

Since the Assembly was established under the 1998 Belfast Agreement, there has never been a by-election. A small number of MLAS have died in office in that time, and were replaced by co-opted party colleagues without the need to involve voters in any way.

The Assembly also has no official opposition, although the seven-member Alliance Party does try hard to punch above its weight.

The SDLP and UUP attempt to oppose the DUP–Sinn Féin axis on occasion, but this is hardly a sustainable long-term position while they remain in the Executive at the same time. However, expecting them to simply walk away from places in government and hand even more power to their rivals also seems unrealistic.

Any new political force trying to break through in Northern Ireland will face severe barriers. Politics—and the media coverage of it—is dominated by the four governing parties, as they jostle and bicker while running the place at the same time. Opportunities for mobilising public opinion against the Executive on specific issues will be strictly limited. Stormont policies will continue to be fixed to a significant degree from Westminster.

Parity with Britain on key issues like public sector pay, benefit levels and taxation will presumably continue to be the best deal possible for Northern Ireland. In addition, the nature of the Executive coalition will inevitably push policies towards a predictable, centrist approach. Ministers will do some things better than their Direct Rule predecessors. They will also do some things worse. If any measures prove particularly unpopular with the public—like the long-delayed introduction of water charges—MLAS can always blame the Brits.

The next Assembly election will in all likelihood follow the path set for the 2009 European poll. Once again, the DUP will seek to rally unionist voters on the alleged risk of Sinn Féin getting more votes than anyone else. And Sinn Féin will use the same message to mobilise its supporters.

The next Executive is unlikely to be very different from the current administration, in terms of the parties involved and the number of ministerial posts they hold. The entire system can be summed up in the immortal words of the Bonzo Dog Band: 'No Matter Who You Vote For, The Government Always Gets In.'[1]

The status quo is also further copper-fastened thanks to the taxpayer. Public expenditure is under severe pressure in this recessionary age, but large sums are still being channelled towards Northern Ireland politicians and their parties. This also helps them maintain their grip on the political scene, both provincewide and at local level.

Each MLA can claim in the region of £72,000 annually to run constituency offices.[2] That sum, drastically increased from the £48,000 a year available before devolution was restored in 2007, can keep advice centres and satellite offices going in different locations. Such centres are not just about helping pensioners fill in complicated benefit forms. They also act as promotional—some would say propaganda—stations. They advertise the MLA's name and all the work he or she is doing for the community. Staff within them can be mini-spin doctors, liaising with local reporters to help ensure that a constant stream of press releases is regurgitated in weekly papers.

Sixteen MLAS, including a number of Stormont ministers, are also MPS. This provides them with up to £107,700 a year or so each in office-running and staffing expenses.[3] Sinn Féin MPS get this cash, along with other Westminster allowances, despite not taking their Commons seats. As the controversy over the Paisley office in

Ballymena showed, there have been no regulations in place to limit the size of the Assembly-funded constituency offices. All this publicly funded support helps the sitting MLAs to maintain their profile and dominance.

Further helpings of public money are dished out to the parties at Stormont.[4] At Westminster, there is a party-funding system called 'Short Money' which allocates sums to opposition parties. This was established to help them conduct parliamentary business, including policy research. The aim was to redress the imbalance caused by the governing party having access to the full machinery of Whitehall—civil servants, special advisers, researchers, etc. At Stormont, however, the party funding system actually favours the bigger, governing parties. The more seats a party has, the larger the annual sum it receives. The DUP therefore had a party allowance of £138,000 from the Assembly in 2007/08, plus other, smaller allowances adding up to £29,776. That gave it a total of £167,776. Sinn Féin's share came to £136,000 while the UUP received £116,105, and the SDLP £121,828. This funding is spent on subsidising the now sizeable party backroom teams. Once again, taxpayers' money is being used to beef up the ruling political class.

The DUP and SDLP also get 'Short Money' from Westminster, even though their actual contribution to the Opposition role in the Commons is negligible. The DUP's 'Short Money' allocation for 2008/09 was £162,524, while the SDLP's was £60,572. A separate, similar scheme has been created at the Commons for Sinn Féin to get round the small matter of them not taking their Westminster seats. This came to £95,958 for 2008/09. The DUP and SDLP also receive 'policy development grants' from the taxpayer-funded Electoral Commission. In 2007/08, this worked out at £154,754 each. Every little helps.

The Northern Ireland parties can swell their coffers further by fundraising from private sources. Unlike in the rest of the UK or the Republic, donations do not have to be publicly declared. An exemption from transparency legislation that affected British parties from 2001 was brought in by the Northern Ireland Office (NIO) and subsequently extended to 2010 at the earliest. The official total for secret donations to the province's four main parties in 2007—Assembly election year—came to £744,529. In the previous year, when the return of devolution seemed unlikely to many, the grand total was just £296,115.[5]

The ongoing lack of transparency on donations means the public has had no idea who was helping to bankroll the governing parties. While powers under devolution are limited, Stormont decisions—in terms of regulatory approval or financial support— could still turn lowly businessmen into millionaires. And these lowly businessmen could have first dipped into their pockets to help out a governing party. There is, it must be emphasised, no evidence that this has happened to date. But the fact that it is even possible—and could happen in total secrecy—is surely a cause for concern.

Such matters need not unduly trouble the British government. Bombs are not going off in London, security spending is down and the place is largely back at arm's length again. The fact that it may be something of a ghettoised political slum in accountability terms is obviously unimportant to Whitehall by comparison.

IS THAT IT?

So where does that leave those of us actually living here?

Northern Ireland is self-evidently a better place to live in now than in the dark days of the Troubles. Only a fool would argue otherwise. But that does not mean the Stormont structures or politicians should be exempted from all criticism. It's entirely right to question the in-built bias in favour of the current ruling parties—in terms of the substantial subsidies they receive and the way the restricted focus of politics and policies works in their favour.

For the purposes of truly completing the peace process, more space should surely be created for alternative forms of politics. That's because the prospects for breaking down age-old divisions will be limited while politics remains fixed in the old unionist– nationalist ruts.

Putting up with a less-than-perfect devolved system would be more acceptable if it delivered good government. Unfortunately, the outlook there is not particularly encouraging. Environmental policy provides a perfect example of Stormont's shortcomings to date. It might have been thought that the DUP would learn some wider lessons from the Giant's Causeway visitor centre debacle. Its attempt to approve a private sector approach in this sensitive location backfired badly, to the embarrassment of the party. The controversy also led to Paisley Jnr's fall from power. So it should surely have been recognised that the environment is a politically important and sensitive subject. It also has national and international dimensions, as the UNESCO factor in the Causeway centre debate illustrated. In addition, there is a very strong economic case for environmental protection, as Northern Ireland's landscape is one of its few unique tourism selling points.

In the end, Seymour Sweeney's private sector Causeway centre plan was turned down by a DUP minister and an alternative scheme tabled by the National Trust was subsequently given approval.[6] Otherwise, however, the DUP has seemed largely content to stick to its old short-sighted approach on the environment—complete with hostility to conservation campaigners.

The chief demand from the province's environmental non-governmental organisations (NGOs) was for a new environment protection agency, operating independently from government. This proposed reform would have brought the province into line with practice elsewhere in the UK and in the Republic. Its main impact would have been to move the environment up the political agenda, by creating a watchdog to speak up on its behalf without ministerial interference. The demand was backed in a major 2007 report by an expert panel that had been appointed by a Direct Rule minister. But in May 2008, DUP Environment Minister Arlene Foster threw out the recommendation.

This surprised no one, as the Ulster Farmers' Union had led the fight against a new agency. The agricultural lobby is one of the most powerful in Northern Ireland politics, and heavily influences DUP thinking. The Environment and Heritage Service, a wing of Foster's department, was given a reprieve. Instead of being replaced by an independent body, it was simply re-branded the Northern Ireland Environment Agency.

Foster's colleagues lined up to applaud her Assembly announcement, just as they had done the previous September when she declared that she was 'of a mind' to approve the Sweeney Causeway centre. MLA Sammy Wilson, one of the party's leading development enthusiasts, accused NGOs like Friends of the Earth of making 'frenzied demands' for an independent agency. Foster also rounded on the same target during the debate, saying: 'I look forward to the day when those people put themselves up against me for election; to see what the people of Northern Ireland believe is the best way to achieve better regulation and better governance.'[7]

Greeted by a chorus of 'hear, hear' from the DUP benches, this was a nonsensical statement by the Minister. It is hard to imagine anyone having ever voted for Foster's party on the basis of its environmental governance policies. That's not what Northern Ireland politics is about—especially in Foster's own constituency of Fermanagh–South Tyrone, where maximising the evenly divided unionist and nationalist votes is the focus of elections.

To be fair, it is not just the DUP that has relegated the environment well down the Stormont priority list. Despite being officially in favour of an independent protection agency, Sinn Féin did nothing of any value to challenge Foster's refusal decision within the Executive. Indeed, the Environment Minister told the Assembly that two Sinn Féin ministers—Michelle Gildernew at Agriculture and Conor Murphy at Regional Development—had opposed the reform model proposed by the government-appointed expert panel.

When it came to restrictions on housing development in the countryside, another key policy issue at the Assembly, the DUP actually favoured greater planning controls than Sinn Féin or the SDLP.

In a thoughtful article in 2008, Friends of the Earth's Northern Ireland director, John Woods, concluded that devolution was failing the environment.[8] He also described the system of government at the Assembly as 'dysfunctional', adding:

In more conventional democracies the electorate can choose to change the Government at the next election. Critically, in Northern Ireland we have no equivalent of the official opposition at Westminster. It is left to a small number of MLAS outside the coalition, NGOS and the media to fulfil the role of an opposition. But what they can't do is perform the main role of opposition: to offer an alternative Government.

By this stage, the DUP's attitude to the environment was helping to make Stormont look ridiculous. Shortly after blocking an independent protection agency, Arlene Foster was promoted to the Department of Enterprise in a ministerial reshuffle by new leader Peter Robinson. She was replaced at Environment by Sammy Wilson, who had made no secret of his hostility to green issues and his antagonism to planning regulations that delayed economic development.

Wilson was no sooner in office than he was denouncing the agenda of 'bearded, sandal-wearing, *Guardian*-reading, muesli-eating environmentalists'.[9] He also went on something of a personal crusade to promote his scepticism about climate change science. This is not the place to examine the scientific evidence on climate change as a man-made phenomenon. It should, though, be recorded that the expertise of Wilson, a former economics teacher, on the subject has not yet been validated.

His supporters argued that he was entitled to his personal views. However, he had fought the 2007 DUP election on a manifesto that stated: 'It is important that we in Northern Ireland not only look after our own environment but also play our part in global issues such as tackling climate change.' The DUP supported a UK-wide Climate Change Bill at the House of Commons. Wilson went against his party's policy to oppose it.

The Stormont Executive's Programme for government for 2008–2011, meanwhile, states: 'It is clear that climate change is one of the most serious problems facing the world. While we recognise that it requires action internationally, we are determined to play our part in addressing this challenge by reducing our impact on climate change.' This is the government programme under which Sammy Wilson was serving as a minister. His climate change scepticism might not have mattered that much if he was Minister for Paperclips. But he was Minister for the Environment—while not believing in the policies of his government and his party on the most significant environmental issue of the age.

In any normal democracy, that would be a resigning or sacking matter. But First Minister Peter Robinson made it pretty clear at an early stage that he was more than relaxed about his Environment Minister's anti-green credentials. In his leader's speech to the DUP's annual conference in November 2008, Robinson said:

> New ministers are often accused of going native when they take over a department. I think it's safe to say that, so far at least, Sammy seems to have resisted that temptation. However, I wasn't prepared to accede to his suggestion of changing the logo for the Environmental and Heritage Service to a depiction of a JCB.[10]

THE TIMES THEY AREN'T A-CHANGING

Sinn Féin and the DUP could conceivably share power together for many years, providing they don't spectacularly mess it up between them. It's in their interests—and the interests of London and Dublin—that the status quo continues. So they will probably have to find a way to live together, with perhaps an occasional public row or two around election time to keep up appearances.

A telling phrase was repeatedly uttered in the second half of 2008, when the Executive was not meeting and concerns were growing about the possible collapse of the administration. Those in the know predicted that the parties would eventually sort something out as they had 'nowhere else to go'. So it proved.

'Nowhere else to go' could be the motto for the new Northern Ireland. It's hardly inspirational, but it seems to capture the tightly fixed nature of political life. Chapter 4 of this book quoted from the poem 'The Coasters' by John Hewitt, on the 'noisy preacher' Paisley. This poem, from the early days of the Troubles, also refers to permanent government being 'sustained by the regular plebiscites of loyalty'.[11] It adds:

> *Faces changed on the posters, names too, often,*
> *but the same families, the same class of people.*

It seems Stormont has not altered very much since then. The political class in charge these days has a cross-community hue, which is progress. Its system of government looks pretty permanent too. The same families might even still be in charge many years from now, given the number of MLAs employing their children in their backroom teams. Some will inevitably move up into high-profile elected roles in future.

There's also a danger that the voting public will grow increasingly uninterested and disenchanted. A fractious, underperforming and costly devolved institution is hardly going to attract a new wave of future leaders to enter politics. Some at the Assembly believe the lure of power—and maybe some higher salaries—will bring in a better calibre of candidates in future. But the risk is that Northern Ireland's communal form of politics will continue to act as a major deterrent.

On a visit to the province in May 2008, New York Mayor Michael Bloomberg spoke of the poisonous consequences of sectarian division.[12] In a speech largely on economic matters, Bloomberg highlighted the need to bring down the 'peace' walls and fences that divide Protestant and Catholic communities. There are currently dozens of these physical divides in Belfast. The most recent addition to the list was constructed in the grounds of an integrated primary school some seven months into the new power-sharing era at Stormont. Bloomberg warned: 'The fact is the best and the brightest don't want to live in a city defined by division. They don't want to live behind walls. And they don't want to live in a place where they are judged by their faith or their family name.' Unfortunately, the sad truth is that Stormont politics continues to be 'defined by division' and seems likely to remain that way for many years.

The 'best and the brightest' can for the most part be expected to steer well clear of it. Among the younger generation, many will leave for university courses or other opportunities in Britain and not come back. For those who stay, the most favoured option may involve getting on with their lives and paying little or no attention to what's happening at the Assembly.

The current Stormont bosses might think they have little to fear from such public disaffection. It's not as if they are going to be voted out of government and onto opposition benches. Not while politics has nowhere else to go.

Chapter 16
The Fall of the House of Robinson?

'Pride goeth before destruction, and an haughty spirit before a fall.'
PROVERBS 16:18

The DUP should have started 2010 in a relatively upbeat mood, preparing for a General Election. Instead, it began the year consumed by an astonishing scandal involving the politician wife of the party leader and First Minister Peter Robinson.

It was revealed—thanks to a BBC Northern Ireland 'Spotlight' investigation—that Iris Robinson had had an affair with a teenager in 2008. This occurred around the same time that the MP and MLA was crusading against the 'abomination' of homosexuality. She had also procured cash from two friendly property developers to help the youth set up a new café business. The shocking revelations brought a swift end to Mrs Robinson's political career and placed her husband's position in immediate jeopardy.

The development is significant enough to warrant this additional chapter of *The Fall of the House of Paisley*. The abrupt departure of Ian Paisley as First Minister in 2008 had provided a dramatic and symbolic end point for the original book. But in terms of sheer drama, it has now been surpassed by the fall of Iris Robinson.

It can all be seen as part of a wider story—the slow crumbling of the Paisleyite movement that blended uncompromising politics and religion and wielded a powerful influence over Northern

Ireland. Damaging disclosures on how DUP politicians treated taxpayer-funded expenses have played their part. So too have personal failings, hypocrisy, arrogance and bad luck. The House of Paisley will never return to the pomp of its brief time in charge of Stormont. And the Robinson 'family firm' that rose to the top through Paisleyism has been ripped apart. It is by any standards a remarkable story. The full extent of the fall-out is not yet known but it can be safely assumed that the DUP will never be quite the same again.

As a starting point, it is also worth noting that the Iris Robinson scandal could hardly have come at a worse time for her party.

2009: ANNUS HORRIBILIS

Given the disastrous start to 2010, DUP supporters could be forgiven for looking back on the previous year with nostalgia.

In truth, 2009 was a very tough period for the party. Not as bad as having one of your senior politicians embroiled in a sex-and-money scandal. But it was nevertheless a bruising time—in no small part because of key issues examined in this book. The 'ghost of Paisley past' came back to haunt the party in the shape of Jim Allister's anti-agreement TUV party. As a result, the DUP suffered a major setback in the European elections, failing spectacularly in its declared aim of preventing Sinn Féin from topping the poll. Meanwhile, the issue of expenses created a fully fledged crisis for the UK's political class, with serious knock-on effects for Stormont.

There were also ongoing problems for the Paisleys. Ian Paisley Jnr continued to insist to anyone who would listen that he had been 'vindicated' over the controversies that had forced his ministerial resignation. He appeared to have convinced himself—and quite a few in his party—that he was the victim of a groundless and malicious vendetta from elements in the media. A motivation for this alleged campaign of character assassination was never given. Maybe he thought it was just because he was a Paisley. Or perhaps it was all the work of lazy journalists attacking God's anointed leader via his son.

The facts continued to get in the way of such conspiracy theories. These included the empirical reality that Junior was no longer a government minister, plus the defeat of Seymour Sweeney in the Giant's Causeway planning battle.

In May 2009, a long-awaited investigation report by Assembly Standards Commissioner Tom Frawley was finally published. It examined complaints made in February 2008 under the Stormont code of conduct against Paisley Jnr by SDLP MLA Declan O'Loan.[1]

Paisley Jnr had always maintained that his links with Seymour Sweeney were nothing out of the ordinary, merely an example of an MLA working for a local businessman and constituent. Frawley's report, however, stated that the connections were 'such as to establish a close association', including 'recreational, social and political contacts together with property dealings'. He concluded that these connections warranted a declaration in the Assembly register of interests as they constituted 'a greater level of interaction with a single constituent than is normal'.

This verdict was blocked by a six–five majority on the Stormont Standards and Privileges Committee. The four DUP and two old guard Ulster Unionist members on the body provided the votes in Paisley Jnr's favour. The verdict of the Standards Commissioner nevertheless remained a matter of public record. In the real world, the views of a man like Frawley with his deep experience of public life carry much more weight than those of six minor backbenchers on a Stormont committee.

The Frawley report also found that the taxpayer-funded rent being claimed by the Paisleys for their Ballymena constituency office was 'significantly' above the normal market rate, and that the money was creating a 'property asset' for the party. It was concluded that no rules had been broken, not least because there were no rules on the subject. The Standards and Privileges Committee—including its DUP members—agreed with Frawley that the expenses rulebook should be urgently reviewed. It said this was necessary 'in the interests of public accountability and securing public confidence' and 'for the integrity of the Assembly'.

The DUP did not seem unduly worried that its Ballymena

office—owned by a DUP-linked company—was being funded through rent expenses well above the market rate.

There was some speculation that Paisley Jnr might even make a return to the party's ministerial ranks in a 2009 summer reshuffle by leader Peter Robinson.

In the end, he had to make do with the post of chair of the Assembly Agriculture Committee—and hopes of succeeding his father as north Antrim MP.

By mid-2009, the standard political-class expenses excuse—'no rules have been broken'—had been comprehensively discredited by events at Westminster. A disc containing uncensored details of MP expenses dating back to 2004 was leaked to the *Daily Telegraph*. A subsequent wave of revelations exposed outrageous claims made by Tory and Labour politicians, particularly under the second home allowance for staying in London on parliamentary business.

Northern Ireland MPs and MLAs also became the subject of increasing public anger on such issues as employing family members and double jobbing between Westminster and Stormont. The House of Paisley suffered some of the pain. The Ballymena rent issue continued to fester. It was also revealed that Ian Paisley Jnr had billed taxpayers £950 for a single chair through the Assembly office expenses system.[2] He defended himself by saying that his office furniture had been 'purchased nearly a decade ago' and 'is still used today'. Presumably, a cheap and cheerful £500 chair would have fallen apart long ago.

Paisley Senior faced more serious criticism, over food allowance payments from the House of Commons.[3] Under this arrangement —now scrapped—MPs were able to claim up to £400 per month for food while in London. No receipts were required, but the honourable members had to sign a declaration each month saying the costs were incurred 'wholly, exclusively and necessarily to enable me to stay overnight away from my only or main home for the purpose of performing my duties as a Member of Parliament'.

Paisley was revealed to have had one of the highest food expenses bills in the Commons, repeatedly claiming the full £400 even in parliamentary recess periods.

Maximum sums were paid out to him throughout the year 2004/05, during which he had been seriously ill. The full £4,800 annual total was also claimed in 2007/08, when he had a somewhat busy workload back at home as Stormont's First Minister. The *Daily Telegraph* included Paisley's name in a list of 32 top MP food claimants under the heading 'Who ate all the pies?'[4]

Sinn Féin also faced intense criticism over the fact that its five MPs had claimed up to £100,000 a year between them on the second home allowance, with the money largely going on the rental of two shared properties in London. The five were naturally enough infrequent flyers to the city, due to the small detail that they do not take their Commons seats. Newry and Armagh MP Conor Murphy confirmed this rather bluntly, saying of the London accommodation provided for him by taxpayers: 'I have been in that house once in the last year.'[5]

Of all Northern Ireland politicians, DUP golden couple Peter and Iris Robinson suffered the biggest fall-out from the expenses disclosures. London tabloid newspapers latched on to the fact that the Robinsons had four relatives—their three children and a daughter-in-law—on their MP payrolls. Rough calculations were also carried out showing that the pair's combined annual salaries and expenses total from politics came to over £500,000. Like other husband and wife MPs, they were each entitled to claim full second home allowances as part of their expenses. That meant sizeable mortgage interest payments had been obtained from the Commons for their Docklands apartment in London. Their other property holdings included a villa in Florida and a richly furnished family home in Belfast, complete with themed rooms. An old jibe coined by Ulster Unionists about the 'Swish Family Robinson' suddenly started to stick.

Peter Robinson did not help his cause with some crass attempts to defend himself.

When it was revealed that the MP food expenses he and his wife had been claiming added up to around £30,000 over four years, the First Minister said: 'I think if MPs slept on a park bench and starved themselves that would still be too much for some people.'[6]

He also claimed the food expenses total only came to £73 a week. That calculation included months when Parliament was in recess. It also overlooked the fact that the two Robinsons spent a significant chunk of their time at Stormont, attending to their other jobs in the Assembly.

To make things worse, it was disclosed that Iris Robinson had tried to bill the public purse for a £300 designer Mont Blanc pen under the parliamentary expenses system. The fact that it was turned down by Commons officials did not provide much comfort to hard-pressed taxpayers suffering through a serious recession.

The expenses debacle of 2009 caused great damage to the reputation of politics across the UK. It was not an ideal time to be on the campaign trail for the European election.

The DUP's choice of Diane Dodds—wife of deputy leader Nigel—to fight the June 2009 poll might have seemed like a good idea at the time. The expenses controversy, however, brought the issue of DUP dynasties to the fore—with critics referring to a Dodds dynasty joining the Paisleys and the Robinsons.

The DUP's election strategy also backfired badly. It attempted a modern variant of its old 'Smash Sinn Féin' platform, arguing that only a big vote for Dodds could prevent the nightmare scenario of Sinn Féin's Bairbre de Brún claiming top spot.

This, of course, jarred somewhat with the reality that the DUP was in a power-sharing government with de Brún's party.

Having finished first in every previous European election in Northern Ireland, the DUP had a poor result. De Brún topped the poll comfortably with 126,184 votes, a 26 per cent share. The DUP's vote share fell from 32 per cent in the previous European election to 18.2 per cent—88,346 votes. That was down to TUV leader Jim Allister receiving a 13.7 per cent share with 66,197 votes. After second preferences in the PR election had been counted, Diane Dodds had to content herself with the third and final seat, finishing behind de Brún and UUP veteran Jim Nicholson, who ran on a joint Ulster Unionist–Conservative ticket. Turnout slumped to 42.8 per cent from 51.7 per cent, suggesting a serious level of voter disenchantment.

The European result proved that the Dromore by-election of February 2008 was not a fluke. It's impossible to say just how many people backed Allister as a protest against expenses, dynasties and uninspiring devolved rule. But his vote undoubtedly contained a core element that still believed everything Ian Paisley had preached over the years—on how power-sharing was wrong in principle and having republicans in government was morally unacceptable. Allister's strong electoral showing provided a major worry for the DUP and helped destabilise power-sharing at Stormont.

The DUP also had a major credibility problem when it came to putting the case for partnership government. It could point out that Northern Ireland is a divided society that needs shared institutions. However, that is a hard argument to make convincingly when you have spent decades not only rubbishing it but lambasting its adherents.

Meanwhile, Sinn Féin was becoming increasingly impatient over a lack of progress towards devolving policing and justice powers to the Assembly. With the spectre of the TUV lurking and a General Election approaching, the DUP was in no hurry for a deal. That added to a rancorous mood at Stormont, and the prospect of a cohesive Executive working together for the common good receded yet further.

FIGHTING BACK

If Peter Robinson and the DUP could be counted on for one thing above all else, it was to fight their corner with maximum aggression. After a period of internal reflection following the European election, the party looked to be regaining some of its old confidence in the final months of the year. There was talk of taking the battle to Jim Allister and of private polls showing a recovery in DUP support levels. A glossy new brochure, *Building on Success*, was published to belatedly make the case for the 2007 power-sharing deal. In an interview with *Belfast Telegraph* political correspondent Noel McAdam, Robinson admitted: 'We should have spent more time to stop and sell before we took the step.'[7]

There were some grounds for optimism for the party at this

stage. Both the UUP and TUV were lacking teams of big name candidates for the Westminster election. And the DUP seemed to be gaining an advantage in the tug of war with Sinn Féin. Robinson was under no obligation to agree to the transfer of policing and justice powers, no matter how much Martin McGuinness sulked. DUP strategy was to exploit the situation to win concessions for unionism. Its wish list included making it harder for nationalist objectors to prevent Orange marches passing through disputed routes.

In his speech to his party's annual conference in November 2009, Robinson also pledged that his party would not walk away from the Assembly. With beaming wife Iris and Ian Paisley Snr among those on the platform behind him, the First Minister proudly warned Sinn Féin: 'Threatening the DUP is just dumb.' Robinson's conference speech was enthusiastically cheered by Union-flag-waving delegates, who were then led in a chorus of 'Peter is our leader, we shall not be moved' by MP William McCrea. The DUP was giving every impression of itching for an electoral rematch.

However, in another part of town . . .

IRIS UNDER THE 'SPOTLIGHT'

It is now known that from late autumn 2009, a whistleblower was talking to BBC Northern Ireland's 'Spotlight' documentary team. His name was Selwyn Black, a former clergyman who had been a member of Iris Robinson's staff. The information he had was so explosive that 'Spotlight' chiefs launched a 'lockdown' operation to guard against leaks. A small team including reporter Darragh MacIntyre was moved out of the programme's normal office to a separate location. Work began on a story that would rock not just the DUP but the whole Stormont set-up.

It is believed that in the final weeks of the year, the Robinsons started to suspect that Black had gone overboard. On 28 December, with politics in its normal Christmas-period lull, a shock announcement was issued through the DUP press office. Iris Robinson was quitting politics, citing 'serious bouts of depression' as well as physical health problems. 'The stress and strain of public life comes at a cost and my health has suffered,' she said.

While expressions of sympathy were naturally voiced, there was puzzlement at the timing. Although Mrs Robinson's health had been the subject of speculation for months, the resignation had still come as a major surprise, even to senior party colleagues. In a newspaper interview published just the previous month, she had dismissed the idea of retiring. 'I can do a day's work to match any man,' she added. 'I don't like bringing gender into any equation, but I've so much still to do and so much want to be part of the political life because I see good times ahead. When you love what you do it's a gift.'[8]

At that point, 'Spotlight' was not on the brink of screening its special programme.

Speculation about the Robinsons intensified over the New Year period, following her departure announcement. The First Minister was criticised after taking almost three days to issue condolences following the death of Cardinal Cahal Daly, a former Catholic Primate of Ireland. When asked if he would be attending Daly's funeral, a DUP spokesman said Robinson would be 'out of circulation' for the rest of that week to attend to 'family circumstances'. Rumours were flying by this stage—including suggestions that he was also quitting, or that he was separating from his wife.

On 6 January, the First Minister spoke to TV cameras and four hand-picked journalists in the study of his home. This was not the cocky DUP leader the public was used to seeing.

It was revealed that his wife had had an affair, and subsequently tried to take her own life in March 2009. She did not appear before the cameras, but a detailed, guilt-ridden statement from her was released. With his voice occasionally cracking with emotion, Robinson spoke of having forgiven Iris and of trying to save his marriage.

Behind him on a shelf, a small sign said: 'Dad no matter how tall I grow I will always look up to you.'

The interview was hard to watch. The agony experienced by

Robinson, an intensely private man, in having to bare his soul was clearly extreme. But there were political considerations at work too. By that stage, he and his wife had received a series of written questions from 'Spotlight' based on its investigations. Robinson's career was at stake as well as his marriage.

His interview was met with cynicism in some quarters, but with a large degree of public sympathy generally. However, if the game plan had been to get his retaliation in first and spoil 'Spotlight's' exclusive, it did not work. The full story was about to come out, solving the mystery of why the DUP leader had chosen that particular moment to share family secrets with the world. The BBC changed its programme line-up for 7 January and Darragh MacIntyre's documentary was eagerly watched in homes across the province.

It told a sordid tale of sex and money.

The first staggering revelation was that Iris Robinson's lover, Kirk McCambley, had been just 19 at the time—40 years younger than her. She had promised his dying father that she would look after him, and referred to him at one stage as 'the other son I would have loved to have been a mother to'. The relationship turned sexual in the summer of 2008, close to the time when the high-profile MP was taking to the airwaves to denounce homosexuality and argue that governments should be upholding God's laws. Her infamous use of the word 'abomination' was a quote from the Old Testament book of Leviticus. It also advocated death for adultery.

The 'Spotlight' documentary included interviews with McCambley and whistleblower Selwyn Black. Its account was supported by a series of text messages sent by Mrs Robinson to Black, which had been automatically stored on his phone.

The programme told how the MP had identified a business opportunity for her young gentleman friend—a new riverside café outlet built as part of a Castlereagh Council visitor centre development. Mrs Robinson was a member of Castlereagh Council. She also set about securing him start-up finance, procuring £50,000 from two property developers. One of the benefactors was Fred Fraser, one of Northern Ireland's leading housing tycoons, who had died in August 2008 just weeks after providing £25,000. A further £25,000 came from Ken Campbell, who ran a building firm and was a family friend of the Robinsons. Campbell had also made a donation to the DUP in the past, while the party stonewalled questions on whether it had ever benefited from Fraser's money.

According to Kirk McCambley, Iris Robinson took a £5,000 cut in cash from the £50,000. The summer of 2008 saw her lobbying in favour of a proposed County Down housing development by Campbell. She also attended the Castlereagh Council meeting where the lease for the café was formally released to McCambley— and did not declare an interest. Nor did she declare her involvement with the property developer money in the registers of interests at the Assembly and House of Commons. Text messages indicated that she retained a level of control over the finance after it had been received by her teenage lover. There was a reference in one message to a plan for her church to receive a third of the café's profits.

Towards the end of 2008, the relationship with McCambley soured and she demanded repayment. Her initial plan was apparently for £25,000 to go to her and £25,000 to her church.

But 'Spotlight' said First Minister Peter Robinson intervened around the turn of the year to insist that the money go back to the developers. He did not learn of the affair with McCambley until early March 2009, on the night of his wife's overdose bid.

MacIntyre argued that Robinson had been obliged under the ministerial code to report his wife's non-declarations to the Commons, Assembly and Castlereagh Council. He firmly denied that, insisting he had acted properly at all times. There was also the associated question of why he had not persuaded his wife to make belated declarations of the money once he had become aware of it. The separate MLA Code of Conduct, for its part, required members to register any gift received by their partners that 'in any way relates to membership of the Assembly'. Various inquiries were initiated in the wake of the 'Spotlight' programme and the police also announced a criminal investigation into allegations against Mrs Robinson.

This book has documented serious accountability gaps in Northern Ireland politics and these provided a contaminating background factor in the scandal. Northern Ireland parties had been allowed to keep taking secret donations from business interests, unlike their counterparts in Great Britain and the Republic. In addition, the code of conduct for councillors in the province was for guidance only, with no repercussions if its principles were flouted. And there was no independent procedure for assessing alleged breaches of the Stormont Ministerial Code. That meant the 'Spotlight' allegation against Peter Robinson on the Ministerial Code could not be swiftly referred to an established process, free from government involvement.

Having strict rules on standards in public life does not stop politicians misbehaving. But it can at least send out the message that ethics are important. Instead, the impression was given for years that Northern Ireland politicians were a special breed, who did not have to worry about rules that applied elsewhere. Complacent London ministers must have taken the view that trifling matters of accountability could be ignored, so long as everyone stayed on board the peace process wagon.

Peter Robinson survived the initial period after the 'Spotlight' broadcast. Party colleagues publicly rallied behind him, unified in part by their traditional enmity towards the media. It was also announced that Mrs Robinson was in a residential facility receiving acute psychiatric care.

The Paisleys declined to take up a number of opportunities to voice their personal support for their party leader. A report in the *Sunday Tribune* quoted sources saying that Paisley Snr was 'beyond fury'. It was not denied.[9] Free Presbyterian clergyman Rev. David McIlveen said publicly that Robinson's position was becoming untenable due to the 'heavy burden' placed on him by private family matters. McIlveen, one of Paisley Snr's closest associates, emphasised that he was voicing his own personal opinion and no one else's. When asked if he had talked to Paisley on the matter, he replied: 'I speak to him about pastoral work generally every week.'[10]

On 11 January, Robinson temporarily stepped aside from some

of his First Minister duties, for a period of up to six weeks. He returned around half way through that timeframe, although the main standards investigations in the case had barely started.

If the normal laws of political gravity applied, the best years of Robinson's long political career were behind him.

PETER'S PLIGHT

Aside from specific questions about what Peter Robinson should or should not have done about his wife's actions, there was the bigger issue of the political fall-out for him. He and Iris had been packaged and promoted as a team for many years. When she stood in her first election, for a seat on Castlereagh Council in 1989, the local DUP manifesto said: 'Being married to DUP deputy leader Peter Robinson means she is no newcomer to the political scene.' His name helped her early career, but having a successful MP wife boosted his image too. It was stated that she had persuaded him to improve his appearance in more recent years, with the help of a new hairstyle and contact lenses. Joint photocalls were also arranged for the media, including a toe-curling kiss for the cameras when he became First Minister in June 2008. Her authorised 2006 biography—*Iris: An Intimate Portrait*—was full of warm anecdotes about their married life together.[11] His party conference speeches affectionately name-checked her, and his website noted that they were 'the first husband and wife team ever to represent Northern Ireland at Westminster'.

There is nothing remotely surprising or wrong about any of this. Family friendly images have long played a part in political marketing. But the years of 'Team Robinson' meant that he could not possibly be fully shielded from the serious scandal that engulfed his wife at the outset of 2010. For the foreseeable future, every time he appeared in front of a TV camera, voters would be reminded of the sleaze allegations around her.

There was compassion in some quarters for what was clearly a family nightmare at the heart of the saga. But it must also be recorded that black humour was in plentiful supply. Comedian Keith Law attracted many YouTube hits with a clever parody of the

Simon and Garfunkel hit 'Mrs Robinson'. And countless obscene jokes about the unlikely affair between the DUP granny and the teenager flew between mobile phones.

None of this was good news for a First Minister who had always given the impression of taking himself very seriously indeed.

A HOUSE IN RUINS

Sex-and-money scandals are bad news for any political party.

But this was the DUP, with its roots deeply embedded in a stern, censorious brand of evangelical Protestantism. That's why the news of Iris Robinson's affair and sugar-mummy routine with developers' cash was so toxic for her party and the Paisleyite legacy. It also explains why sympathy over her public humiliation and mental health problems was not as strong as it might have been.

She and other party figures had been vigorously preaching at others for years. Whether it involved what people could do on Sundays or in their bedrooms, they had believed their views should prevail. The Robinsons were not Free Presbyterians, but for years they were very much part of the Paisleyite world, where dogmatic religion and politics were mixed. When Iris Robinson launched her salvos against homosexuality in 2008 she might have caused some embarrassment to her more media-savvy colleagues. She was in fact staying true to the traditions of her party.

Indeed, when she first entered political life in 1989, the DUP manifesto in Castlereagh carried a message from leader Ian Paisley under the heading 'For God and Ulster'. It also stressed the party's opposition to 'immoral practices' and referred to 'recognising the laws of God and the inherent benefits of the Ulster Sabbath as part of our heritage'.

Iris Robinson clearly believed she had divine approval for her entire political career. Her authorised biography makes it clear that she only stood in 1989 in the first place after receiving direct guidance from God through the Bible. It quotes her saying: 'When I received a word from the Psalms that assured me of victory, I submitted my name and then I told Peter!' On winning a seat, she recalled: 'I had taken God at His word and proved Him faithful. It was incredible to witness how God takes control. The glory had to go to Him.'

Likewise, she told her biographer about a pretty powerful ally when being elected to the Commons 12 years later: 'If there's one lesson I've learned in life, it is that God doesn't make mistakes. I loved the work He had first given me in 1989 but I knew there was more for me to do. When the opportunity arose again in 2001, I had no doubt that this time God would open the door.'

By the beginning of 2010, the door was closed in her face. The DUP made it known that she had been expelled from the party, even though she had not had any opportunity to defend herself publicly or counter allegations against her. Her immediate resignations from Westminster, Stormont and Castlereagh Council were announced on her behalf. The DUP was in full damage limitation mode, and crisis talks with Sinn Féin on the policing and justice powers stalemate seemed to provide a welcome distraction.

There were also some tentative suggestions about the long-term realignment of unionism. One of the chief purposes of the DUP had always been to denounce the rival Ulster Unionist Party as traitors. That could hardly work when they were both supposed to be in the pro-power-sharing camp. Fundamental questions could be asked on exactly what the point of Paisleyism was any more, especially if events had undermined any prospect of DUP politicians moralising in future.

With Peter Robinson taking his break from government duties to tend to family matters, 39-year-old MLA Arlene Foster temporarily took over as the party's Acting First Minister. She had started her political career in the Ulster Unionist Party. And she is a member of the Church of Ireland—a denomination long vilified by Ian Paisley as being in league with the Pope.

Things aren't what they used to be.

Notes

Unless otherwise stated, sources quoted will have been interviewed directly for this book. Likewise government documents will have been obtained directly by the author, normally through freedom of information disclosures, but sometimes through leaks. DUP manifestos are sourced from the party's website or the Linen Hall Library's invaluable Northern Ireland political collection. Paisley Jnr press releases are archived on his own website.

Introduction (pp IX–XIII)

1. This official verdict was delivered in 1969 by the government-appointed Cameron Commission on street disorder linked to the civil rights movement. The report condemned counter-rallies involving Paisley and an ally of his called Major Ronald Bunting. It said the two men and their supporters 'must bear a heavy share of direct responsibility' for serious instances of disorder.

Chapter 1 (pp 1–9)

1. 'The Stephen Nolan Show' interview, BBC Radio Ulster, 4 April 2007.
2. Ian Paisley's full statement on the deal is archived, among other places, on the *Guardian*'s website. The BBC website has the statements by both him and Adams.
3. '"Chuckle brothers" enjoy 100 days', BBC Northern Ireland website, 15 August 2007.
4. *Belfast Telegraph*, 8 June 2007.
5. The Smithsonian Institute's Folklife Festival in Washington, D.C.
6. Office of the First Minister and Deputy First Minister (OFMDFM) press release, 27 June 2007, entitled 'Northern Ireland wows Washington'.
7. BBC Northern Ireland website, 27 June 2007.
8. OFMDFM press release, 14 June 2007.
9. Ian Paisley Jnr and Conor Murphy quotes on junior minister roles from *Belfast Telegraph*, 16 December 1999.
10. 'Nolan Live' interview, BBC1 Northern Ireland, 4 April 2007.
11. Interview with *Hot Press* magazine, 13 June 2007.
12. *Belfast Telegraph*, 30 March 2007.
13. *Ibid.*
14. *Belfast Telegraph*, 29 March 2007.
15. *Observer*, 11 March 2007.

Chapter 2 (pp 10–26)

1. An Ian Paisley sermon on 6 January 1980 in his Martyrs Memorial Free Presbyterian Church, quoted in the February 1980 edition of the church magazine *The Revivalist*.
2. *Portadown Times*, 13 July 2007.

3. Interview with the author.
4. Interview with the author.
5. *Ballymena Times* online video report, 1 February 2008.
6. *Belfast Telegraph*, 4 June 2007.
7. Comments made during 'Nolan Live' on BBC1 Northern Ireland, 4 April 2007.
8. *Belfast Telegraph*, 27 October 2006.
9. *News Letter*, 23 January 1974.
10. Comments after Assembly eviction sourced via BBC's online 'On this day archive' for 24 June 1986.
11. See Henry McDonald, *Gunsmoke and Mirrors* (Gill & Macmillan, 2008).
12. Ian Paisley speech to north Antrim DUP dinner, November 2004. Extracts from the speech are reproduced on the Cain web archive service.
13. Ian Paisley Jnr speech to Queen's University DUP Dinner, May 2007. Sourced from his website.
14. *News Letter*, 6 March 2007.
15. *Belfast Telegraph*, 22 February 2006.
16. *Irish Independent*, 6 February 2006.
17. Hansard, 25 June 2001.
18. Ian Paisley Jnr speech to DUP conference on policing, 6 February 2006. Sourced from his website.
19. The Patten Commission on policing was headed by former Conservative Party Cabinet Minister Chris Patten. Its 1999 report led to a number of reforms including a 50/50 (Protestant/Catholic) recruitment policy and a name change from the Royal Ulster Constabulary (RUC) to the Police Service of Northern Ireland (PSNI).
20. Report on UTV website, 12 June 2006.
21. The d'Hondt system allocates seats in the Executive according to party strength in the Northern Ireland Assembly. It is named after a Belgian lawyer called Victor d'Hondt.
22. *News Letter*, 23 January 1974.
23. *News Letter*, 2 January 1974.
24. Quoted in Gordon Gillespie, *Years of Darkness* (Gill & Macmillan, 2008), p. 131.
25. *Independent*, 13 February 1997.
26. *News Letter*, 16 May 1998.
27. The full-page ad appeared in the *News Letter* edition of 20 May 1998.
28. Quoted in Ed Moloney, *Paisley* (Poolbeg Press, 2008), p. 360.
29. *Ibid.*
30. *Belfast Telegraph*, 7 March 1998.
31. *Belfast Telegraph*, 14 March 1998.
32. *The Revivalist*, April 1981.
33. *The Revivalist*, July/August 1983.
34. Interview with BBC Northern Ireland, 30 May 2008.
35. *Belfast Telegraph*, 13 July 2007.

Chapter 3 (pp 27–38)
1. *New Humanist*, July/August 2007.

2.   *Sunday Tribune,* 3 June 2007.
3.   *Irish News,* 7 October 1995.
4.   *Hot Press,* 13 June 2007. The contents of the *Hot Press* interview were made public ahead of the magazine's publication.
5.   Ian Paisley Jnr press release, 20 September 2004.
6.   *Belfast Telegraph,* 31 January 2005.
7.   Ian Paisley Jnr press release, 7 February 2005.
8.   *Belfast Telegraph,* 1 June 2007.
9.   BBC Northern Ireland News online, 31 May 2007.
10. Report to the Northern Ireland Assembly Standards and Privileges Committee, published 12 September 2007.
11. *The Revivalist,* September 1977.
12. *Belfast Telegraph,* 3 May 2007.
13. *Belfast Telegraph,* 2 May 2007.
14. *Belfast Telegraph,* 4 May 2007.
15. *Irish Independent,* 19 November 2005.
16. 'The Stephen Nolan Show', BBC Radio Ulster, 6 June 2008.
17. 'The Stephen Nolan Show', BBC Radio Ulster, 17 July 2008.
18. See, for example, *Times* report on Belfast City Hospital research work, 20 June 2007.
19. Column for *News Letter,* 19 September 2007.
20. *Belfast Telegraph,* 31 October 2008.
21. Ian Paisley sermon quoted in *The Revivalist,* March 1972.
22. Figure obtained from the OFMDFM under freedom of information (FOI).
23. *The Revivalist,* June 1982.
24. *Belfast Telegraph,* 25 February 2008.
25. BBC Northern Ireland news website, 6 March 2008.
26. OFMDFM press release, 7 March 2008.
27. Sermon quoted in *The Revivalist,* March 1986.
28. Comments on Elton John quoted in a *London Independent* interview, 22 May 1998.
29. Ian Paisley sermon, 22 January 2008. Recording sourced via the website *www.ianpaisley.org/*.
30. Ian Paisley sermon, 30 March 2008. Recording sourced via the website *www.ianpaisley.org/*. This particular sermon was the featured sermon on the website in February 2009.
31. Commons Hansard record for Delegated Legislation Committee proceedings, 27 March 2008.
32. OFMDFM has confirmed the £100,000 total in a FOI disclosure. That left a further £80,000 still to be allocated by the Department with Robinson as its First Minister.

Chapter 4 (pp 39–59)

1.   Children's Sunday School chorus based on a gospel parable.
2.   BBC Northern Ireland news website, 26 March 2007.
3.   *Irish Times,* 12 September 2008.

4. Treasury press release, 2 November 2006.

5. Gordon Brown and Peter Hain comments were reported on BBC Northern Ireland news website, 1 November 2006.

6. BBC Northern Ireland website report, 2 November 2006.

7. *Belfast Telegraph*, 17 November 2006.

8. *Ibid.*

9. Department of Finance and Personnel's 2008–11 budget document, published 22 January 2008.

10. Sir David Varney, *Review of Tax Policy in Northern Ireland* (HM Treasury, December 2007).

11. From a talk in Oxford by Dr Bradley reported in the online Border Ireland Discussion Forum, 25 November 2008.

12. Department of Finance and Personnel press statement issued 9 May 2008.

13. *Belfast Telegraph*, 7 May 2008.

14. Article in *Irish Voice* online edition, 29 March 2007.

15. *Irish Independent*, 2 August 2007.

16. The Nationwide housing market reports referred to here are archived at *http://www.nationwide.co.uk/hpi/*.

17. Department of Finance and Personnel's 2008–11 budget document, published 22 January 2008.

18. *Belfast Telegraph*, 28 November 2007.

19. *Irish News*, 22 October 2008.

20. *Sunday Tribune*, 8 August 2004.

21. Graham Turner, *The Credit Crunch* (Pluto Press, 2008), p. 3.

22. Annual Report of the Citizens Advice Bureau Dealing with Debt service for 2006/07.

23. Speech by Mark Langhammer at a debate on the Northern Ireland Executive's budget, held at the Belfast Unemployed Resource Centre on 20 March 2008.

24. Sydney Elliott and W.D. Flackes, *Northern Ireland: A Political Directory, 1968–1999* (Blackstaff Press, 1999), p. 225.

25. Peter Robinson speech, from June 2006, is sourced from the 'key speeches' section of his website *www.peterrobinson.org*.

26. From John Hewitt, *Selected Poems* (Blackstaff Press, 2007).

27. *News Letter*, 17 January 2009.

28. Northern Ireland Assembly Official Report, 2 October 2000.

29. Douglas McIldoon made this comment in a letter dated 27 October 2008 accompanying a review he had been commissioned to conduct for his successor as energy regulator.

30. Peter Robinson's speech was issued in a DUP press release, 10 October 2008.

31. First Trust Bank, Economic Outlook and Business Review, September 2008.

32. *Belfast Telegraph*, 18 September 2008.

33. Nigel Dodds interview on BBC Northern Ireland's 'Hearts and Minds' TV programme, 27 November 2008.

Chapter 5 (pp 60–78)

1. Northern Ireland Assembly Official Report, 11 September 2007.

2. Northern Ireland Tourist Board website.
3. Department of Enterprise, Trade and Investment (DETI) press release, 11 October 2005.
4. This memo was released under FOI. All other government documents quoted in this chapter were obtained through the same route, unless otherwise stated.
5. Department of the Environment (DOE) press release, 10 September 2007.
6. Northern Ireland Assembly Official Report, 11 September 2007.
7. *Belfast Telegraph*, 25 September 2007.
8. Article for *Belfast Telegraph*'s Business Telegraph section, 24 September 2007.
9. Figures for objections and letters of support from DOE Planning Service file submitted to Minister Foster on 1 June 2007.
10. *Belfast Telegraph*, 24 October 2007.
11. *Belfast Telegraph*, 11 June 2007.
12. Northern Ireland Assembly Official Report, 11 September 2007.
13. DOE press release, 11 September 2007.
14. Northern Ireland Assembly Official Report, 24 September 2007.
15. *Belfast Telegraph*, 17 October 2007.
16. Northern Ireland Assembly Official Report, 24 September 2007.
17. *Belfast Telegraph*, 27 September 2007.
18. *Belfast Telegraph*, 11 September 2007.
19. Correspondence released under FOI.
20. *Belfast Telegraph*, 29 October 2001.
21. UNESCO's 'Report on the mission to Giant's Causeway and Causeway Coast (United Kingdom) from 16 to 19 February 2003'.
22. *Belfast Telegraph*, 27 November 2007.
23. This email was placed online by the Department of Culture, Media and Sport (DCMS) as a FOI disclosure.

Chapter 6 (pp 79–100)

1. 'The Stephen Nolan Show', BBC Radio Ulster, 11 September 2007.
2. Statement issued by Seymour Sweeney through his PR company, 11 September 2007.
3. *Belfast Telegraph*, 12 September 2007.
4. *Irish News*, 15 September 2007.
5. 'The Stephen Nolan Show', BBC Radio Ulster, 25 October 2007.
6. 'Spotlight', BBC Northern Ireland, 23 October 2007.
7. 'The Stephen Nolan Show', BBC Radio Ulster, 24 October 2007.
8. Northern Ireland Assembly written answers, 16 November 2007.
9. 'Spotlight', 23 October 2007.
10. Planning Service document, 5 July 2002—obtained from open file on Ballyallaght application.
11. Memo dated 25 July 2002, also obtained from open file.
12. Planning Appeals Commission report on the hearing was issued on 8 August 2007.
13. 'BBC Newsline', BBC Northern Ireland, 19 September 2007.
14. Leaked document.
15. Information on licence changes disclosed by Fisheries Conservancy Board.

16. *Belfast Telegraph*, 11 September 2007.
17. 'Spotlight', 23 October 2007.
18. Department for Social Development press release on conviction, 8 May 2006.
19. FOI disclosure.
20. *Belfast Telegraph*, 20 May 2008.
21. FOI disclosure.
22. Ian Paisley Jnr press release, 18 December 2005.
23. *Belfast Telegraph*, 3 March 2003.
24. Planning Appeals Commission report on the hearing was issued on 21 March 2005.
25. *Belfast Telegraph*, 25 September 2007.
26. Seymour Sweeney made the statement in documentation obtained by the author.
27. *Belfast Telegraph*, 4 October 2007.
28. 'BBC Newsline', BBC Northern Ireland, 5 October 2007.
29. 'Spotlight', 23 October 2007.
30. *Belfast Telegraph*, 24 October 2007.
31. This email was placed online by the DCMS in relation to an FOI disclosure.
32. BBC Northern Ireland website report, 4 September 2004.
33. Northern Ireland Assembly Official Report, 8 October 2007.
34. *Belfast Telegraph*, 10 October 2007.
35. *Ibid.*
36. The DETI FOI disclosure with 13 lobbying examples was reported in detail in the *Belfast Telegraph*, 1 November 2007.
37. Planning Appeals Commission report issued 27 June 2002.
38. Northern Ireland Audit Office report, *The Private Finance Initiative: A Review of the Funding and Management of Three Projects in the Health Sector*, issued 5 February 2004.
39. Moyle Council document was leaked to the author.

Chapter 7 (pp 101–112)
1. *The Times*, 10 September 2007.
2. *Belfast Telegraph*, 10 September 2007.
3. *News Letter*, 10 September 2007.
4. *Belfast Telegraph*, 10 September 2007.
5. *Sunday Life*, 9 September 2007.
6. BBC News, 8 September 2007.
7. Ian Paisley sermon, 9 September 2007. Recording sourced via the website *www.ianpaisley.org/*.
8. *Belfast Telegraph*, 31 May 2007.
9. *The Revivalist*, May 2007.
10. *Belfast Telegraph*, 6 September 2007.
11. *Belfast Telegraph*, 4 September 2007.
12. *News Letter*, 8 September 2007.
13. *News Letter*, 10 September 2007.
14. *Irish News*, 25 September 2007.

15.   Northern Ireland Assembly Official Report, 11 June 2007.
16.   Northern Ireland Assembly Official Report, 18 September 2007.
17.   Northern Ireland Assembly Official Report, 8 October 2007.
18.   Northern Ireland Assembly Official Report, 10 December 2007.
19.   Northern Ireland Assembly Official Report, 12 November 2007.
20.   Northern Ireland Assembly Official Report, 25 October 2007.
21.   UTV news website, 18 April 2007.
22.   UTV news website, 25 September 2007.
23.   'UTV Live', 6 November 2007.
24.   *News Letter*, 9 December 2007.

Chapter 8 (pp 113–125)

1.   Northern Ireland Court of Appeal ruling issued 16 February 2007 on a dispute between some of the developers planning to buy the Ballee land.
2.   A sheaf of Department for Social Development (DSD) papers was issued under FOI to the author on the Ballee case. All quotes from government documents and Ian Paisley Jnr correspondence with the DSD in this chapter are from this FOI material, unless otherwise stated.
3.   Northern Ireland Assembly written answers, 12 December 2008.
4.   *Belfast Telegraph* and 'BBC Newsline', BBC Northern Ireland, 6 December 2008.
5.   'BBC Newsline', BBC Northern Ireland, 6 December 2008.
6.   *Belfast Telegraph*, 10 December 2007.
7.   *Belfast Telegraph*, 18 January 2008.
8.   *Belfast Telegraph*, 21 January 2008.
9.   Northern Ireland Assembly written answers, 16 May 2008.
10.   Northern Ireland Assembly written answers, 13 June 2008.
11.   *Belfast Telegraph*, 18 January 2008.
12.   Northern Ireland Assembly website, Standards and Privileges Committee section.
13.   *Ibid.*
14.   Northern Ireland Assembly Official Report, 4 February 2008.

Chapter 9 (pp 126–136)

1.   *News Letter*, 5 December 2007.
2.   OFMDFM press release, 5 December 2007.
3.   *The Times*, 13 December 2007.
4.   *Independent*, 1 January 2008.
5.   *Irish Voice*, 3 January 2008.
6.   *Belfast Telegraph*, 31 December 2007.
7.   *Derry Journal*, 1 January 2008.
8.   *News Letter*, 28 December 2007.
9.   David McKee, *Two Monsters* (Andersen Press Ltd, 2005).
10.   Slugger O'Toole, 17 May 2007.
11.   Speech quoted in David Bleakley, *Faulkner* (Mowbrays, 1974), pp. 186–96.
12.   *Belfast Telegraph*, 7 November 2007.
13.   *Daily Mirror*, 15 December 2007.

14. *News Letter*, 27 April 1964.
15. Kirk Session statement and Ian Paisley sermon, 20 January 2008. Recording sourced via the website *www.ianpaisley.org/*.

Chapter 10 (pp 137–146)
1. Unless otherwise stated, all government documents referenced in this chapter on the St Andrews lobbying were made public by MEP Jim Allister.
2. Press release, 15 January 2008, archived on his website.
3. 'BBC Newsline', BBC Northern Ireland, 15 January 2008.
4. *Ibid.*
5. In an article for the *Belfast Telegraph* published on 27 February 2008, former BBC Northern Ireland security editor Brian Rowan stated: 'It was Paisley Jnr who asked me to send a camera to record his father's words that night although he did not give me any advance information on the speech.'
6. 'The Stephen Nolan Show', BBC Radio Ulster, 16 January 2008.
7. *Belfast Telegraph*, 16 January 2008.
8. 'BBC Newsline', BBC Northern Ireland, 15 January 2008.
9. *Belfast Telegraph*, 16 January 2008.
10. *News Letter*, 17 January 2008.
11. 'The Stephen Nolan Show', BBC Radio Ulster, 16 January 2008.
12. Statement issued by OFMDFM press office to author.
13. *News Letter*, 17 January 2008.
14. 'The Politics Show, BBC Northern Ireland, 1 February 2008.

Chapter 11 (pp 147–168)
1. See Larry Elliott and Dan Atkinson, *The Gods That Failed* (The Bodley Head, 2008), pp. 251–2.
2. *Belfast Telegraph*, 21 February 2008.
3. Document leaked to the author.
4. Annual Reports of Assembly pension trustees.
5. *Belfast Telegraph*, 2 November 2006.
6. *Belfast Telegraph*, 8 December 2006.
7. *Belfast Telegraph*, 2 May 2006.
8. *Belfast Telegraph*, 1 June 2007.
9. *Belfast Telegraph*, 9 February 2004.
10. Commons Standards and Privileges report published 30 October 2001.
11. *Belfast Telegraph*, 2 March 2007.
12. Disclosures made in party press releases.
13. *Belfast Telegraph*, 22 February 2008.
14. *Belfast Telegraph*, 8 May 2008.
15. *Belfast Telegraph*, 22 February 2008.
16. *Belfast Telegraph*, 6 February 2008.
17. *Belfast Telegraph*, 21 February 2008.
18. John Lyon's response obtained by the author.
19. Hay Group report published by Senior Salaries Review Body on 3 December 2008.

20. *Belfast Telegraph*, 13 February 2008.

21. *Belfast Telegraph*, 11 April 2008.

22. Details summarised in *Belfast Telegraph*, 6 June 2008, with actual rental figures obtained through FOI.

23. *Belfast Telegraph*, 22 February 2008.

24. *Belfast Telegraph*, 30 July 2008.

25. *Ballymena Times*, 20 November 2007.

26. Seymour Sweeney's involvement with Sarcon 250 was detailed in the *News Letter* and *Belfast Telegraph* editions of 16 February 2008 and 18 February 2008. All quotes from Ian Paisley Jnr in the remainder of this chapter are from those editions.

27. *Belfast Telegraph*, 19 December 2008.

Chapter 12 (pp 169–181)

1. Aesop's Fables.

2. *Dromore Leader*, 1 January 2008.

3. 2005 result from the website *www.ark.ac.uk*.

4. *Banbridge Chronicle*, 19 December 2007.

5. *Banbridge Chronicle*, 6 February 2008.

6. *News Letter*, 8 December 2007.

7. *Belfast Telegraph*, 11 January 2008.

8. *Banbridge Chronicle*, 23 January 2008.

9. *Belfast Telegraph*, 7 February 2008.

10. *Sunday Tribune*, 10 February 2008.

11. Result statistics sourced from the Electoral Office for Northern Ireland website.

12. *Belfast Telegraph*, 14 February 2008.

13. Jim Allister and Basil McCrea were both interviewed for this book.

14. *Belfast Telegraph*, 15 February 2008.

Chapter 13 (pp 182–203)

1. *Belfast Telegraph*, 18 February 2008 (morning edition).

2. *Belfast Telegraph*, 18 February 2008 (early lunchtime edition).

3. *Ibid.*

4. *Irish News*, 19 February 2008.

5. BBC Northern Ireland website report, 18 February 2008.

6. *Derry Journal*, 16 February 2008.

7. *Belfast Telegraph*, 19 February 2008.

8. Comments from Daithí McKay, Declan O'Loan, David Ford and Shaun Woodward were all reported on the BBC Northern Ireland website report, 18 February 2008.

9. Press release issued through his PR company, 18 February 2008.

10. *Belfast Telegraph*, 19 February 2008.

11. 'Spotlight', BBC Northern Ireland, 19 February 2008.

12. *Irish Times*, 19 February 2008.

13. *Irish Times*, 17 January 2008.

14.   BBC Northern Ireland website report, 21 January 2008.
15.   See Chapter 9 for a fuller account of this sermon.
16.   *The Herald*, 21 February 2008.
17.   *Belfast Telegraph*, 20 February 2008.
18.   *Guardian*, 21 February 2008.
19.   *Irish Times*, 21 February 2008.
20.   *Sunday Tribune*, 24 February 2008.
21.   *Belfast Telegraph*, 27 February 2008.
22.   Gordon Brown and Paula Dobriansky quotes sourced from BBC Northern Ireland website report, 5 March 2008.
23.   Press release posted on Ian Paisley Jnr's website.
24.   Interview with UTV's Ken Reid, 4 March 2008.
25.   Comments from Sir Reg Empey and Peter Robinson from *News Letter*, 6 March 2008.

Chapter 14 (pp 204–219)

1.   All quotes on these proceedings are from the Northern Ireland Assembly Official Record, 5 June 2008.
2.   *Belfast Telegraph*, 27 September 2004.
3.   *Irish Independent*, 23 August 2005.
4.   Northern Ireland Assembly Official Record, 5 June 2008.
5.   Jonathan Powell, *Great Hatred, Little Room* (The Bodley Head, 2008), p. 118.
6.   Powell, *Great Hatred, Little Room*, p. 258.
7.   Comments in this chapter by Seamus Mallon, David Trimble, Anthony McIntyre, Danny Morrison and Clifford Smyth were all made directly to the author.
8.   Paisley interview with BBC Northern Ireland political editor Mark Devenport, 30 May 2008.
9.   'The Late Late Show', RTÉ, 30 January 2009.
10.   Quoted in BBC Northern Ireland website article by historian Dr Eamon Phoenix on classified government files released under the 30-year rule, 29 December 2008.
11.   Paisley's machinations around this time were detailed in a 1981 pamphlet by the left-wing *Workers Weekly* paper, provocatively entitled 'Paisley on the Lundy Trail'.
12.   Ed Moloney, *Paisley* (Poolbeg Press, 2008), p. xiii.
13.   Line-dancing was publicly condemned by the Free Presbyterian Church in 2001.
14.   House of Commons Public Accounts Committee report, *Improving literacy and numeracy in schools (Northern Ireland)*, published 8 December 2006.
15.   Eamonn Mallie's comments were made to the public affairs magazine *agendaNI*, September 2008 edition.
16.   *The Revivalist*, February 1972.
17.   Detailed in a press release issued by the Evangelical Alliance (Northern Ireland), 10 December 2007.

Chapter 15 (pp 220–235)

1. This timeless classic includes the refrain:

   Heigh ho! Don't worry
   Pop your cross in the bin
   (Heigh ho! Heigh ho!)
   No matter who matter who you vote for, the Government always gets in.

2. It was increased from £48,000 to £70,000 in 2007 and then up to £72,660 in 2008—*Belfast Telegraph*, 30 April 2008.
3. House of Commons expenses figures for 2006/07—up to £20,440 for office running and £87,276 for staffing.
4. Party grant figures obtained from Assembly and Electoral Commission under FOI and from Commons publications.
5. *Belfast Telegraph*, 31 July 2008.
6. Department of the Environment press release, 27 January 2009.
7. Northern Ireland Assembly Official Record, 27 May 2008.
8. Friends of the Earth Northern Ireland newsletter, Autumn 2008.
9. *Irish Times*, 23 June 2008.
10. *Belfast Telegraph*, 3 November 2008.
11. From John Hewitt, *Selected Poems*.
12. Press release issued on 8 May 2008, sourced from City of New York website.

Chapter 16 (pp 236–250)

1. Frawley's report is published on the Assembly website, along with the conclusions of the Standards and Privileges Committee.
2. *Belfast Telegraph*, 3 June 2009.
3. Details of all MP expenses, including the Paisley and Robinson food allowances and the Sinn Féin rental sums, are published on the House of Commons website.
4. *Daily Telegraph*, 18 June 2009.
5. 'The Stephen Nolan Show', BBC Five Live, 10 May 2009.
6. BBC NI News, 15 June 2009.
7. *Belfast Telegraph*, 20 November 2009.
8. *News Letter*, 2 November 2009.
9. *Sunday Tribune*, 10 January 2010.
10. 'Sunday Sequence', BBC Radio Ulster, 10 January 2010.
11. *Iris: An Intimate Portrait* by Lorraine Wylie, Ambassador Publications, November 2006.

Index